GLOBAL CITIES AND URBAN THEORY

SAGE was founded in 1965 by Sara Miller McCune to support the dissemination of usable knowledge by publishing innovative and high-quality research and teaching content. Today, we publish over 900 journals, including those of more than 400 learned societies, more than 800 new books per year, and a growing range of library products including archives, data, case studies, reports, and video. SAGE remains majority-owned by our founder, and after Sara's lifetime will become owned by a charitable trust that secures our continued independence.

Los Angeles | London | New Delhi | Singapore | Washington DC | Melbourne

GLOBAL CITIES AND URBAN THEORY

DONALD MCNEILL

Los Angeles | London | New Delhi
Singapore | Washington DC | Melbourne

Los Angeles | London | New Delhi
Singapore | Washington DC | Melbourne

SAGE Publications Ltd
1 Oliver's Yard
55 City Road
London EC1Y 1SP

SAGE Publications Inc.
2455 Teller Road
Thousand Oaks, California 91320

SAGE Publications India Pvt Ltd
B 1/I 1 Mohan Cooperative Industrial Area
Mathura Road
New Delhi 110 044

SAGE Publications Asia-Pacific Pte Ltd
3 Church Street
#10-04 Samsung Hub
Singapore 049483

Editor: Robert Rojek
Editorial assistant: Matthew Oldfield
Production editor: Katherine Haw
Copyeditor: Neil Dowden
Proofreader: Rebecca Storr
Marketing manager: Sally Ransom
Cover design: Stephanie Guyaz
Printed and bound by CPI Group (UK) Ltd,
Croydon, CR0 4YY

© Donald McNeill 2017

First published 2017

Apart from any fair dealing for the purposes of research or private study, or criticism or review, as permitted under the Copyright, Designs and Patents Act, 1988, this publication may be reproduced, stored or transmitted in any form, or by any means, only with the prior permission in writing of the publishers, or in the case of reprographic reproduction, in accordance with the terms of licences issued by the Copyright Licensing Agency. Enquiries concerning reproduction outside those terms should be sent to the publishers.

Library of Congress Control Number: 2016938535

British Library Cataloguing in Publication data

A catalogue record for this book is available from the British Library

ISBN 978-1-4462-6706-6
ISBN 978-1-4462-6707-3 (pbk)

At SAGE we take sustainability seriously. Most of our products are printed in the UK using FSC papers and boards. When we print overseas we ensure sustainable papers are used as measured by the PREPS grading system. We undertake an annual audit to monitor our sustainability.

CONTENTS

ILLUSTRATIONS

ABOUT THE AUTHOR

Donald McNeill is Professor of Urban and Cultural Geography at Western Sydney University, having previously lectured at King's College London, Southampton and Strathclyde. His books include *The Global Architect: Firms, Fame and Urban Form* (Routledge, 2008), *New Europe: Imagined Spaces* (Arnold, 2004) and *Urban Change and the European Left: Tales from the New Barcelona* (Routledge, 1999).

ACKNOWLEDGEMENTS

My employers, Western Sydney University, have been thoroughly committed to supporting urban and humanities research for many years, and they deserve significant acknowledgement for allowing time to complete projects such as this. I'd like to thank my colleagues, particularly in the Institute for Culture and Society, for their collegiality and inspiration.

At SAGE, I am grateful to Robert Rojek for his support for this project, to Keri Dickens, Matthew Oldfield and Katherine Haw for their help during the production phase, and to the proposal reviewers who provided important early feedback and encouragement.

Some of the work has been published previously. Sections of Chapter 1 first appeared in D. McNeill (2003), 'Rome, global city? Church, state and the Jubilee 2000', *Political Geography* 22: 535–56; 'Airports and territorial restructuring: the case of Hong Kong', *Urban Studies* 51 (14): 2996–3010; and in, 'Caput Mundi? St Peter's and the deterritorialised church', in D. Arnold and A. Ballantyne (2004) (eds), *Architecture as Experience: Radical Change in Spatial Practice*. New York: Routledge, pp. 134–52. The Australia Hotel study in Chapter 3 is excerpted from D. McNeill and K. McNamara (2012), 'The life and death of great hotels: modernity, disrepair and demolition in Sydney's "The Australia"', *Transactions of the Institute of British Geographers* 37 (1): 149–63; the case study of Hong Kong airport in Chapter 4 is excerpted from D. McNeill (2014), some of the material on IBM and smart cities in Chapter 6 has been drawn from D. McNeill (2015b), 'Global firms and smart technologies: IBM and the reduction of cities', *Transactions of the Institute of British Geographers* 40 (4): 562–74, and the discussion of San Francisco and Uber was drawn from D. McNeill (2016), 'Governing a city of unicorns: tech capital and urban politics in San Francisco', *Urban Geography* 37 (4): 494–513.

My thanks and love to Carol, Kim and Maya.

INTRODUCTION

BRIGHT LIGHTS, GLOBAL CITIES

The global city has been with us for some time now. At some point in the 1990s, it became clear that the imagined geography of the nation-state was being challenged by the likes of New York, Tokyo and London, that cities were making impacts on the world disproportionate to their territorial footprints and that the apparently inexorable suburbanization of economic activity was faltering. More recently, Asia Pacific cities such as Shanghai, Singapore and Sydney began to be mentioned in a similar vein as they grew rapidly in both stature and size. The symbols and signifiers of these cities were often presented in the media with both bravado and disdain: scurrying crowds of suited bankers, gleaming office towers, luxury brands, extravagant bonuses.

Many working to promote this image were far from disinterested. It has been increasingly obvious that consultants seeking global brand recognition see cities as a universal field of understanding. And so, the long-established Brookings Institution partners with the investment bank JP Morgan to develop global cities benchmarking; the management consultancy Accenture produces its Global Cities Strategy; the architecture and engineering firm Aecom launches its own Global Cities Institute; the giant information technology firm IBM promotes smart cities strategies which seek a universal systems-based solution for urban issues. Then there are the seemingly endless lists of city rankings, often promoted by media brands: the magazine *Monocle* produces its own quality of life urban rankings, *The Economist* orders cities according to ease of doing business. The list could go on, but the point should be clear: even speaking about global cities is an industry in its own right. And, above all, there is a sense that cities are always involved in practices of comparison, self-assessment and promotion for reasons that are sometimes very practical, and sometimes highly nebulous.

The response within scholarship has been widespread and varied. Globalization as a theory has been gathering in significance across the social sciences and humanities since the 1970s (James and Stenger 2014). Saskia Sassen's *The Global City: New York, London, Tokyo* (1991) brought this to the study of cities, arguing that the mere possession of corporate headquarters was not enough for cities to 'command and control' the increasingly financialized world economy of the 1980s. Rather, it was the co-presence or agglomeration of interacting producer services firms that gave cities their ability to influence global flows. From the UK, a cluster of scholars working within Loughborough University generated both significant theoretical framings of a world cities network (for example, Beaverstock et al. 2000; Taylor 2004), as well as hosting the the Globalization and World Cities (GaWC) website which gathered a diverse range of working papers and reports from scholars worldwide. The landmark *Global Cities Reader* (Brenner and Keil 2006) runs to 50 extracts from a wide range of perspectives including fields of representation, cultural identity, and the nature of the concept as a sociological and geographical problematic. The field continues to be expanded and developed, both in terms of an explicit exploration of global cities as a concept (for example, Acuto and Steele 2013; Bassens and van Meeteren 2015), but also through ongoing debates about the nature of 'city' and 'urban' as explanatory concepts (for example, Robinson 2006; Brenner and Schmid 2015; Davidson and Iveson 2015a, 2015b).

My focus here is on exploring a set of quite diverse literatures which together explain, or call into question, what, exactly, could be called global, what constitutes a city, and what objects and practices are involved in putting the two together. A number of theorists have worked to provide contrasting entry points to the world cities and global cities literatures: Richard Smith (2003a, 2003b), who provided some early, radically post-structural set of analyses to the field; Jenny Robinson (2002, 2005, 2006, 2011, 2013), whose 'ordinary cities' motif sees the global ascription as being part of a categorizing impulse rooted in Western modernity; and anthropologists who explore the nature of local knowledge and contingency (e.g. Roy and Ong 2011). My purpose in the book is to work across these different literatures in a dialogue with my own empirical observations over the years (e.g. McNeill 2003, 2009a, 2010, 2014, 2015a, 2015b). I have also like many been influenced by the work of actor-network theorists, and especially Bruno Latour, whose 'flat' ontology of networks is well known and aggressive in its opposition to scalar analysis; as one commentator summarized, 'the actor does not pre-exist the network but arises as a product of it ... the actor [is] a relational effect ... it does not take actors' capacities as pre-given black boxes but problematizes the very process and precariousness of assembling them' (Müller 2015: 72).

Throughout, I have focused on a series of objects or sites that serve to *concentrate* the city. Their material density means that a small number of sites have a disproportionate effect on the surrounding urban territory and have powerful, long-lasting, durable impact on their relations with other places, objects and peoples. Through a wide range of urbanized practices such as sacralization, ordering, governmentality, indexicality, hospitality, air conditioning and prediction, these cities are being both composed and acted upon in a material way. However, just listing and describing these practices, devices and sites is not sufficient in itself, and the book works with several standpoints of origin: the importance of cultural and political economies of cities; the significance of the material density of global cities, and their concentration of devices; and the nature of how people and objects, the socio-material, act together to produce these spaces.

Certainly, following materiality through to its logical conclusion could be as exhausting as it is exhaustive. So in these chapters, I follow the materiality of key techniques in the production and programming of big city space. By production,

I am alluding to Lefebvre's broad-based discussion of Marxian forms of space development, with its underpinnings of land value, architectural space shaping, modes of maintenance, leasing and redevelopment. By programming, I refer more specifically to the ways in which space is organized for analysis in various ways:

> The notion of programmes, or the realm of the programmatic, refers to all those designs put forward in a wide range of more or less formal documents by those who seek to configure specific locales and relations in ways thought desirable. Philosophers, political economists, philanthropists, government reports, committees of enquiry and so on all seek to re-present the real as something programmable, susceptible to diagnosis, prescription, improvement, and even cure. (Mennicken and Miller 2012: 17)

To do this, each of the chapters makes reference to a range of sites within 'big cities' to form a stage where a set of tales might be set forth that can build to an urban theory of global cities. They include Rome, Paris, Hong Kong, London, Mumbai, San Francisco, New York, Singapore and Sydney. These cities are of interest precisely because they have massive 'hinterland' effects, both as models to be copied, but also as centres of influence.

While there is a perception that global cities are linked everywhere, all the time, always on, specifying their power is a lot more elusive. Moreover, economically powerful cities may be far less significant than cultural and political centres. It is important to think about cities like Jerusalem, which pervades any discussion of the Middle East, the political division of Berlin during the Cold War, the status of Washington, DC and Brussels as places with, perhaps, the greatest number of accredited journalists in any one city, or, in one case I examine here, the role of Rome as the secular container for the world's smallest sovereign state, but the home of the largest global institution in terms of active membership. In getting to grips with this global and local dilemma, I draw on Latour's far-reaching observations, on networks, relations and interactions. I discuss this more in Chapter 2, but for now, consider the following argument:

> no interaction is what could be called isotopic. What is acting at the same moment in any place is coming from many other places, many distant materials, and many faraway actors ... no interaction is synchronic ... and interactions are not synoptic. Very few of the participants in a given course of action are simultaneously visible at any given point. (Latour 2005: 200–1)

The aim is, then, to zoom into some of the key engineering sites in the concentrated city. To be more specific, each chapter in the book illustrates some kind of urban technology and city material: the cathedral of St Peter's, itself a machine for expressing power; the sometimes clunky apparatus of the state, with its files, surveyors' offices, litter-bin warehouses and traffic engineers; airports, skyscrapers, glasshouses and hotels.

The mundane operations of these urban spaces are sometimes taken for granted, but are underpinned by calculative practices which value, monitor, and order how people and objects co-produce cities.

It is increasingly fashionable to present the city as having floated free from the nation-state as a site of both prosperity and cosmopolitan identity. Texts such as Ed Glaeser's *Triumph of the City* (2011) or Richard Florida's *The Rise of the Creative Class* (2002) surf upon simplified metanarratives of what cities are and where they are going. By contrast, scholars such as Aihwa Ong (2006), working in a post-developmental context, have argued that many nation-states have been reconfiguring many of the existing power relationships within nation-states and creating a 'graduated sovereignty' of rights and territories. Anderson (1996) explores the possibilities of a 'new medieval' approach to territoriality that conceives of political power as being expressed through multiple organizational forms, some of which are territorial, and some of which are not. In a similar vein, Elden traces the evolution of the concept of territory as being a calculative construction:

> Since the seventeenth century, the predominant ontological understand-ing of the world has been its calculability. If we are to make progress in understanding the geographies of globalization in relation to their ter-ritorial, deterritorialized and reterritorialized aspects, it behoves us to understand what their conditions of possibility are. The point is where to begin. (2005: 16)

Elden doesn't explicitly discuss cities in this essay, but he does give some indications about how we might conceive them. On the one hand, cities lie completely within state borders: they appear to be safely territorialized, showing up in censuses, with a city government that sits within a neatly scaled hierarchy of authority. On the other, they are famously porous and unruly due to their density and sheer population size: they are often described as difficult, problematic to govern, unstable. As Elden has argued elsewhere, territory 'is a process, not an outcome … a political technology, or a bundle of political technologies, understanding both political and technology in a broad sense: techniques for measuring land and controlling terrain' (2013: 36).

The purpose of the book is to identify some specific processes, practices, devices and sites that help to position the term. This involves getting beyond the scalar trap that often dominates debate:

> Especially within the social sciences, it has been common to encounter fundamental splits in terms of scale: discussions are often organized in terms of the micro, macro, and meso, for example, as well as local and global. Often rancorous disputes are organized around a host of similar-sounding dual-isms: micro/macro, large/small, global/local, particular/general, near/far, and so on … Typically, adherents to 'micro' analysis are criticized for their resistance to broad generalization. Those in the 'macro' camp are criticized

for their vagueness, for lack of rigour and for the ease with which they jump
from particular examples to general conclusions. (Thrift et al. 2014a: 2–3)

For this reason, many scholars are now turning to a range of practice-based measures
to work out how cities and globalization are brought into being, on a continual
basis. In what follows I tell some stories of cities – or sites, better said – because of
their uniqueness, but also processes that are by their nature highly generalized. It isn't
either/or, but both.

Furthermore, this means that the sites of the formation of global cities cannot be
assumed, or parodied, or glossed. It requires a textured and fine-grained discussion of
how sites such as airports are far from being non-places, but are rather constructed
through intense specialist practices and workplace sociality that enable and enact both
short- and long-distance mobilities; that offices are so important to societies and economies that they might, in aggregate, be regarded as 'territories'; that hotels of all types
and standards act as a motor for the essential circulatory nature of global capitalism;
and that cathedrals, mosques and temples and their associated buildings are influential
organizational sites in shaping wider societal attitudes to the world. From this we can
see that there are key individuals who use these sites as a way of ordering societies and
capitalism: the CEOs and executives of firms, the engineers, designers and managers, the
theologians and preachers.

Similarly, these human actors work with objects and devices, together making or performing the economies of these sites (Barnes 2002, 2008; Christophers
2014). Timothy Mitchell, whose book *Rule of Experts* (2002) charts the formation
of the territorial Egyptian state, suggests the need to provide a 'genealogy of the
economy' (p. 83), focusing on the tools and techniques deployed to build the state.
A growing population had to have certain services provided; to provide the services, revenues for taxation had to be raised. Without knowledge of who owned
what piece of land, rent collecting was very patchy. And so, the Egyptian government developed a mapping office which was combined with a set of calculative,
statistical practices in order to provide a 'scientific' reading of the economy. As
Mitchell says:

> New forms of architecture, engineering, science, schooling, statistical
> knowledge, finance, commerce and government were ordering up a world
> in which buildings, educational establishments, technologies, commercial
> houses and the 'visible institutions of the state', in Simmel's phrase, presented
> to the individual what now looked like an 'objective culture'. (2002: 97)

And yet, the techniques of measurement and division – fairly crude – were subject
to material degradation and disrepair, affecting government's ability to be performed.
An absence of trained surveyors would hinder the speed with which the territory
was established as a stable object of governance. Little has changed in the context of
the global city.

CULTURAL AND POLITICAL ECONOMIES

> Cities – and for that matter other spatial formations – are not purposeful or
> bounded economic entities, but sites where the full variety of the 'economy
> in general' is made visible and juxtaposed, but with crucial effects resulting
> from the particularities of 'placement'. The urban is not just a microcosm
> of the world, a window through which the economy can be read, but also
> a forcing house with considerable power to drive and shape the economy
> through its gatherings. (Amin and Thrift 2007: 150)

In two significant commentaries, Ash Amin and Nigel Thrift (2002, 2007) set out to
reorient ways of theorizing cities as being driven by a performative, experimental
capitalism. Their particular interest here is the city as an economic engine, not as an
'economic sphere in its own right', but instead as a 'composite space with compositional capability' (2007: 150). In some ways, this could be seen as a cop-out: the
ill-defined city with a vague sense of agency. Nonetheless, they are correct in identifying 'the need to grasp a phenomenality that cannot be known through theory
or cognition alone' (p. 9). 'An everyday urbanism', they argue, 'has to get into the
intermesh between flesh and stone, humans and non-humans, fixtures and flows,
emotions and practices' (p. 9).

Amin and Thrift have provided an important stimulus to understanding the
concept of 'cultural economy'. This term has moved beyond the early 'additive'
model ('in which all that was attempted was to add a cultural element to an
economic explanation'), to a 'hybrid model in which the two terms, culture and
economy, are dispensed with, and instead, following actor-network theory and
similar approaches, attention focuses on different kinds of orderings' (2004: xiv).
Read in conjunction with the broader shifts in economic sociology and political
philosophy that underpinned their book, they made a significant attempt to bridge
the cultural and the economic, often seen as two very different epistemological standpoints. Three of their keywords were transitivity ('spatial and temporal
openness of the city', 2007: 9), rhythms (a Lefebvrian, or perhaps James Joycean,
emphasis on everyday encounter and multiple and parallel time-spaces of daily
life) and footprints, a simpler metaphor that dealt with the presence of things left
behind, either from many years hence, or the split second of anteriority that can
be cognized by the urban user.

However, this opening to a fuller sense of the cultural sometimes underplays
the important structuring role of specific firms and business coalitions in the constitution of urban economies. In diverse ways, firms large and small channel many
of the objects and experiences that we understand as urban culture. In this book
we encounter several of them, from the software products of Uber and IBM, to
the portfolio strategies of property developers, to the hotel-management practices of the likes of Hilton and Marriott, to the increasingly commercial practices
of airport operators. While many discussions of the flow of goods and ideas

through cities have focused on state action, there is little doubt that there is a suite of global service firms that seek to standardize sets of practices, standards and norms that enable the global harmonization of trade, investment and transactions (Beaverstock et al. 2013; Faulconbridge 2006; Boussebaa et al. 2012).

In particular, a relatively small world of accountancy firms – the 'Big Four' audit firms of KPMG, Ernst & Young, Deloitte and PwC – along with major management consultants such as McKinsey are present in many cities worldwide, and normalize business standards through a 'zonal' establishment of rules, procedures, and norms (Barry 2006). Similarly, major IT and computing firms such as SAP, IBM and Apple seek to produce economies of scale in selling their products, and increasingly seek to actively produce the markets they are operating in, by shaping consumer loyalty and satisfaction, as well as by selling more quantity or diversity of products (Rossiter 2016).

To make sense of this requires a reinvestment of time into an understanding of numbers. Barnes and Hannah (2001) have argued that 'the inscription of figures, and later their joining to probability calculations within a burgeoning set of both commercial and statist networks, produced worlds to be organized, controlled, manipulated, studied, and known' (p. 379). Here, the gathering, categorization and deployment of numbers, and an understanding of the work they do to fix a particular thing in place, is an important task that requires an analyst who understands statistical practice per se, but also the representational tropes that it deploys. And it also requires attention to the visualization of complex numbers, as in the intense world-making calculative practices being undertaken through human–screen interactions within cities on a daily basis (Pryke 2010; Zaloom 2010).

MATERIAL TURNS

This book aims to build out an argument about materiality in the construction and operation of global cities. It takes as its starting point a coalition of work that sets out to understand the materiality of cities in their widest sense, which includes the nature of their capitalist economies, an ontology of actors and networks, and an ethnographic epistemology of the state (Amin and Thrift 2002; Latour and Hermant 2006; Bennett and Joyce 2010; Farías and Bender 2010). Through these works, it is proposed that we can approach these big, global cities in a slightly different way, one in which we can hold down, provisionally, a very complex assemblage of facts, theories, observations, artefacts, anecdotes and practices. This partly requires an engagement with the ontology, practice and performance of capitalist society, and in turn an engagement with what is meant by the urban economy.

However, while most scholars are happy to accord some degree of importance to materiality, there are significant differences as to how this is actually theorized. As Chris Otter has pointed out in an insightful essay, the range of diverse traditions that contribute to urban analysis have very significant differences between them:

> With urban sociology, the material is a *background* or *arena* within which social forces act and social structures are formed. With capital, the material is an *outcome,* but also a *medium* through which capitalist social relations are reproduced and an *obstacle* to later capitalist development. With culture, the material is a *text* to be decoded or a *symbolic* bearer of meaning. Obviously, material things and systems *do* often function as background, arena, outcome, medium, obstacle, text or symbol. However, every one of these functions leaves materiality itself – the forms, states and qualities of matter – analytically underexplored. (2010: 43, italics in original)

By extension, explanations of why cities grow, and why they fare differently, would have to address this point. As Otter (2010) continues many theories of the urban dematerialize our understandings of cities *on purpose.* He identifies three distinct theoretical approaches that have done this for different reasons. For early twentieth-century sociologists such as Simmel or Park, new modes of social organization – dense living, for example, and crowded streets – 'made' people socialize differently. For Marxists such as Lefebvre, Castells and Harvey, the urban was 'the site for, and medium of' (p. 40) social relations based on access to capital. And for cultural theorists the focus shifted towards semiotic strategies that tried to decode and decipher landscape, space and building and 'read off' their representational power.

In this latter approach, influenced by the impact of post-structuralism in the humanities, social identities are seen to be mediated and produced through different texts. Otter (2010) suggests that the re-emergence of materialist interpretive frameworks was a response to this 'cultural turn' in urban theory, where a focus on meaning, representation and interpretation – especially in visual terms – became the dominant mode of urban critique. As Otter notes:

> Material things ... were never entirely ignored in such analyses, but they remained undifferentiated and black-boxed. Little serious attention was devoted to physical qualities: molecules, forces and textures. In urban sociology, material space was primarily a backdrop for social action ... The cultural turn threatened a wholesale, reductive dematerialization of the city. (2010: 43)

Otter introduces three alternative modes of interpreting materiality. The first, 'thing theory', provides an abstract understanding of how the materiality of objects lead to different human understandings and moral judgements, related to mystery, excess, innate potential, consumption and so on. This object-oriented philosophy was popularized through influential books such as Jane Bennett's (2010) *Vibrant Matter,* which advocates a 'molecular' level of material analysis, either a fundament or a triviality depending on your viewpoint. The philosophical intricacies of this are not my main focus here, though it is important to recognize the significance of Immanuel Kant and Martin Heidegger in debates over how to theorize the separation of human intention from objects. Arguably, this has helped drive the continuing 'backdrop' or 'blackboxing' of urban technologies that has gone on through generations of social theory.

The second approach, material agency, is often linked to science, technology and society (STS) approaches or actor-network theory (ANT). Here, matter generates agency even without intent or consciousness. There is an affinity between these literatures and the practice of researching the city because of the importance of large infrastructural networks in the constitution of the urban. As David Madden suggests: 'some qualities of cities themselves might make urban studies particularly fertile territory for ANT. Where subway lines can be shut down by distant signal failures and architects take into account the behavioural tendencies of rats, the idea of nonhuman agency is intuitively plausible' (2010: 585). And so, what attracts and appeals about ANT is its basis of 'irreducibility and infinite combinability':

> Despite the word 'theory' in its name, ANT is not a theory. It is a method for framing field sites and research objects … Staunchly opposed to essentials of any sort, ANT sees the world as immanent, contingent, absolutely heterogeneous, and as ontologically flat, disclosing no other levels, final explanations or hidden core. (Madden 2010: 584)

Urban technologies are, at first sight, obvious: the things that save us time, make us safer, or save us from chaos as we crowd in our cities, such as elevators, smoke alarms, traffic lights, and so on. We nowadays associate technology with automation, though we might also think about simpler manual devices – keys, combs, park benches – in this vein. But we can also include representational tools such as stained-glass windows, maps and guidebooks, all of which help communicate ways of thinking about cities. So while there is much current discussion about smart cities and their technologies, it is important to account for the role of objects in holding cities together. We should also bear in mind the recent debates in this field regarding the 'affordances' of objects, and their variable abilities to sustain, enhance or weaken urban life (Otter 2008; Bennett and Joyce 2010).

Third, there is the political economy tradition, which – although politically heterodox – can be seen to be extending Marx's concept of historical materialism, where societies develop through the manipulation, circulation and accumulation of capital of various forms. And so there has been a plethora of important works based around the materiality of infrastructure, such as water, waste, power and so on, and its structuring influence on urban life and city form. Graham and Marvin's *Splintering Urbanism* (2001) provided a comprehensive overview of these trends, offering a relational ontology of the urban which showed how unequal access to basic services in many cities is. Others, working in a Lefebvrian tradition, have extended this to explore how this might be a 'planetary urbanization' where the exploited value of scarce natural resources is redistributed into cities, thus linking the most extreme anti-urban regions of the planet, such as Antarctica, into our global urban present (Brenner and Schmid 2013, 2015; and see the response by Walker 2015).

So, how can these various material approaches be applied to global cities scholarship? First, there have been a set of works that seek to chart how the global is constituted by moving objects. Here, we can see attempts to provide an inventory of 'global objects'; there are books that gather together apparently disparate phenomena as gap years, university graduation ceremonies, barcodes, containers, cut flowers and so on (see Pile and Thrift 2000; Thrift et al. 2014b). Second, if we could all agree on a set of 'global cities' and add up all their material components (such as in a 'footprint' approach) it would soon become clear that they constitute only a fraction of the world's 'stuff'. However, we would also find that we could locate many of the people who ordered, designed and financed the production of that stuff in these global cities. Third, in attempting to take objects and materiality seriously, some hard thinking has to be done about – as Otter puts it – the 'molecules'. There can be a tendency to think of materiality as stuff in cargo containers, and these are important of course. But there are other forms of materiality, including code, air and speech, which are more elusive. Fourth, there is a growing interest in the power of the animal world to shape territories; Timothy Mitchell's (2002, Chapter 1) influential attempt to retell the modern history of Egypt in *Rule of Experts* is a case in point: 'Can the mosquito speak?', he asks, in his insect-centred economic narrative. More specifically, there has been a macrohistorical and philosophical interest in examining the power of – apparently lifeless and human-controlled – objects as generators of significant social changes, as in Jared Diamond's *Guns, Germs and Steel* (1997) and Jane Bennett's *Vibrant Matter* (2010) respectively.

Aside from the guns and the germs, though, there is also a story of urbanization that is boring in its nature but world-making in its impact. The spread of standards, norms, templates, forms, languages and anything that seeks to make things 'seamless' or inter-operable is a major story of the last few hundred years. Processes such as the ongoing production of clean water involves a linked set of 'routine practices' which involve water-treatment plants, compliance to remote set standards, laboratory testing and pipelines. Yet while this is often a fairly localized or national process, it can be brought into a global framework that allows countries to be measured and ranked against each other: 'it is in the laboratories that the sample is transformed into a number on the computer screen and can finally be compared to the global standard' (Zeiss 2014: 107).

There is also a very real set of materialities surrounding the movement of bodies. There is definitely a need to understand the 'geographies of the super-rich' (Beaverstock et al. 2004), as well as the role of intermediaries such as recruitment agents in their promotion of a 'global war for talent', typically to fill the ranks of globally operative corporations. Set against this is the 'commoditization' of labour, with posts that require little training or even contractual obligation (Hill 2015; Mezzadra and Neilson 2013). And so we might think of global cities, so often conceived as cosmopolitan sites of mixing, as being at the sharp end of border technologies, structured by the often competing desires of firms, on the one hand, who only really have to consider the wage relation with their employees, and governments, on the other, who are increasingly driven by the technological costs of processing and maintaining migrant bodies.

THE ORGANIZATION OF THE BOOK

Each chapter of the book tells a very distinct tale of how these practices have played out in particular places. An important point to flag here is that although many of these practices are transferable, they have a point of origin or strength, a *genius loci*, that generates its own momentum, sometimes called path dependence. The book aims to convey a sense of the spatial political economy of why some cities have been more influential than others, and why some parts of cities have become central to the organization of global practices, concentrated zones of ordering, developing, curating, designing, engineering, accounting, worshipping.

To progress along these lines, the book begins in Chapter 1 with a discussion of what could be called the 'original global city', Rome, and its particular association with one of the most obvious and most influential of global institutions, the Catholic Church. Religion is a key structuring force of contemporary cities, but it is often absent from the global cities literature, and has been associated with a perceived secularization of urban life. How it comes into being as a spatial phenomenon has rarely been studied. In this chapter, which outlines a spatial ontology of Roman Catholicism, I use Rome to provide an express route through some of the key problems faced in attempts to theorize global cities, which includes 'methods of long distance control' (Law 1986, 2004), and the existence of non-economic forms of global identity. This is the site of the world's largest global institution, and its smallest sovereign state, after all, and the institution has exploited its territorial inheritance of the Roman Empire in various ways. But it also relies on material devices and technologies to sustain its globality: the theological interpretations of the Bible, the architecture and design of cathedrals, and the Popemobile are all mechanisms by which the Vatican *attempts* to exert its control of a global Church, even while many Catholics seek to generate their own, culturally specific practices of worship and everyday life.

While Chapter 1 speaks of centrality and attempts to impose and sustain hierarchy, Chapter 2 comes from a radically different approach: one that sees flatness, rather than scale or hierarchy, as the best way to understand how cities are in fact assemblages of power. This moves the discussion to another European city, Paris, which is inextricably linked with two often combative traditions of urban theory: the political economy traditions of spatial theorists such as Henri Lefebvre and David Harvey, and the actor-network theory of Bruno Latour. In *Paris, Ville Invisible* (2006), Latour and his colleague Emilie Hermant provide an absorbing journey through Paris. This work is in many ways an urban field guide to Latour's *Reassembling the Social* (2005), and applies the tenets of actor-network theory to the study of a single city. Latour's focus is on disaggregating the casual knowledge that is held about such apparently stable signifiers as 'Paris', revealing the objects, humans and actants that are constantly revitalizing it, reassembling it through networks and objects in a series that he terms 'sequences'. In many ways, the terrain of struggle here is as much about how far a single site can speak to a global process, and how far the aggregation of site-specific arrangements of institutions, markets, objects and practices – which Latour presents as a kind of localized mesh of networks – can then be recomposed in a way that specifies, rather than assumes, how cities exist as a set of network ontologies.

Chapter 3 develops this by concerning itself with the ordering mechanisms and practices that place cities within hierarchies and ranks. The chapter explores a debate between those who seek a 'metageography' of globalization as composed by inter-city links, and a literature that is sometimes known as the 'ordinary cities' perspective. The latter group of scholars tend to perceive a Western or Euro-American bias in the dominant theoretical perspectives that have framed the study of global cities. However, while undoubtedly true, my argument is that standardization is a process that requires many hands, and so the chapter explores the embodied knowledges, objects and technologies that standardize cities, such as hotels and air-conditioning systems.

By now, with studies of Rome, Paris and various 'ordinary cities' under discussion, the discussion moves towards a more extensive, distanciated consideration of the structured practices of global mobility. In Chapter 4 the discussion explores what has been called 'logistical territories', material systems for organizing global navigation. It considers what the concept of 'port ontologies' might offer for the study of global cities, and does so by considering two 'machinic complexes' that organize the circumnavigation of the globe, ships and airports. In this sense ports are a key machinic complex for the reorganization of cities (Amin and Thrift 2002), but also require a take on 'surface' and territory, because how these maritime and aerial launch-pads are configured is crucial to capitalist economies.

However, the study of intense and fast flows between cities can obscure the fact that while economic activity is dispersing globally, this actually increases the need to concentrate the people responsible for its co-ordination and calculation. This insight, which is the cornerstone of Sassen's global city thesis, means that we might see global cities as actually referring to a very small footprint – office territory – within the cities of London, San Francisco or Shanghai. Chapter 5 further develops the actor-network concept of 'centres of calculation', describing various examples of the embedded calculative practices of contemporary capitalism, and different ways of narrating this. It places the material organization of office geographies at the centre of this approach, suggesting that these are specific spatial arrangements that provide the constitutive power of global city status. In doing so, it seeks to reinvigorate the concept of the central business district, or CBD, using it to gather a set of ethnographic research sites that can illuminate practices of global city making, positioned between radical flatness and overbearing hierarchical power.

Having set out a case for the fine-grained study of the work going on in corporate offices and central business districts, Chapter 6 moves the optic back to a mobile, relational ontology by considering how these are zones of embedded knowledges which are 'world-making'. It examines the spread of 'global' business knowledge through individual 'gurus' such as Richard Florida and Ed Glaeser, but also through the structured marketing of knowledge by management consultancies. The chapter then sets out some of the 'experimental' and 'exhibitionary' city platforms that have emerged in recent years, from eco-cities to smart cities. These are key elements in the ongoing reproduction of urban policy and city-focused products, key elements in the erasure of difference between cities. These have their own business models, and the chapter briefly profiles how San Francisco acted as a launch-pad for Uber, sitting within a few kilometres of Silicon Valley, perhaps the world's most concentrated innovation system.

I began this book with the well-worn cliché of 'bright lights, big cities'. And in many ways, this is a very biased book in its focus on the things that are exciting about globalization. The mysteries of the Boeing 747 are as great as those of the miracles of Roman Catholicism, the micro-geographies of offices and the new urban maps of Uber are fundamental underpinnings of the 'essential' city, and the big things of the study – Silicon Valley, Hong Kong International Airport, the Vatican, the City of London – become more and more interesting when they are interpreted as a rather looser aggregation of practices than is often assumed.

1

CENTRALITY

We can view global cities as being about concentrations of power and influence, that gain their power from their ability to organize distance. They have a certain centrality or capitality in relation to other spatial formations. The purpose of this chapter is to explore how organized religions – their institutions, buildings, leaders, civil services, standards, and practices - have long been a key force in the governing of distance-based communities. This chapter focuses on one particular religion, and one particular branch of Christianity: Roman Catholicism. It does so because for several centuries, this religion has organized itself around a single city, Rome, with a leader, the Pope, that gains legitimacy from its biblical, locational genealogy. It uses this as the basis of both its territorial power and its claim to cosmological significance. In some ways, this has its parallels in the role of Mecca for Islam, a gathering place of both sacred relics and a place of pilgrimage whose meanings have been consciously curated, altered and rearranged over centuries by territorial governments (Sardar 2014). Such sites, and cities, are central to global city scholarship in their revelation of how particular worldviews have been sustained and ritually performed for centuries.

Moreover, in the context of urban theory, the chapter pursues the idea that a study of Rome reveals many issues surrounding centrality, and how sites are gathered and configured in a way that relates both highly localized material and human relationships, as well as long distance, and virtual, identification. It seeks to unpack the long-noted tension between a Rome-based hierarchical conception of the Church, and the contrary 'collegial' model demanded by many Catholics as a key means of adapting theology and religious practice to culturally specific contexts. Here, the city is important in three ways: *theatrically*, as a performance space for the Pope, as a site of embodiment of worship and religious devotionalism; *mythically*, as the representationally and materially constructed capital of the world, *Caput Mundi*, based on St Peter's locational choice of Rome as a site to found the Church; and *institutionally*, as the location of the key decision-making forces within the Catholic Church, particularly the doctrinal councils of the Curia, the Vatican's bureaucracy.

CAPUT MUNDI: CAPITAL OF THE WORLD

Volumes and volumes have been written on Rome. As a religious 'capital', it struggles with all of the problems that the secular world presents: the complex and often corrupt politics that characterizes the Italian nation-state that also claims Rome as its capital; the maintenance and conservation of some of the world's most fascinating and fine architectural monuments, and ruins, while actively encouraging the world to pay it a visit; the problems faced in negotiating territorial miniaturism with spiritual massiveness. This is a city that houses the leadership of the world's largest institution in terms of actively identifying members; a city that has given its name to arguably the most successful form of imperial control; a city that has inspired imitators in architecture, culture and art; and it is a city that is, almost by definition, a *locus classicus*. It is surely impossible to speak of Rome in 'general terms'. But if we admit this is the case, then does that mean we can speak of any cities in anything other than 'local' terms of reference?

One way in which this has been rendered is through portraying the city as 'microcosmic'. Krieger (1971: ix) has described the nineteenth-century historian Gregorovius's history of medieval Rome as:

> an early example of urban history in the microcosmic sense that is now standard for the genre. Like the histories of cities being prosecuted today, Gregorovius's Roman history is an attempt to write general history by focusing upon a circumscribed, manageable framework which is either the embodiment or the crossroads of general movements. For Gregorovius the city of Rome was precisely such a crossroads in the middle ages: as the seat of the papacy, as the basis of the Empire, and as the pivot of Italy, his Rome witnesses the crucial events of European history from the schism of east and west through the duel of pope and emperor to the end of the Italian Renaissance and the start of the modern age of liberty. These events, moreover, lose their abstract character and take on palpable and dramatic forms when they appear on the Roman scene. Gregorovius shows the big events in their local impact and he shows the expansive effects of superficially local events: but always what concerns Rome concerns the world at large. The choice of Rome as the urban microcosm was especially appropriate to the middle ages, when most men were vitally committed both to the local and to the universal, to the familiar and to the absolute, and only vaguely to the intermediate levels between them – and Rome was the one locality that was the home of both universal medieval institutions, papacy, and Empire.

In his layered historiography of Rome, Bosworth (2011) draws attention to how Gregorovius suggests that the choice of the city as the capital of the newly founded Italy from 1870 would lead to its historical decline in importance. After this time, Rome became a historical resource rather than a city of universal significance: 'it was a Rome of the mind that mattered, and therefore one Rome or other of the past' (p. 102).

Here, we need to consider several things: the nature of Rome itself – what is it? Where does it begin and end? Who is claiming it? Who owns it? Who speaks of it, and how? How does it fit into its nation-state, for it is both the Italian capital as well as the home of the Vatican. How does it figure within the restructuring of Roman Catholicism? What lessons can be drawn from its classical remains, and how important is its Renaissance legacy? And how might it speak to a global geography that is both urban and involved in its escape into a spiritual dimension?

THE 'ORIGINAL GLOBALIZER'? CITIES AND TERRITORIALIZED RELIGION

> The idea that religion is 'the original globalizer' destabilizes the more common assumption that markets are the primary force for globalization. It also stands in contrast to the assumption that globalization abolishes frontiers and leads to homogeneity. In economics globalization does mean homogenization in the sense of drawing far-flung agents into a competitive world market, and although that notion also needs a great deal of refinement, we can take for granted that it does pull down barriers to trade and competition. By contrast, religion breaks through frontiers and in the same process throws up new frontiers because religions ancient and modern, monotheistic, polytheistic and totemic, with their apparatus of ritual practices and internal, proprietorial, self-sufficient codes, are demarcators and markers of difference rather than similarity and homogeneity. (Lehmann 2002: 299–300)

This is a striking claim when considered in the context of global cities. The idea that markets may be subordinate to religion as a driver of globalization is an intriguing one. The development of a schematic spatial ontology of Roman Catholicism, the Papacy, and the Vatican can reveal some significant insights about urbanity and globalization. First, by tracing its geographies, we can get an insight into a drastic shift in the place of the Vatican in the world. Throughout the last century there has been a gradual de-Italianization of the Church, reaching its logical conclusion with the appointment of the first non-Italian Pope for centuries, John Paul II, followed by a German, Benedict XVI, and most recently an Argentinian, Pope Francis. This had an explicitly global motivation: John Paul II dramatically increased the number of cardinals in the Church, particularly from the huge – urban – growth areas in the 'global South', in parts of Africa, Asia and Latin America. For example, the Catholic columnist John L. Allen has suggested that:

> The shift from north to south in terms of the center of gravity in the church is like when St. Paul left Palestine in the first century and took Christianity to Greece, and ultimately to Rome, and made it a new religious movement in the Greco-Roman world, utterly transforming it. We are living in one of those

transformative moments right now. ... In the 21st century, places like Abuja in Nigeria and Jakarta and Manila will be what places like Paris and Milan were in the 15th and 16th centuries – that is, they will be the primary centers where new theological ideas, new pastoral models, new political priorities emerge. (2010)

The question this poses, however, is one that is central to globalization studies: how to understand, measure and conceptualize spatial 'reach', how to maintain influence over distance, and how to integrate this with the 'deterritorializing' effect of near instant global communication and social media networking.

Second, Catholicism has been challenged by the secularizing tendencies of modern urban societies, where countries from Italy to Ireland have passed legislation contrary to Church teaching on issues such as divorce and abortion. Wealthy modern cities have been fertile sites for theologies of 'prosperity Christianity' which has replaced the convictions of the after-life encompassed by images of hell and damnation (Woodhead 2002: 177). As Lanz (2014) has suggested, secularism has had its effect on how cities have been studied:

> Urban theory ... considers that modern urbanity, as the end product of the city's long spiritual decline, can be equated with secularity ... Beyond this, urban religion was seen as a social reminiscence, a sign of urban backwardness, linked to (poverty) zones in 'Third World Cities' captive to their traditions, or to migrant millions not yet fully urbanized. Even here, urban theory overlooked, for example, the major importance of liberation theology on the intellectual level, as well as their grassroots congregations, as religious, social and political actors in Latin America's poor urban districts. (Lanz 2014: 21–2)

Rome provides an important driving force in this re-engagement with the religious.

Third, religion as an experience has been restructured and reorganized, with the rise of charismatic – even celebrity – preaching, and televangelism undoubtedly influencing the Church's increasing openness to, for example, television and the internet. Lehmann distinguishes between 'cosmopolitan' globalization, where the hierarchy of established, pre-modern churches try to integrate the culture of colonized societies within their own church's history; and, on the other hand, the rise of 'fundamentalist' or 'charismatic' forms of religion that are the fruit of an intensification of individual knowledge of religious choices (that some have characterized as 'supermarket' or à la carte religion). Lehmann sees Roman Catholicism as the exemplar of religious cosmopolitanism, where

> a religious culture, identity and institution expand across cultural and political frontiers accompanied by a 'theory' of the other. Such globalization involves the very modern idea that religious practices are embedded spatially and temporally, that they express the location of a people in time and space, and that changing others' beliefs requires an understanding of that embeddedness. (2002: 302)

Thus, through the notion of 'inculturation', the Vatican has sought to incorporate and absorb the 'local' residues of non-Christian religious practices (such as quasi-pagan cults of saints) into its liturgy and policy.

Fourth, there has been a battle between those who seek the concentration of 'command and control' in Rome, the Papacy, and the Vatican civil service (the Curia), and those who – before and after the Second Vatican Council of 1962 to 1965 – have sought to decentralize the Church towards either national, or 'base' communities (in the case of Latin American liberation theology). This Council, a rare reconsideration of theological issues, had prefigured the growing power of non-European Catholic communities, and had made many progressive statements on how Catholicism was practised. And yet many of the advances made at the Council were never implemented: 'Some [bishops] feared that once they went home, the Roman curia would again become dominant in the church, a fear that proved prophetic' (Reese 1996: 42). As with any major governmental organization, the role of bureaucratic office is fundamental in implementing policy.

THE CATHEDRAL AND THE GLOBAL CITY

To create solid and stable convictions in the minds of the uncultured masses, there must be something that appeals to the eye: a popular faith, sustained only on doctrines, will never be anything but feeble and vacillating. But if the authority of the Holy See were visibly displayed in majestic buildings, imperishable memorials and witnesses seemingly planted by the hand of God himself, belief would grow and strengthen like a tradition from one generation to another, and all the world would accept and revere it. (Pastor 1923, in Duffy 2008: 181)

So Nicholas V announced in 1455, from his deathbed, that Rome should be reshaped to reflect the glory of God. It would not be until 1506 that Pope Julius II decided to destroy the original St Peter's, which had lasted for over 1000 years and which was 'cluttered with nearly a hundred tombs, altars, and chapels added over the centuries' (Partridge 1996: 50). In its place, and centred around the tomb of St Peter, a succession of Popes and architects – Bramante, Sangallo, Michelangelo, della Porta and finally Bernini – shaped the current basilica, and the famous colonnade and central square. Its timing coincided with the Church's reaction to the Reformation, where 'the grandiose architecture, sculpture, painting and music of the baroque were an expression of the reinforced claim to rule of an *Ecclesia militans et triumphans*' proclaiming a re-Catholicization of Europe that 'would be carried through politically wherever possible and with military force wherever necessary' (Küng 2001: 146, 147). With a glorious Rome on the one hand, and the Inquisition on the other, Catholicism re-emerged as a powerful force both in statecraft and in shaping the lives of individuals across Europe.

The reconstruction of St Peter's created what would now be called a 'mega-church' of great prominence among followers. The city's centrality in Church history is owed to the notion of the Petrine lineage, as the actual terrestrial site where St Peter is told to make a church by God. By the time of the Renaissance, this centrality is actively worked into urban space, with Sixtus IV's papal bull of 1480 seeing Rome as:

> the city consecrated to Christ through the glorious blood of the Apostles Peter and Paul, and [that] has been made by the Most High head of the Christian religion and the seat of His vicar. This civitatis sacerdotalis et regia (royal and priestly city) is caput mundi, and in consequence draws multitudes of the faithful from all parts of the earth to visit the basilicas of the Apostles and to gain indulgences, especially during Jubilee Years. For these reasons, a more decorous and beautiful city was vital. (Stinger, 1998: 32)

And so the size, arrangement and design features were all communicative devices:

> The enormous basilica was meant to demonstrate the Church's triumph over schism, heresy, the abnegation of her Sacraments and interference in her affairs by emperors, kings and councils. It was to be a concrete testimony of her powers of withstanding the tempests of a hostile world. It was the loud proclamation of papal supremacy over the universal Christian Church. Nearly every component of St Peter's is symbolic of this great boast. The marble relief of Bonvicino over the central door to the portico pictures Christ handing the keys to Peter. This is the initial reminder to those about to enter that divine authority has been committed to the papacy. Lest the visitor should be in any doubts, the relief by Bernini over the central door into the church itself next brings to his eyes and understanding the doctrinal incident, 'Feed my Sheep'. It lays emphasis upon the spiritual leadership given by God to Peter and his successors. The basilica was meant then to be not only a colossal token of victory but an instrument of propaganda. (Lees-Milne 1967: 327)

Such religious spaces are also microcosmic in the sense that they express a complex ontology in a spatial format. Margaret Visser provides an eloquent, book-length articulation of one small church in Rome, and uses it to work through how the individual detailing of this singular space addresses the far larger themes contained in religious identities:

(Continued)

(Continued)

The Cross, the human body, and destiny are three of the ideas that have informed the traditional design of many churches for centuries. A church is often cross-shaped – that is, in the form of a human body, with the arms constituted by the transept, the head by the apse, and the heart by the altar. A strong directionality is commonly expressed: a door, then a narthex, and then the long main body of the church or nave, heading directly to the altar and the rounded apse wall beyond it. The people in the church are on a journey, the 'journey of life', towards their destiny, which is God. Time – the life of the group, the lifetime of each individual person – is expressed as space. (Visser 2001: 32)

This miniaturized organization of space is connected to a much more expansive religious geography, linked to practices of pilgrimage, as discussed below.

From the fifteenth century onwards, Church historians note an intensification of the Vatican's desire to shape the topography and built space of Rome as a means of fusing imperial myth with papal power. Here, relics and tombs (such as that of St Peter), a Marian piety and belief in miracles, and the strong belief in the significance of doors (such as those in St Peter's and the Lateran) strengthened the link between the Church's understanding of the materiality of Christ's time on earth and Rome as a sacred site.

FIGURE 1.1   The packed crowds at a Papal Mass in St Peter's Square in the Vatican demonstrate how Rome pulls religious tourists and pilgrims to a central point

Source: Alessia Pierdomenico / Shutterstock.com

THEOLOGICAL CENTRALITY

One of the key moments in the emergence of Rome as a global city came in 1870. The location of the capital of the new Italian Republic – chosen for its geographical centrality and symbolic richness – provided a direct challenge to the Church, which saw itself engulfed by the new secular state. Throughout the twentieth century, and despite the reconciliation between church and state in 1929, there was an on-going tension between the 'two capitals', the one serving as seat of government and bureaucracy of the secular Italian state, the other the spiritual home of Roman Catholicism as well as its institutional and theological nerve centre. The rapid secularization of Italian society has not, however, softened claims on Rome, particularly during the theologically active primacy of John Paul II. Furthermore, the collapse of the post-war Italian party system in the early 1990s, combined with increased Mafia tension and separatist movements from the North, has reopened debates over the nature of Italy itself, and Rome's place as its capital.

The foremost achievement of Vatican II, the far-reaching theological gathering of the late 1960s, was in popularizing an ancient conception of the Church: the Council affirmed that each group of Christians gathered around its bishop is in that place, 'the fullness of the Church, the Spirit's temple, sacrament of Christ' (Cornwell, 2001: 19). It is in this that many reformers, unhappy at the increasing conservatism and centralization of the Church in Rome have sought to remake the role of the global Church. In many ways the debate was an echo of the key question facing all faith communities at a time of technological progress, declining church attendance, and changing moral values – the issue of secularism, and in particular the question of the Vatican's role in the Church's response. The difficult nature of the financing of the Church, and a more elusive commodification of pilgrimage, has raised interesting and troubling questions over the 'worldliness' of the contemporary Church.

This becomes particularly tense when the Vatican intervenes in global affairs, particularly since John Paul II's role in Cold War geopolitics, and more recently Pope Francis's interventions in a range of issues such as climate change. During the period running roughly from the loss of temporal power to the opening of Vatican II, the Vatican was markedly Italian and defensive (Pius X had, after all, declared himself a prisoner in the Vatican, and Pius XII had pursued a strongly contested policy of defensive accommodation to the forces of fascism (Cornwell 2001)). John Paul II changed this dramatically, and in two ways. First, he actively sought a role for the Vatican in the destabilization of communism, drawn on his militant Polish Catholic nationalism (Hanson 1992). Second, after the decline of state communism, he and his aides turned their attention to cultural relativism, the fear of organizational fragmentation and an attack on the moral absolutism of the Church (and the teaching of the Pope) by, for example, demands for freedom of choice on birth control, ordination of women priests and issues of gay rights. The powerful liberation theology movement was tackled through the excommunication of many of its key members, such as Leonardo Boff. In terms of sexuality, the lack of recognition of the right to be Christian and homosexual has had enormous impact in liberal parts of the USA, especially big cities; the banning of contraception has, of course, been instrumental in the population explosion of many parts of the developing world, particularly Latin America. As a response to many of these problems, local congregations and priests have developed plural interpretations of the faith, and in some places whole new political practices.

POPEMOBILE: UNIVERSALITY AND VISIBILITY

The possibility of meeting the Pope has always been an important element of pilgrimage to Rome. Papal Masses are a central part of how the Pope's presence is projected within the space of the Vatican. But during his period in office, John Paul II actively sought to reinforce the spatial reach of Roman Catholicism, frequently travelling around the world to visit cities with large Catholic populations. He saw this as central to a project of universalism, an important theological riposte to the culturally plural forms of Catholicism that had been emerging in various places.

> The problem about the Universal Church is how to make it more visible. There are tendencies in theology and above all in the Orthodox Church to reduce everything to the level of the local church. But the church was born universal from the moment it began in Jerusalem. Saint Paul's travels, Saint Peter's coming to Rome, the Apostolic tradition, everything confirms the Petrine tradition of giving the church its universal dimension. And it seems to me that my travels help to make it more visible. (John Paul II, cited in Willey 1993: ix)

Yet this was combined with an embrace of modern means of display and communication, showing a clear conviction of the importance of spectacle in the televisual age, perhaps reflecting the need to actively compete with other global religions.

For many centuries, the Pope was almost a mythical figure, rarely travelling beyond Rome and certainly not undertaking international evangelization tours. The arrival of reliable air travel opened up new possibilities, however, which John Paul II was quick to spot:

> More alert than his aides, the pope quickly recognized the sheer dramatic power of his office. No other world leader celebrated open-air triumphs against such unabashedly theatrical backdrops. No secular leader could routinely address hundreds of thousands of citizens in mass meetings anywhere on earth. The forceful personality of John Paul II lit up the TV screen. Images of him standing in the popemobile, arms extended in greeting, of him kneeling to kiss the ground of yet another country swept the television screens of the world. Without TV the 'Wojtyla phenomenon' of the 1980s could never have existed. ... Beneath the eye of the camera,

his global evangelization came to life. John Paul II was the first pope to understand the television era, the first one who mastered the medium, who could handle a microphone, who was used to performing in public. People watched him against the backdrop of exotic panoramas: sailing down tropic rivers, standing on slopes of sacred volcanoes, or walking in the shadow of soaring skyscrapers – like some omnipresent Master of the Universe. (Bernstein and Politi 1997: 398–9)

This global evangelization project required a significant amount of bodily effort, and it also reframed the papal body in several ways. For centuries, the Pope had been carried short distances on a raised seat. Popes had used automobiles for several decades when travelling through crowded city spaces. But John Paul II popularized several variants of what became known as the 'Popemobile', ranging from an armored truck while visiting Cold War Warsaw, to the more typical Mercedes-Benz convertible. But the advent of the Popemobile helped to mark an apparent closing of the gap between Pope and faithful. The assassination attempt on John Paul II in 1981 served to reconfigure again how Popes travelled, with the addition of the technology known as bullet-proof glass.

FIGURE 1.2 A mural of Pope Francis, New York City, 2015. The bodily image of the Pope, linked biographically to Rome, has always been an important element in how the Church travels

Source: Ivan Cholakov / Shutterstock.com

CREATIVE GLOBALIZATION? PILGRIMAGE PRACTICES

> Celebration of the millennium is an act of creative globalization which universalizes the Western, Christian space-time that underpins a largely secular geographical imagination. In order to be enacted, the meanings of millennialism – death and renewal, origins and ends, memory and desire – have not only to be attached to a specific calendrical moment, but also to be mobilized at particular locations across the globe ... These celebrations seek to universalize complex meanings, memories and desires through concrete interventions: buildings, spectacles, and performances, and to animate historic genius loci in determinate locations within a contemporary global context. (Cosgrove and Martins 2001: 169)

John Paul II marked the turn of the millennium, in 2000, with a Holy Year or Jubilee. From its origins, the Church has actively used such events to make its presence in Rome in both space and time. The figure, body and institution of the papacy was increasingly woven into the theatrical and mediated space of Rome. Drawing legitimacy from the martyrdom of the apostles Peter and Paul led to the introduction of the Bishop of Rome – the Pope – being seen as the direct inheritor of the keys to the Church of Rome. For Küng (2001), this occurred in the fourth and fifth centuries, when the Bishops of Rome established the attributes that many today still see as being 'originally Catholic', including the exploitation of the Matthaean 'rock' as apostolic seat, and the promotion of a more understandable version of the Bible; the initiation of the title of 'Pope', 'the process of a Roman monopolization of titles' drawn from the Eastern bishops; the beginnings of the imposition of a universal liturgy; and the first attempts to declare papal pronouncements as binding (Küng 2001: 51–2).

Through the centuries, other techniques – combined with the growing military and political power of the papal states – would further reinforce the centrality of Rome, as in Charlemagne's introduction of a common Latin liturgy, which led by the eleventh century to a full 'Romanization' of the Church. This was accompanied by the gradual, but increasingly sophisticated, development of a worldwide network of churches, materially linked through the promotion of Latin; the physical sending of messengers to communicate new theological determinations; the establishment of a management class of bishops and cardinals; the standardization and repeated revision of a Roman missal that determined the format and timing of Mass; and the training of priests. In the case of American Catholicism, for example, Peter d'Agostino describes the intense efforts of Leo XIII between 1878 and 1903 to develop a permanent organizational presence in the USA: the appointment of nuncios (diplomats) to foreign governments, of apostolic delegations to national churches: 'Catholic schools and seminaries inculcated an appreciation of the importance of the Roman Question. Producers of Catholic culture – clergy, sisters, lay congresses, editors, mothers in their homes – conveyed sentiments of protest against Liberal Italy and taught the necessity of temporal power' (2004: 53).

However, the Catholic Church has paid particular attention to practices of pilgrimage, such as Jubilees or Holy Years. This is often ignored in more formal historical accounts of religion. Hecht (1994: 184), studying the inter-religious tensions that surround the Church of the Holy Sepulchre in Jerusalem, argues that:

> The history of religions … has come to understand that the sacred manifests itself at specific places and moments, making them, for all purposes, sacred for all time. It has then created an 'aesthetics' of sacred space and time which it conveys through a rich, metaphorical language. Its analyses of sacred space and time are largely devoid of conflicts over their organisation and meaning.

The staging of the Jubilee has been interpreted as central to John Paul II's theology and mystique, as a means of closing (or arguably reversing) many of the ideas that came from the Second Vatican Council. On a global scale Roman Catholicism was being increasingly challenged by other religions, a phenomenon that has seen religious groups adopt the values of marketing and advertising in an attempt to 'sell God' in a 'cultural marketplace' (Chidester 2000: 590). As such, the Roman Catholic Church – as with most other religions – has had to become increasingly worldly in its attitude to capitalism, a stance further exacerbated by the severe financial crisis that it faces. Furthermore, this has taken place at a time in which neo-conservatives have battled progressives for the 'soul' of Catholicism, in terms of attitudes to changing social attitudes and secularization (Hebblethwaite 1987; Cornwell 2001).

The practice of holding Jubilees has always been indissociable from the secular–sacred divide in the city. Based on Old Testament practice (Leviticus 25:8–55) where slaves were freed and land returned to its original owner, Nicholas V (Pope between 1447–55) instituted the modern practice of plenary indulgence for pilgrims. As Stinger (1998: 44) summarizes:

> What in the Old Testament conception of the mystery of the Jubilee Year belonged to the remission of the world and the restitution of properties is to be understood by Christians in a spiritual manner. Thus all people, even those guilty of the most serious sins, provided they are truly repentant, have confessed, and have visited the four major basilicas in Rome, should receive a plenary indulgence for their sins.

This began a practice of shortening the gap between such Holy Years to twenty-five years, and marked an increasingly close relationship between the urban form of the city of Rome and the process of pilgrimage and spiritual belonging. During the Jubilee, visitors to Rome are awarded preferential time-off in purgatory if they visit a specific number of Roman churches. Yet the nature of pilgrimage in the year 2000 contrasted sharply with the traumas and dangers faced by medieval pilgrims in attending the Jubilees. Now, as Chidester (2000) has also noted, pilgrimage is increasingly indistinct from the practices of international tourism, where the privations, cost and dangers faced in past times have largely been superseded.

In this context, the years leading up to 2000 were characterized by an increasingly tangled relationship between the secular city council and senior figures in the Holy See. First, Rome – as both capital and sacred city – became an exhibition space for a commercially, as well as spiritually, minded Church. Second, the church–state separation enshrined in the Lateran Treaties of 1929 (and revised in 1984) were being informally smudged by what we could call a 'growth coalition' between Vatican, city council and Italian state. Third, some critics attacked the irresponsibility of inflicting a huge human event on the fragile streets and ruins of Rome. Local and national media were full of foreboding in the months running up to the event, with the anti-clerical news weekly *L'Espresso* proclaiming that Rome was 'Kaputt Mundi', a pun on the Church's Renaissance claim that Rome was '*Caput Mundi*', 'capital of the world'. The huge impact of tourist and pilgrim coaches on the crowded streets, the pressure on accomodation, and the general disruption to daily life in the city caused significant local discontent.

The Jubilee also raised another important issue: the ability of the Vatican to govern the conduct of individuals, whether practising Catholics or not. A fundamental tenet of the post-Vatican II return to conservative theology has been a very restrictive biblical interpretation on homosexuality, derived from the sacredness attached to sex as procreation. The clearest statement of the Church's renewed viewpoint came in Cardinal Ratzinger's 1986 'Letter to the Bishops of the Catholic Church on the Pastoral Care of Homosexual Persons':

> Although the particular inclination of the homosexual person is not a sin, it is a more or less strong tendency ordered toward an intrinsic moral evil; and thus the inclination itself must be seen as an objective disorder. Therefore special concern and pastoral attention should be directed toward those who have this condition, lest they be led to believe that the living out of this orientation in homosexual activity is a morally acceptable option. It is not. (In Fox 1995: 148–9)

In 2000, the Mario Mieli pressure group organized a global 'Gay Pride' demonstration in Rome. Cardinal Sodano of the Vatican noted that 'the government knows that Rome is a sacred city, a unique city due to the presence of the Pope' (29 January). The social democrat government leader Amato noted that a march was 'inopportune in the Holy Year'. Silvio Berlusconi, as leader of the (then) opposition right-wing alliance deemed the event 'mistaken both for the timing and backdrop chosen'. Finally, on the day after the march, came the strongest voice of all – from the Pope himself. 'In the name of the Church of Rome I cannot fail to express sorrow for the affront caused to the Great Jubilee of the year 2000 and for the offence against Christian values of a City that is so dear to the hearts of all the Catholics of the world' (in La Rocca 2000: 2). Re-emphasizing the substance of the Ratzinger statement above, his intervention restated the deeply held attachment to Rome's sacred status felt by the Pope. With estimates that 200,000 had marched (though some sources put this closer to 70,000) the event was generally hailed as a success by the gay community (partly welcoming the hostility of the Vatican and right).

Perhaps hostility to the march was greater because it disrupted the Vatican's own choreography of the city during the Jubilee, where St Peter's and other holy sites acted as a magnet for huge numbers of pilgrims. Indeed, the number of visitors became so huge that at certain times of the year extra sites in Rome had to be found, such as the staging of the mammoth youth Jubilee on the city's periphery in August 2000. As such, Roman space became strongly contested, with issues of marching permits, media coverage and the varying political discourses that surrounded both events, representative of the sensitive nature of 'sacred' Rome.

THE BIBLE AND THE GLOBAL SOUTH

Globalizing processes have produced a variable geography of religious experience, where, for example, the exponential growth of Catholicism in Africa has seen the incorporation of non-Christian rituals and cults into Christian worship, leading to the challenge of 'inculturation'. Here too, the challenge of the 'ecclesiocentric and Christocentric conditions for salvation had erected barriers that separated Christians from other religions' (Chidester 2000: 597). The theological challenge posed by inter-faith dialogue and an apparent increase in inter-religious (and even inter-Christian, such as in Yugoslavia and Ireland) intolerance and warfare remains central to the Vatican's concerns.

The key device which underpins Christianity as a globally communicated phenomenon is, of course, the Bible. And yet it is mistaken to see this as a singular object. As Visser explains:

> The Bible is not a history book. It has history in it, certainly, but it contains all sorts of other literary genres too: poetry, myths, stories, prophecies, canons of law, commentaries, ethical pleading. The word 'Bible' is, in fact, a plural noun (Greek *ta biblia*, 'the books'), and that is what the Bible is – many books, many historical periods, many points of view. (2001: 35)

How the Bible has travelled, and continues to travel, and how it is read, spoken about, and interpreted remain a vital social practice. Jenkins (2006) provides a fascinating account of how the Bible is read in the global South, in a way that transposes contemporary urban life with the pre-modern settings of the scriptures:

(Continued)

CASE STUDY

(Continued)

> Read Ruth, for instance, and imagine what it has to say in a hungry society threatened by war and social disruption. Understand the exultant release that awaits a reader in a society weighed down by ideas of ancestral curses, a reader who discovers the liberating texts about individual responsibility in the book of Ezekiel ... Or again, read Revelation with the eyes of rural believers in a rapidly modernizing society, trying to comprehend the inchoate brutality of the megalopolis. (Jenkins 2006: 187)

This is a crucial issue, because as Jenkins later argued in *The Next Christendom: the Coming of Global Christianity*, the demographic changes occurring in Africa, Asia and Latin America mean that the established geographical dominance of the 'old' imperial Catholicism is rapidly diluting: 'If we imagine a typical Christian back in 1900, we might think of a German or an American; in 2050, we should rather turn to a Ugandan, a Brazilian, or a Filipino' (2011: xi). Gone are the days of missionary diffusion of theology, fanning out from the religious centres of the North, and instead the key decision-making body of the Vatican, the College of Cardinals, is increasingly populated by cardinals from archdioceses from the global South. In 1939, 55 per cent of Cardinals were Italian; by 2015, the Archbishops of Cologne, New York and Florence had been joined by those from Abuja, Manila and Buenos Aires, to name but a few.

In many ways, this is a reflection of the grassroots organization of spaces of worship that look nothing like what we might think of when we hear of 'church' or 'mosque', and which in turn are driving very important urban changes. Consider contemporary Nigeria, a site of intense application of Christian and Islamic practices as a central part of urbanization. As Ukah (2014: 179) describes, 'Pentecostal Christianity, and to a lesser extent Pentecostal Islam, is precipitating large-scale urban renewal in and around Lagos in the form of the construction of prayer camps and religiously-owned real estate.' Ukah goes on to describe how the Redeemed Christian Church of God, founded in 1952, has shifted from a 'temporary site of prayer to a permanent living, working, and production site ... With a population of between 7000 and 10000 persons – with an additional 4000 university students and staff – "Redemption City" is no longer simply a ritual site; it represents a formidable strategy of spatial and territorial domination and resource capture' (p. 179). Under the leadership of Enoch Adejare Adeboye, this church, sited on the largest private estate in Nigeria, has become a major element of territoriality in Lagos, and is 'arguably the largest physical environment dedicated to the production, circulation and consumption of religion in Africa' (p. 180). Interestingly, Ukah suggests that there is a connection between this transformation and the wider processes of neo-liberal economic reform at the national level in Nigeria.

FIGURE 1.3 The Popemobile: replacing the chair that they were once carried on, Popes have favoured this converted car as a means of travelling rapidly through urban space while waving to huge crowds.

Source: miqu77 / Shutterstock.com

★★★★

The aim of this chapter was to consider some of the links between urban theory and the globalization of religion as a set of organized practices with a central point of power. Rome itself might be seen as 'microcosmic', which has a double meaning: literally, it refers to the Vatican's understanding of its own location within space, which is understood as both worldly (temporal), universal, and extratemporal or spiritual. And so there has long been a profound centralizing process which has used Rome as political technology to hold together – and enact – Catholicism as a global movement. It is important to emphasize that this has been a tense process: there has been an expression of regional and local forms of Catholic worship and identity – often referred to as 'relativist' by the conservative Popes – that seek to provide a theologically driven way of living. One of the most important of these, the Latin American liberation theology which was bound up with an anti-imperialism, was firmly closed down by John Paul II. And space precludes an extended discussion of how Catholic communities in cities around the world have very different views of birth control, bodies and ways of living a religious life. So the analysis of Rome as a religious global city raises several ontological challenges.

First, the chapter has attempted to sketch out a basic spatial ontology for the understanding of contemporary Roman Catholicism. It has stressed that the Church itself has embraced materiality, signification and relational sociality as its theological basis. It has operated with an apparently pure form of global–local organization, with little interest in national politics (with some important exceptions). It has an explicit praxis regarding the co-existence of the local (the parish-based forms of community) with the global (the papacy, its lineage, and the Vatican and its manufacture of theology and its artefacts). This structure creaks all the time, and the reluctance of two recent Popes to intervene in, for example, child-abuse cases has been a very significant, though sadly predictable, fault-line within its governance. As such, globalization has emerged as a major challenge for contemporary Catholic theology, and has been used as a pejorative catch-all term for many of the threats to the orthodox theology coming from the Vatican under John Paul II and Benedict XVI. Yet it might be more accurate to see it as an early 'universalizer', given that the focus of its message was otherworldly, cosmological, in much the same way that Mecca emerged as a site of otherworldly performance. The aim of the papacy – if not the Church broadly understood – is to enact its theological praxis of underpinning the centrality of the Pope and Rome as the centre of Roman Catholicism. This is a political project, and this is why the varying proclamations of John Paul II and the current Pope Francis have been at odds with their intercessor, Benedict XVI, who was arguably in favour of a smaller, more coherent Church.

Second, the Church has always been a key agent in developing the materiality of globalization. With its early modern construction of pilgrimage routes, veneration of saints' relics, sites of apparition and so on, the Church has facetiously been referred to as the world's first travel agent. The construction of cathedrals, including the use of stained-glass windows as a means of communicating the Bible to an illiterate congregation, became an important element of early mobilities of skilled architects and stonemasons. Furthermore, Rome's ability to 'command and control' its network of dioceses and parishes is in no small part due to its vast global real-estate portfolio. The use of emissaries to visit dioceses in order to summon or admonish errant clergy was an important, embodied exercise of centralized power, long after the end of the Pope's so-called 'temporal' powers to enforce militarily its will. It has been noted by McBrien (1997) that Catholic theology is based upon three key elements: sacramentality, signification and communion. It is interesting that these connect with recent relational and material theories of sociality within social science. Sacramentality – that the Church exists through bread and wine, for example, through transubstantiation – is as devoted a position regarding the importance of materiality as one can surely have. Both signification (that Catholicism involves a mediated encounter with God, delivered through many communicative devices and through a small number of delegated apostolic ministers), and communion (that the Catholic Church is at root a relational, social religion) provide clear demonstrations of how a global institution gathers power through an aggregate of tiny, everyday practices.

Third, there is the issue of territoriality and sovereignty. The territorial base of the Vatican has been of great importance to the Catholic Church: relegated to a tiny patch of land within Rome, the Vatican's mode of operation has always been a heuristic of the ontological questions surrounding national territorial sovereignty, raising questions such as do nation-states need armies? Do they have autonomous economies? What are their legal obligations over their citizens? It has been argued that, indeed, contemporary sovereignty is now unbundled (were it ever coherent) into a neo-medieval patchwork of overlapping jurisdictions and powers (Anderson 1996). The decisions that affect everyday life are only partially determined by elected national governments. In the same way, developments in digital media have threatened to undermine the Vatican's brief period of comfort with modern technology that came with John Paul II's televisual mastery. An important element of this is social networking, and the growth of so-called 'cyberparishes', web chatrooms where 'Catholics find the things parishes have traditionally offered in virtual form – a sense of community, good preaching, inspired music, opportunities for charitable service and social justice advocacy, faith formation, Bible study, and all the other forms of ministry associated with parish life' (Allen 2009: 295). The Vatican, unsurprisingly, remains rather more attached to Web 1.0 than its subsequent variants.

To conclude, we might ask how the Church as network holds shape as it moves. This is important, because a common-sense ontology of Roman Catholicism would have it not moving, given the fixity of its huge cathedrals, the largely unchanged material nature of its Bibles and liturgies, and the sheer age and fragility of its artefacts. The papacy is the longest continuous office of any type in the world, cunningly parlaying pre-Christian Roman geographies: 'all roads lead to Rome' as we know from the Milliarium Aureum, the monument in the Forum of Ancient Rome from which all distances to the various cities of the Roman Empire were measured. During the centuries of European imperialism, it set out the civilizing way as it saw it. We might ask how the Church is mapped. Certainly it has its own territorial geographies – somewhere in the Vatican there will be Euclidean maps of parishes, dioceses and so on. And we might consider how the mythic, essentialized nature of sacred Rome mobilizes hundreds of thousands of visitors and pilgrims; this aspect is in turn relational in that it ties Rome into networks of faith communities in all parts of the world. Actor-network theorists would point to its many agents acting for it at a distance, and the role of the Vatican as an 'obligatory point of passage' in the orchestration of its network.

FLAT CITIES

ACTOR-NETWORKS AND POLITICAL ECONOMIES

> At first it seemed simple: to encompass all of Paris in a gaze we simply needed to be high up, to stand back. But where should the camera lens be put? At the top of the tower of Montparnasse? No, the view would be too squashed. At the top of Montmartre – which would have the advantage of not seeing the hideous Sacré-Coeur? Yes, but the partial view would be too oblique. At the bottom of the catacombs? We'd see only a narrow corridor, partially lit. From the blind eye of a satellite camera? We'd get only one view. From the prime minister's window, at Matignon? We'd simply see a well-tended garden and not France, even though he governs it. From the balcony of the Mairie de Paris, at the Hôtel de Ville? An empty and cold square, cluttered with ugly fountains; nothing that gives life to this metropolis. Does that mean that Paris is invisible? 'Move on, there's nothing to see.' Well yes, let's do just that, let's move and then, suddenly, Paris will begin to be visible. (Latour and Hermant 2006: 28–9)

This chapter is about the social scientific framing of cities – how they can be 'seen', ordered and categorized. After the discussion of Rome, it shifts the focus to another city that has been central to urban thought for a long time: Paris. More specifically, it looks at a very unusual book produced by the sociologist Bruno Latour and his photographic collaborator Emilie Hermant, called *Paris, Ville Invisible* [Paris, Invisible City], published in French in 1998 and with an English translation in 2006. Latour was a central figure in the formation of actor-network theory (ANT), a body of theory developed by other key thinkers such as Michel Callon, John Law and Anne-Marie Mol to produce a reading of society that doesn't privilege human agency or reify structures and institutions. His key works such as *Laboratory Life* (Latour and Woolgar 1986), *Science in Action* (1987) and *Reassembling the Social* (2005) set out a radical view of how scholarly work often fetishizes things like 'the city' or even 'Society' itself.

And as the quotation above shows, Latour takes issue with many of the things that are taken for granted in urban theory. As Farías (2010b: 1) argues, introducing a set of papers that apply ANT to urban theory in various ways, the shift towards 'relational, symmetrical, and even flat perspectives' on cities provides the first 'significant theoretical quantum leap in urban studies' since the arrival of the structural Marxist accounts of the 1970s associated most closely with Manuel Castells and scholars such as Doreen Massey and David Harvey. This latter stream of thought, often referred to as urban political economy, has been remarkably influential and stolid, girded by a political reaction to the neo-liberal policies that have influenced city government in a widespread way since the 1990s. It has also been seen as reductionist, placing too strong an emphasis on the undifferentiated power of the state, or the unitary operations of social classes, to accurately capture the nuance of urban life.

The relevance of ANT to urban theory has been given extensive discussion, from Richard Smith's early overview (2003a), to Graham and Marvin's *Splintering Urbanism* (2001), to the aforementioned set of essays in *Urban Assemblages* (Farías and Bender 2010). Oddly enough, *Paris, Invisible City* as a book has rarely been given an extended scholarly treatment, perhaps due to its unorthodox and uncompromising narrative style. But it contains many important insights that uses ANT to frame some of the practice-based forces that shape contemporary global cities, such as the concept of 'centres of calculation' (Latour 1987). In an otherwise sceptical essay, Madden has made the following perceptive observation:

> Arguably, ANT's encounter with urban studies is not a new introduction so much as a reunion. ANT's attention to the interrelationships between humans and nonhumans, its attraction to the mechanic and the technical; its curiosity about what happens behind the closed door or the laboratory or the trading floor; its focus on infrastructure, linkage and decay – in a variety of ways, ANT could be considered a twin, or even a mutant outgrowth, of urban studies itself. (2010: 584)

And so, we might consider how urban scholarship often combines accounts of nature, technology and economy to a networked reading of place. At one point, Latour refers to Cronon's study of Chicago, *Nature's Metropolis*, as being a 'masterpiece of ANT because no hidden social force is added to explain the progressive composition of the metropolis itself' (2005: 11).

The chapter begins, however, by describing how *Paris, Ville Invisible* works as an experimental travelogue of sorts that breaks apart and then recomposes Paris in a variety of ways. It then briefly compares this to the spatial economies of the Marxist geographer David Harvey, many of whose key theoretical works are also focused on Paris. Latour and Harvey clearly share a great deal of enthusiasm for Paris, but they use it in strikingly different ways, and this difference can reveal much about the process of 'narrating' a convincing urban theory. The chapter then moves through the core idea of ANT, the significance of 'flat ontologies' of society (and cities) to

Latour's wider project and the importance of key terms such as 'figuration' and 'actant'. It considers the problem of conceptualizing the city in ontological terms, and traces how Latour sees the role of objects in holding together, or composing, the thing we know as Paris, hooking together human and non-human agents into the project of constructing the city.

A PARIS JOURNEY; OR, THE PROBLEM OF THE 'ZOOM'

> They [the panoramas] are all over the place; they are being painted every time a newspaper editorialist reviews with authority the 'whole situation', when a book retells the origins of the world from the Big Bang to President Bush; when a social theory textbook provides a bird's eye view of modernity; when the CEO of some big company gathers his shareholders; when some famous scientist summarizes for the benefit of the public 'the present state of science'; when a militant explains to her cellmates the 'long history of exploitation'; when some powerful architecture – a piazza, a skyscraper, a huge staircase – fills you with awe … What is so powerful in these contraptions is that they nicely solve the question of staging the totality, of ordering the ups and downs, of nesting 'micro', 'meso', and 'macro' into one another. But they don't do it by multiplying two-way connections with other sites – as command and control rooms, centers of calculation and, more generally, oligoptica do. They design a picture which has no gap in it, giving the spectator the powerful impression of complete control over what is being surveyed, even though they are partially blind and that nothing enters or leaves their walls except interested or baffled spectators. (Latour 2005: 187–8)

The original French version of *Paris, Ville Invisible* uses collage on its over-sized pages to try to convey the tension between text and word power (which is really the core device that Latour uses) and that of graphical and photographic representation. The photos here, blown up so their pixels are dramatically large, are of mundane places: a small office, for example, or bollards. Newspaper cuttings and headings are 'pasted' onto the authorial text. Press clippings are superimposed on photographs, with Latour's text squeezed and woven in and out of the pages. For many non-French speakers, the first contact with the book is via the rather prosaic free English translation available on the web as a PDF. This is quite an interesting issue in itself: it says in a box at the start, in red, that 'the text is not understandable without the pictures' (Latour and Hermant 2006: 1). I don't think this is strictly true, but it certainly helps to get a sense of the book's unusual presentational strategy, and its rationale. As Conley has observed, it is central to Latour's application of ANT, and so we might also see *Paris, Ville Invisible* (which also has a website) as a way of 'routing' knowledge:

The visible does not reside either in one image alone or in something outside of that image. In the second world in which we live the image exists only as a montage and in a … routing, a traversal of sorts, less through nature – as in the first world – than along an ever-bifurcating pathway through different photographic angles. Images give form and introduce relations. Phenomena as such do not appear in the image. They too become visible only through what is being transformed, transported and deformed from one image to the next. Images are linked by a trace that enables humans to come and go, to circulate along a path both laterally and transversally. In order to see and to make a reference, we must follow the movement or perceptions of this trace through all the gaps and hiatuses of its transformation. (2012: 116)

The book begins: 'Paris, the City of Light, so open to the gaze of artists and tourists, so often photographed, the subject of so many glossy books, that we tend to forget the problems of thousands of engineers, technicians, civil servants, inhabitants and shopkeepers in making it visible' (Latour and Hermant 2006: 1). The material form of Latour and Hernant's book is thus something of a performance of ANT, the photographs offering traces of networks.

The architecture of the book follows a set of four 'sequences' which, broadly speaking, correspond to an ANT method: first, the problem of *visualizing* Paris;

FIGURE 2.1   The practice of the panorama: Bruno Latour sees technologies such as this telescope on the Eiffel Tower as one way to try to capture the 'totality' of the city.

Source: Hadrian / Shutterstock.com

second, as an attempt to engage with its *size and shape*; third, to understand how it is *distributed* as a network of actants; and, fourth, to provide a sense of the challenge of *recomposition*. Each of these terms is used by Latour to indicate a specific mode of theoretical city-making.

It is necessary to run quickly over the sites visited in the book that construct, or rather sequence, their account, though it is a lot more fun to take the time to read it oneself. The first sequence, that of visualization, deals with the problem of finding a convincing, authoritative viewing point with which to capture a city as a total-ity. For Latour, this is an impossibility, and he is scathing about social scientists who think they can do so. So much of this sequence is about looking for the kind of places that *deign* to capture totalities. They begin at the famous nineteenth-century Samaritaine department store, where one can access a rooftop 'panorama' – an area set aside with display plates showing an annotated set of markers pointing out key buildings on the skyline. This is an apparently suitable vantage point to try to make claims about envisioning the 'whole' city, the cityscape, but one which for Latour is immediately impossible to sustain. The narrative quickly shifts onto the city's left bank and on to a small office in the École des Mines, occupied by a Mrs Baysal, who is responsible for planning the room timetabling of the school's classes. Here, the university's lecture halls are meticulously set out on a set of spreadsheets or diagrams: Mrs Baysal can't see them as physical spaces, but through her files she has total obser-vance of them from her office. Next, Latour and Hermant follow a Mrs Lagoutte, a tourist in the city, as she is guided by the blue plaques of street names that sit on the walls: 'Without the establishment of these relays, these affordances or props, Mrs. Lagoutte would never be able to use the street guide (that she can carry in her bag and hold in her hand) to help her find her way in the real Paris' (p. 12). They then pay a visit to the office of the STDF, the Ordinance Survey department, the land surveyors, key figures in the establishment of governable territory, processing, filing and making available to other organs of the state the means necessary to value, tax, measure and monitor the land uses of the country and city. This is the agency, and building, that produces the tiny identity cards that sit in the pocket or purse of every French resident, a key motif in the social definition of the individual, an object that mediates between the state's knowledge of its inhabitants, and one that other state agents – traffic cops, perhaps – can oblige the carrier to show. And then there is the first glimpse of the urban economy: a trip to the famous Left Bank Café de Flor (p. 18), with its theatrically gruff waiters who observe the occupied tables, dispensing coffees and receipts, an action they do hundreds of times a day, almost semi-automat-ically, in a process that can be aggregated out in transaction upon transaction taking place across the city.

Before long, we are steered to a famous Latourian stamping ground, the scientific laboratory, the site of the accretion of formal knowledge, the building that houses experimental practices of the scientific journal paper. Then SOFRES, the survey or opinion polling organization (which solicits the 'views' of the populace on certain matters), and the exhibition space of the Natural History Museum with its ranks of stuffed animals (which formally 'displays' what 'society' knows about 'nature'). Latour and Hermant are picking up pace now and are quickly into the offices of the Parisian water department, with its charts and valves and oversight of the whole system of pipes that keep Paris with a steady supply of water: 'Open Les Lilas! Close St Cloud! Block Austerlitz! Careful at Montmartre!' (p. 27). They come to the end of the first sequence, with a question that should startle all those who are looking for a stable definition of the city, the quotation that opened this chapter: there isn't one. There is no one place that the whole city can be viewed, and there is no way of stopping the city long enough to make it observable. And so, an exhortation to urban theorists: 'let's move and then, suddenly, Paris will begin to become visible' (p. 29).

Urban theorists make use of a range of visual practices, and modes of attentiveness, to make sense of the city (Crary 2001; McNeill 2015a). The first practice that Latour and Hermant utilize here is that of synopsis, an approach used in fields as diverse as meteorology (to describe and aggregate the multiple data points gathered from weather stations to form a simplified, single standpoint), and literary studies (to reduce the multiple key points of a play into a single, brief summary). And Latour sees that as an important metaphor to think about how the social is described: his goal is to argue that the social theorist's all-seeing, panoptic mode of describing the city is always a fiction. This is especially important in accounts that try to move between an overarching view and a grounded, ethnographic perspective:

> All too often social theory still inhabits this utopian world where the zoom is possible. It really believes that we can slide from biggest to smallest, and then wonders how the microscopic – face-to-face interaction – manages to remain meaningful despite the crushing weight of the macroscopic. (Latour and Hermant 2006: 59)

And so as *Paris, Ville Invisible* develops, it becomes strikingly clear that Latour and Hermant's journey is about providing a synopsis of the ontological 'flatlands' of Paris. They are seeking out as many apparently powerful *observational* sites as possible, and make the journey there to meet, observe and note the humans and objects that together fuse to create the city as we think we know it.

It would be quicker, cheaper and analytically more satisfying to make general statements about how 'government controls traffic', but the point is that we don't really know this, we only assume it. However, there are power relations in visual practices, and as a replacement, Latour is happy to refer to the 'oligoptic' construction of the urban. For example, they find themselves in the 'control' room of the Parisian traffic police, standing before multiple screens that stream images from various points on the city's ring-road to the controller, a Mr Henry, who quite literally can see the 'whole' of Paris in diagram, but only a sliver of it, only the roads, not the water system, only aggregated data points of clumps of cars and trucks, not the individual. Latour's point here is to show that actor-network theory is not about eliminating such obvious 'god-like' viewing stations, but rather to insert agency into the visual practice of providing a virtual god-like viewpoint: Mr Henry, whose gaze flicks from screen to screen and interprets what he sees into commands, is described as 'the missing figure of the panopticon' (p. 51), but only with tongue in cheek. On the contrary, as Latour argues in *Reassembing the Social*, such individuals:

> have been given enough space to deploy their own contradictory gerunds: scaling, zooming, embedding, 'panoraming', individualizing, and so on. The metaphor of a flatland was simply a way for the ANT observers to clearly distinguish their job from the labor of those they follow around. (2005: 220)

His point here is that at some point, social (and for us, urban) theorists have to recognize in any explanations of social relations the need to provide some degree of individual intention to prove causation, and how this turns into a composed aggregate:

> You don't have to imagine a 'wholesale' human having intentionality, making rational calculations, feeling responsible for his sins, or agonizing over his mortal soul. Rather, you realize that to obtain 'complete' human actors, you have to *compose* them out of many successive layers, each of which is empirically distinct from the next. (Latour 2005: 207, italics in original)

His concluding point here is this: 'subjectivity is not a property of human souls but of the gathering itself' (p. 218).

So what is the connection with global cities and urban theory? In *Reassembling the Social*, Latour (2005) provides a more abstract discussion of why sociologists should 'localize the global'. By this he means that 'we have to lay continuous connections leading from one local interaction to the other places, times and agencies through which a local site is *made to do* something' (p. 173, italics in original). He demands that big and small places have a defined, evidenced trace, and that by doing so their respective sizes are – in the process – levelled. As he says, 'No place can be said to be bigger than any other place, but some can be said to benefit from far safer connections with many more places than others' (p. 176). It is interesting that Latour has developed this approach from his study of scientific laboratories, because he has something of an obsession with the offices of professional knowledge brokers, which he refers to as 'centers of calculation'. He offers a 'Wall Street trading room' or 'Bill Gates' as exemplars of how to apply oligopticon and panorama in social theory. Both refer to modes of vision and knowing, which is important. The former is important because of its quality: 'From oligoptica, sturdy but extremely narrow views of the (connected) whole are made possible – as long as connections hold' (p. 181). The latter he uses to gather together those moments when someone tries to make sense of 'the whole situation' or the 'Big Picture', things that 'nicely solve the question of staging the totality' (p. 188), whether it be a textbook, a scientist summarizing the field of science for a lay audience, or a CEO addressing a shareholder meeting. Latour's point here goes to the heart of social theory, and the methodological implications this has. The problem for the urban theorist, then, is that of reconciling how their practice is significantly influenced by the ability to secure an observational site from which to view their world. It demands a reflexive interest in the material devices and practices that enhance and enact the visualization of cities.

HOW BIG IS THE CITY?

In the second sequence, Latour and Hermant (2006) continue to glide on through Paris with the aim of working out a few things about its *size and shape*. This is not done without a warning: 'No path leads to either the global context or local inter-action; our social theory metro line stops at neither the "Society" or "Individual" station' (p. 32). And so instead, they try to find the institutions of the city that are charged with the task of understanding really big things. They go to an astrophysics research institute that charts 'unquestionably the "biggest" of all objects' (p. 33): the universe, which we see only through the sky. And 'the sky – galaxies, pulsars, dwarf stars, stars, planets – has to circulate somewhere in Paris, like water, gas, electricity, the telephone, rumours and surveys' (p. 34). But how big is this, they ask: a space of infinite largeness, or something just as big as the institute's 'catalogue of celestial objects ... no bigger than a quadrilateral as wide as two A4 sheets, twelve inches thick' (pp. 35–6)? Our knowledge of the universe, then, is always something that is constructed through such grounded and mundane scientific practices, recently given extra dynamism by the arrival of software and a greater profundity in sifting through the astrophysicists' data points:

> The notion of a circulating referent introduced above enables us to negotiate this gap fairly intelligently. The sky is simultaneously over there, over here, and in our minds. There's no reason to doubt its entire reality, nor to believe that that reality would be any more whole if in one vertiginous bound we could leap into sidereal space. Yet we're not shut up in that office of the Observatory, prisoners for life behind sheets of pixels, dreaming of possible freedom that direct contact with the galaxies would finally guarantee us. No, at the click of a mouse, through a series of links, we're connected to a galaxy that is thus rendered visible and accessible. (Latour and Hermant 2006: 36)

This allows a link to be made with another very big thing, something we know as 'the economy': 'hardly smaller than the sky ... Everything is claimed to be within it' (p. 37). In particular, there is an interest in the formation of markets and prices, something which is often famously seen in neo-classical economics as having a mysterious agency, the 'invisible hand'.

Yet how, Latour wonders, can the Parisian urban economy avoid being fitted neatly within the 'scalar' mindset of how economies are typically understood, as a meshing of the global and the local economy, for example:

> We are said to zoom gradually from the macroeconomic to the microeco-
> nomic, from the unquestionable laws of the international market to the
> microeconomic transactions in which I force myself on Tuesday mornings
> to rationally calculate the price of the apricots I want to buy at the Maubert
> market. (Latour and Hermant 2006: 37)

It is this unwillingness to 'zoom' that characterizes the ANT take on the economy,
with its consideration of how markets are formed and reified (Barnes 2008). This is
a point I return to in Chapters 5 and 6, which discuss the processes of 'actualization'
that underpin the formation of authoritative versions of the 'world'. Underpinning
this is an at times infuriating, though utterly logical, avoidance of claims of causality which begins to make sense quite quickly when one looks at what is sometimes
called the 'real world' that eludes the academic's slick account.

Latour next approaches what are often called the institutions of government, but
probably more accurately the institutions of representative democracy. His concern
is to establish the chain of objects and practices that provide an interface between
the individual and the aggregation that we variously call the government and the
state. He does this with brief acknowledgements of the buildings of city hall, and the
mayor's office, but then spends much more time on the technologies of elections,
such as the polling booth and the voting slip. He captures the work of 'representation'
which has become formalized as electoral process through a captivating vignette,
where he wraps together his chosen individual voter, Alice, with the Mayor of Paris,
Jean Tiberi, whose re-election she is being asked to vote on.

> Nothing binds these two characters, Alice and Mr. Tiberi, particularly strongly,
> except for the fact that they're both on the voters' roll of this neighbourhood
> and that Mr. Tiberi wants to be re-elected. We can't say, for all that, that Alice
> is 'small' and Mr. Tiberi 'big', just because one is a constituent and the other
> a candidate. Yet their respective size is precisely what is at issue: everybody is
> deciding on that today; we'll have the answer after 9 p.m. Developed over two
> centuries of violent change, reforms, adjustments, upheavals, not to mention
> a few revolutions and days of barricades, the entire electoral system must be
> apprehended as a single measuring tool: it concretely resolves the question of
> deciding who is big and who is small – obviously a partial measurement, but
> what measurement isn't? We now know, every panopticon is an oligopticon:
> it sees little but what it does see it sees well. (pp. 47–8)

And so the book describes how our individual Alice crams into a tiny little booth
to make her democratic choice, how the state makes sure no-one is influencing her
or what she is writing on a ballot paper through the deployment of a simple curtain,
before heading home to watch the aggregation of all the booth visits on charts and
diagrams in the election coverage on television. 'Seated on her couch, Alice now
knows what she did, this very morning' (p. 50).

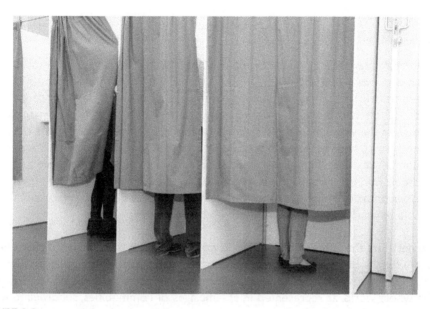

FIGURE 2.2 The voting booth: a simple technology which isolates the individual within the aggregate 'body politic'

Source: Stefano Ember / Shutterstock.com

In these first two sequences of the Paris travelogue, we see an important story emerging about how there are many central points where claims can be made about seeing Paris, or ordering it, or measuring it. This is preparatory work for one of the book's most important claims: that the social, and cities as a kind of extension of that, is constituted by networks whose strength can only be painstakingly assembled through the sorting of traces. This 'flat' ontology (as opposed to many sociological views of different types of 'structure' weighing down and squeezing the 'agency' of individuals) is then elaborated.

WORLD'S FAIRS

Cities have for a long time had places where the national state exhibits its knowledge of the world, an 'exhibitionary complex' located in the World Fair or Expo site. Every few years, the World Expo body reviews bids to host a fair – some are relatively low-key, such as Milan in 2015, but others are of major extent and import, such as that of Shanghai in 2011, which showcased Chinese modernity (Winter 2013). These temporary events do important nation-building, and world-making, work. As Tony Bennett points out:

(Continued)

(Continued)

> In their interrelations, then, the expositions and their fair zones constituted an order of things and of peoples which, reaching back into the depths of prehistoric time as well as encompassing all corners of the globe, rendered the whole world metonymically present, subordinated to the dominating gaze of the white, bourgeois, and (although this is another story) male eye of the metropolitan powers. But an eye of power which, through the development of the technology of vision associated with exposition towers and the positions for seeing these produced in relation to the miniature ideal cities of the expositions themselves, was democratized in being made available to all. (1988: 96)

Bennett lists the other interventions in creating a 'specular dominance over the city' – the use of camera obscura, or panorama. And these also attempted to firmly position the host city within a worldly frame of reference: 'the ambition to render the whole world, as represented in assemblages of commodities, subordinate to the controlling vision of the spectator was present in world exhibitions from the outset' (1988: 96–7). And so when we look at a World's Fair or Expo site, we see an attempt to 'figure' the world through professional practices of curation.

CENTRE OF CALCULATION

At this point, it is useful to pause the Parisian journey, to step back through Latour's biography revisiting one of his major academic interests: the organization of knowledge production in the scientific laboratory. His study of the Salk Institute in California, undertaken with Steve Woolgar, is often regarded as a classic text given its exposition of the 'real life' of the production of scientific knowledge (Latour and Woolgar 1986). In this work, centrality is a key concept, aligned with processes of calculation, where the detailed process of setting up experiments, observing and recording them, analysing and reporting the results has to become concentrated in the ordered, secure space of the laboratory. Jöns summarizes Latour's development of the concept as follows:

> scientific network-building is characterized by a systematic mobilization of human and nonhuman resources, or 'actants', in a few 'centres of calculation' that can afford the expensive 'proof race' of the sciences. His idea that such 'cycles of accumulation' are constitutive of 'centres of calculation' illustrates that knowledge practices displays a complex geography as it is both situated within particular locations and linked to other places through mostly circulatory movements. (2011: 159)

While this work took place in what we might call laboratories with a capital 'L', the process of knowledge production is also linked into the production of imperial knowledge centres (Driver and Gilbert 2003). Scientific disciplines such as archaeology and anthropology were central to this task. Drawing on the account of Bravo (1999), Jöns (2011) traces the origins of colonial geographical knowledge, which includes '"geographical gifts" (geographical knowledge bequeathed through navigation and local people) and "ethnographic navigation" (based on descriptions of people's physical appearance, language, manners, habits and religious ideas as well as on comparisons between differently labelled ethnic groups) which were crucial for generating new geographical knowledge and thus for settling cartographical disputes at home' (p. 160).

Underpinning this are three processes: mobilization of resources, stabilization of new knowledge claims and the extension of knowledge networks. The non-human resources mobilized by scientists must have three properties: 'first, they have to be *mobile* in order to be transported to a "centre of calculation"; second, they have to be *stable* – at least to some extent – in order to be presented and processed in an unchanged way; and third, they have to be *combinable* in order to be aggregated, transformed and connected to other resources in the process of knowledge production' (Jöns 2011: 159, drawing from Latour 1987: 223). The stabilization phase occurs as

> the accumulated resources are systemized, classified, transformed, tied together and re-presented in order to build a strong web of association that makes up a new knowledge claim … Based on comparisons and combinations, reductions, transformations and abstractions, the aim of the work… is to create efficient inscriptions in the form of maps, diagrams, tables, texts and equations that represent comprehensible and well-communicable knowledge claims about much more complex phenomena. (Jöns 2011: 160)

The extension phase occurs when a new scientific argument

> has to prove itself outside its local context of construction in order to become a widely acknowledged fact … Their dissemination relies on the opportunity for and interest of other people to integrate them into their work. The validation, dissemination and preservation of academic knowledge all depend on the actions of other people in other contexts than the formative centre(s) of calculation. (Jöns 2011: 162)

There is an important geographical issue relating to fragility here:

> Widely praised qualities of scientific knowledge such as its presumed universality and the predictability of events depend on the ability to transform places of knowledge consumption in such a way that remaining differences to the context of construction have no significant impact on the

existence of scientific facts and artefacts in these other places. However, as place-specificity makes it impossible to construct the *same* spatial context elsewhere, the application of scientific and technical knowledge is characterised by many complications through missing, failing, or intruding human and nonhuman actants. (Jöns 2011: 162, italics in original)

At this stage, the centre of calculation is being referred to in a rather narrow laboratory context. But it has more general applicability to the understanding of the practices that constitute global cities. The strength of the various stages of mobilization, stabilization and extension is negotiated through a complex network of office-based decision-makers, often housed either in close bodily proximity, or else close infrastructural proximity. I explore these 'office geographies' further in Chapter 5. But for now, it is important to return to how Latour views the congelation of cities, which is sometimes referred to in a rather unreflective way as 'the urban fabric'.

THE OBJECTS THAT HOLD PARIS TOGETHER

The third sequence of *Paris, Ville Invisible*, 'distributing', turns around the nature of what holds Paris together: 'It's to objects that we must now turn if we want to understand what, day after day, keeps life in the big city together: objects despised under the label "urban setting", yet whose exquisite urbanity holds the key to our life in common' (Latour and Hermant 2006: 63). The starting point for our travellers is the inventory of street furniture that represents the municipal state's own bit of Paris, its 400 public toilets to its 9000 benches (p. 64): they pose the problem of crossing the Boulevard Saint-Michel and the bollards and traffic lights that act to 'materialize the municipality's advice' (p. 66). They enter the metro: once the train moves 'I become an average weight that has been the subject of many tests in which I was pitilessly replaced by heavy cast iron dummies' (p. 69). Then pigeons, and ways to control their population; the construction of a parking garage in a historic square; the way in which the *Périphérique* is governed (p. 79); time and measurement of it via wristwatch or clock (pp. 80–1) and weight; safety compliance (p. 83) and standards (p. 84). And so we get an indication of the heft of the objects that inhabit Paris, a visible but ignored population:

> Should we count all those gadgets among the inhabitants of Paris? Partly, because they anticipate all the behaviours of generic and anonymous inhabitants whom they get to do a number of actions, in anticipation. Each of these humble objects, from public toilet to rubbish bin, tree protector to street name, phone booth to illuminated signpost, has a certain idea of the Parisians to whom, through colour or form, habit or force, it brings a particular order, a distinct attribution, an authorization or prohibition, a promise or permission. (p. 64)

Objects also serve to orient narratives about the city. In Paris, as in most cities, there is some alarm when pollution from car exhausts 'peaks'. But:

> Where is this famous peak? In my newspaper. But where does the information come from? The whole of Paris? No, precisely, not 'the whole' of Paris, only certain areas of Paris whose representativeness is a subject of controversy with the ecologists – sensors take samples and transform them, add them up, unite them and return them to the prefecture. (pp. 85–6)

So, an important point about these objects is not their proliferation or even their autonomy: it is the way in which they allow 'alignment' to take place, a sorting of bodies, objects and technologies, as Amin and Thrift help to elaborate:

> In the city, these objects are aligned and made to count through all manner of intermediaries such as rhythms of delivery or commuting, traffic flow systems, integrated transport and logistics systems, internet protocols, rituals of civic and public conduct, family routines, and cultures of workplace or neighbourhood. (2007: 153)

In turn, this should change the way we view the city. Most established sociologies of urban life focused on how individuals interacted with one another in a way that could broadly be described as 'intersubjective', where the apparently autonomous thinking individual has to alter their behaviour in their regular encounters with others, whether friendly, neutral or hostile. And yet, as Latour puts it, intersubjectivity 'isn't appropriate for describing this heterogeneous crowd with such different

FIGURE 2.3 A public toilet in Paris: one of a number of pieces of urban equipment that 'pulls the city together'

Source: Ken Felepchuk / Shutterstock.com

temporalities, such multiple pressures. What about "interobjectivity"?' (Latour and Hermant 2006: 71). In other words, spaces need to be opened for theorizing how social action is driven by practices influenced (though not determined) by traffic jams, sugar intake, turning keys, voting, reading and misreading things, hearing and mishearing things, and money.

It is challenging to capture this, which brings Latour to 'scripting': this is the way in which discourse about Paris works. Again, we are made aware of how easy it is to cut corners and develop a shorthand way of neatly bounding the social: 'being able to reconstruct the shape of Society in the generous roundness of a pumpkin' (p. 87). Even the Eiffel Tower is involved in this, condensing signifiers of modernity, technology, height, the material power of metal structures, the indexical marker; so are the partial totalizations of monuments and plaques, and the words that individuals use to make sense of the totality: 'when, leaning on a bar counter, we make definitive statements to sum up the thread binding us together: "We're in a Republic after all!", "We little guys don't count"' and so on (p. 90).

SMALL PARIS: RECOMPOSITION

> To take it all in at once, to 'dominate it at a glance', to calculate the flows, Paris first has to become small. (Latour and Hermant 2006: 4)

> Armed with such pointers at street level, we can picture the totality from on high and learn to situate events and people within the labyrinthine and kaleidoscopic world of Parisian daily life. (Harvey 2003: 43)

At this point it might be useful to connect this discussion to another very different tradition of urban thinking, that of Marxian spatial political economy. David Harvey is a seminal figure in the construction of this important tradition of spatial theory. His book *Paris, Capital of Modernity* (2003) formed the culmination and consolidation of a long work on the economic geography of late nineteenth-century Paris, a period of political turmoil that had received lot of attention from historians. What Harvey did which was unusual was to examine it from within a spatial frame of analysis, showing how the production of space through capital investment was – crucially – implemented using state actors. Harvey was partly inspired by another key urban theorist, Henri Lefebvre. For now, it is important to think that Harvey and Lefebvre see in Paris, and city-making more generally, the structuring power of capital and state in the production of land markets and the built environment.

For Harvey the Paris of the Second Empire that featured in his work was to be a large canvas that explored even broader social and political relations. But as the two contrasting quotations above illustrate, these two versions – dramatizations – of the city have very different assumptions about what Paris actually is. For Latour, Paris is conceptualized not as the seethingly conflictual spatial formation romanticized by tourist and Marxist alike, but as a rather more mundane world of traffic control centres, mayoral bureaucracies and administrators' spreadsheets. As a social formation, this is an exotic tangle of ordering mechanisms. It is important to acknowledge that Harvey spent a fair amount of time working through the construction of everyday life, and how it was structured by rising rents and downward wage pressures. But this was as ballast for his accounts of revolutionary turmoil and class awareness. For Harvey, Paris is a formation that emerged from French colonial relations, and was a privileged site in the secondary circuit of capitalism. In other words, much of the profit that came from empire had to be reinvested to be valorized, and one of the places to do it was the city's built environment. This partly explains the city's over-endowment with sites of accumulated wealth, whether it be art galleries, museums or the Treasury. In his book *Metromarxism*, Andy Merrifield notes:

> Harvey's Parisian analysis argues that investment in the built environment obeyed a certain logic, having a distinctive pattern and knowable consistency. Periodic gales of 'creative destruction' in the urban fabric devalued capital tied down in space, destroyed its old use value, only to make way for fresh use values and new, increased exchange values. The physical landscape wavered between devaluation and revaluation, crisis and speculative binge, a ravaged built form and a new built form – and a renewed base for accumulation. (2002: 147)

This was an important insight for Harvey, and it provides a good template for under-standing how to analyse the production of space in cities in other times and places. Paris is a place where the state (occupied by forces of capital) has worked to reg-ulate the working class, ensuring that it is reproduced as a factor of production. Nonetheless, some of this work is prone to a reductionism and a 'big society' optic that is strikingly different from that of Latour.

Perhaps to counter this criticism, Harvey provided a close interpretive reading of one of the most iconic sites in Paris, the Basilica of the Sacré-Coeur, which he 'personally hates and want to demystify, ideologically' (Merrifield 2002: 147). This is an important essay in the context of his work (and incidentally also in relation to the study of religious spaces discussed in the previous chapter), in that he identified in the fabric of this huge basilica a portrait of the class contradictions of Parisian society at the time of its construction. Harvey reflected on his own self-consciously totalizing methodological and theoretical approach in *Paris, Capital of Modernity*, as follows:

> a work of synthesis, of the sort I am here attempting, must perforce con-struct its own rules of engagement. It cannot stop at the point of endless deconstruction of the discursive elaborations of others, but has to press on into the materiality of social processes even while acknowledging the power and significance of discourses and perceptions in shaping social life and historical-geographical inquiry. For this the methodology of historical-geographical materialism, which I have for several years been evolving … provides, I believe, a powerful means to understand the dynamics of urban change in a particular place and time. (2003: 19)

For Latour, this kind of reading is inevitably, by definition, a surface level interpretation. As he puts its, 'As soon as we follow the shifting representation of the social we find offices, corridors, instruments, files, rows, alignments, teams, vans, precautions, watchfulness, attention, warnings – not Society' (Latour and Hermant 2006: 17). The core message of *Paris, Ville Invisible* is that the city can be captured as a unity, recomposed. By contrast, Harvey saw the city very differently: 'The capitalist city is necessarily a fetish object … Material relations between people are everywhere in evidence, as are the innumerable ways in which social relations are embodied within things … To construe the city as a sentient being is to acknowledge its potential as a body politic' (2003: 55).

We recall how Latour was interested in Alice, voting about the Mayor, going home, watching from the vantage point of her sofa the aggregate effect of her act, and those of thousands of others, represented via graphs and counters on television. For Latour, this provides the basis for understanding scale. As he asks in *Reassembling the Social*:

> What is the relationship between 'small' Alice and 'France as a whole'? This *path*, laid down by *this* instrument, makes it physically possible to collect, through the circulation of paper technologies, a link between Alice and France whose exacting traceability has been slowly elaborated through two centuries of violent political history and contested voting reforms. (2005: 222, italics in original)

For Harvey, such an account of the composite relations that constitute an election – whether for city hall or a national parliament – would be just a backdrop to more pressing considerations about a class-generated analysis of capitalist economies; despite his enthusiasm and eloquence in his description of the Sacré-Coeur, his sites are never really traced in the same way that Latour understands a flat ontology of standards, metrics, accounts and so on. Whether this is important or not depends on your view of urban theory!

A RUMOUR OF CITIES

> 'Paris has become unbearable', 'the municipality's doing crazy things', 'they have got to consult with the municipalities of neighbouring suburbs', 'the police would do better to patrol the suburbs', 'dog owners should pay heavier fines', 'there are no halls for amateur music': all statements circulating from mouth to media, media to concierges, concierges to co-tenants, co-tenants to petitions, petitions to offices, offices to decrees, decrees to administrative courts … Can we study these myriads of statements? To some extent: on blogs, in newspapers, cafés, dinner parties, squares, SMS. I suppose that the mayor has informers, like the police prefecture has videos and the intelligence services have big ears. A mass of rumours and detached statements whose circulation, from point to point, compose Paris as surely as do cars travelling on the ring road or the millions of users transported daily in the metro. (Latour 2012: 92–3)

This chapter has brought together – through the figure of Paris – two very different traditions within urban research, but which both share the ability to provide synoptic explanation through the use of careful, painstakingly observed and excavated, details. Harvey's mix of historical rental data, read alongside Latour's often funny chains of details and dockets, provide a wonderful contrast into how cities hang together. Read side by side they are a feast: Harvey's search for a grand class-based narrative is tempered by Latour's obsessive search for indeterminacy. From the other side, those unconvinced by Latour's minute focus on the machinations of elections or berry prices can find the big picture in Harvey's political economies.

The utility of ANT has been part of a vigorous debate. For Richard Smith, it had clear benefits in moving on the global city literature through its emphasis on networks and practices:

> with ANT we can make the important switch from studying the nodes in a city network to studying the links between ... This is because ANT requires us to look closely at the traffic, the immutable mobiles, that travel through and in so doing make networks. Indeed, the interesting idea that can be researched by world city scholars is that the nodes and the links are made by that which passes through them. In other words, nodes and links (world city networks) are not viewed by ANT as empty infrastructures that are subsequently filled by immutable mobiles. (2003a: 36)

It has been noted that *Paris, Invisible City* has not been as widely discussed by urbanists as might be expected. Its fourth sequence, which is referred to as 'allowing', is one of the most breathlessly intense pieces of ANT writing that there is, an ontological and historical reading of Parisian experience. Latour offers a simpler explanation in *Reassembling the Social* (2005): the fourth sequence is about recomposition, about finding a city where one can identify the space within which to 'breathe' theory, about finding a way of talking about the ongoing discoveries of theories of cities – of their facts, their smells, their feelings – without crushing them with a prefigured frame. Nonetheless, for all its emphasis on recomposition, to talk about 'big things' is still a challenge for ANT approaches. As Bender (2010: 315) has argued, the goal must be 'to describe the actor-networks in larger, less well-defined domains. This is crucial because for ANT – much like historical narrative – description and explanation are collapsed. In each case, an empirically grounded narrative that includes multiple causal elements becomes an explanation.'

This links to another key idea from ANT: that of 'figuration'. For Latour, it can be understood alongside another key term: actant. He illustrates this with the following point:

> Here are four ways to figure out the same actant. 'Imperialism strives for unilateralism'; 'The United States wishes to withdraw from the UN'; 'Bush Junior wishes to withdraw from the UN'; 'Many officers from the Army and

two dozen neo-con leaders want to withdraw from the UN'. That the first is a structural trait, the second a corporate body, the third an individual, the fourth a loose aggregate of individuals makes a big difference of course to the account, but they all provide different figurations of the same actions. (2005: 54)

This is an interesting solution to what is often known as the structure-agency problem: how to deal with the very obvious macro-social things like 'state', 'economy' and even 'culture', and the far more tangible individuals that apparently make up these terms. But on the idea of individual, Latour has a further point to make: 'no one knows how many people are simultaneously at work in any given individual; conversely, no one knows how much individuality there can be in a cloud of statistical data points' (p. 54).

It is around this point that sceptics begin to see the point of Latour's obsessive search for networks and connections that link non-humans with human action. In his deconstruction–reconstruction of Paris, he is taking on much of the history of sociology itself, which has often sought – for reasons of disciplinary self-preservation, for reason of narrative excitement, and so on – strong explanatory structures. In many ways, Latour suggests, this is all about taking short cuts with what is 'society' and what is the 'social'. And so the 'flat ontology' is actually a call to work much harder as an analyst.

> The totality doesn't present itself as a fixed frame, as a constantly present context; it is obtained through a process of summing up, itself localized and perpetually restarted ... Paris is neither big nor small. Places without dimensions are temporarily dimensioned by the work of rules, files and sums, whose Brownian movement is barely detached from the background of all the other bubbling incessantly agitating the cauldron of the big city. (Latour and Hermant 2006: 51)

This is a neat argument, though it has its limitations, one of which is that Latour doesn't follow his networks as far as they can go.

At one point, he says that 'all networks lead to Paris' and this is an important point. But to find out a convincing ANT explanation for the power of Paris, one would need to go a lot further than the ring-road (*Boulevard Périphérique*) which so conveniently bounds the city's Brownian motion in a test-tube. Interestingly, Latour does acknowledge this to an extent: 'Paris' two thousand-year history has resulted in an accumulation, on a few thousand hectares, of all the passions and agitations that can be activated right down to the centre of this spider web, this central cortex with its neurons crackling in front of us' (p. 53). And so, might we see cities as being calculative panoramas, as much as anything? As Otter suggests:

At this microscale, the operation of power is often better captured through the idioms of norm and capacity ... We are speaking here of the agency made possible by technological networks. The numerous, interlaced vision networks or patterns stimulated and sustained a panoply of individual vision norms and capacities: productive attention, sensory awareness, urban motility, social observation, private reading. (2008: 259)

In this perspective, a characteristic of modern governance is that road users, for example, are fully enmeshed in a network of sociality, sensation and consciousness held together by socio-technical practices of driving, car ownership and so on.

Next, ANT is important in its attention to detail. As Thrift puts it in an interview with Farías in *Urban Assemblages*:

I think ANT works best in strongly defined situations and I think that's difficult to deny, truth to tell. You talked about the laboratory, where in a sense ANT started out. It's moved into the trading room; it's moved into other milieu where you can be very sure of what you are getting, if I can put it that way. There are set apparatuses, set procedures, and you can use ANT to see how these things are built up. (2010a: 112–13)

Yet what is very surprising in all of these accounts of Paris is still the heuristic device used to stabilize the city. Latour, whose method unbounds us from space, still concludes his Parisian 'sociological opera' with a jibe against the 'paralysis of the amusement park' (p. 101). Harvey and Merrifield remain overly obsessed with the working-class arrondissements, failing to grasp the complex post-colonial metropolis that other writers (such as Dikeç 2007) are more comfortable in describing and which, with the events of Charlie Hebdo and the Bataclan, cannot be ignored. The police hunts that formed the aftermaths of these events – which took place deep within the 'traditional' city – traced lines that zig-zagged in and around the city's municipal boundaries, tracing clues that linked violence done to humans by humans with objects.

3

GLOBAL URBAN
ORDER(ING)

So far, the book has looked closely at two cities – Rome and Paris – and various attempts to use very fine-grained study of their constitution to do a number of interesting things: to generalize; to typify; to theorize; to work out their position within what some call a network ontology. In other words, there is always a tension – especially in the case of global theory building – between working through the intricacies of a particular place and attempting to work out the place of cities in the world. Both Rome and Paris would appear in what is often seen as a 'Eurocentric' canon of interpreting, designing and producing cities. This is important to note, because in many ways global city theorization has been dominated by ideas arising from post-colonialism, generating an intense debate about the nature of the global cities literature based around three key problems or biases: economism, ethnocentrism and developmentalism (Edensor and Jayne 2012).

And so, we can see that the global city term has a dual function related to order. On the one hand, it is a vision of orderliness, where certain 'global' standards of healthcare, infrastructure, air quality, personal security and so on, are the norm. On the other, there is a sense of being ordered, as in ranked, where many of the material decisions about whether to visit, locate or invest in a particular city are done using a calculus of comparison.

METAGEOGRAPHIES

In his book *World City Network*, the geographer Peter Taylor employs the term 'metageographies' as a means of building out his own version of what he calls the world city network. By metageographies, he means the 'geographical structures through which people order their knowledge of the world' (2004: 180). Should the world be conceived of as a set of corridors and pathways, for example, which perhaps connote movement and exchange, or a mosaic of discrete national territories and states, which hint at solidity and sovereignty and the power of nation-states?

Interestingly, Taylor has made a key metageographical contribution that has crossed over into city governance and policy-making. Along with other colleagues at Loughborough University, he developed what became known as the 'GaWC' methodology, an abbreviation for 'globalization and world cities'. In truth, the website that popularized GaWC contained many academic papers of a diverse range of theoretical traditions, that drew on both quantitative and qualitative data sources, and which didn't privilege any particular form of representation.

However, the success of GaWC in both reach and impact was its use of relational data sets that tracked economic flows between cities, and then used a hierarchical mode of rating and then ranking cities. This is often cited and examined by city governments as a means of understanding their autogeographical 'place in the world' (see Global Rankings case study on page 55 on how the New South Wales government has referenced it as a benchmarking tool). As with other influential accounts, such as Sassen's *The Global City* (1991), this mode of approaching cities typically led to some key cities of advanced capitalism ranking at the top of the hierarchy, such as New York, London and Tokyo, with a slow descent through some of the prosperous cities of Milan and St Louis to cities with weaker sets of economic data, such as Brazzaville and Kota Kinabulu.

What is notable about this ranking is the use of data about major global firms, otherwise known as transnational corporations, to discern how they ran their business through networks of offices, whether through directly hierarchical 'command and control' management strategies, or more heterogeneous and flexible modes such as joint ventures, franchises, holding companies and so on. The spatial detail of this has been fleshed out in a range of sectors (e.g. Jones 2009; Faulconbridge and Hall 2011), so, it is the impact of major firms that is largely seen by GaWC as determining the position of city governments within a hierarchy. For this reason, cities are often seen as having limited agency, though they can play a significant role in developing good business standards, high-quality office accommodation and efficient infrastructure, be it for data storage or transport.

For Taylor, many of the original scholars of global cities failed to provide an adequate response to 'questions such as "How are cities connected to each other?" and "How can a city's connectivity be measured?" Asking such questions is itself an important step because past concepts used to describe how world cities relate to one another have been notoriously vague in such matters' (2004: 55). As Taylor continues, 'I suggest that it is four agencies – service firms, city governments, service-sector institutions and nation-states – that, taken together, are primarily responsible for shaping the world city network' (p. 56).

Within this framework of agencies, there are two key nexuses that Taylor sees as fundamental in the co-constitution of global cities as networks:

Nexus I draws together service firms and cities in a relationship of mutual reciprocity. Cities need a critical mass of firms to produce the necessary knowledge environment that the firms critically need. This joint reinforcing process is at the heart of definitions of world cities, and indeed of cities more generally. The process has interesting implications in terms of interests: for instance, Japanese and American banks with major offices in London have a vested interest in the future success of London as an international financial centre, while equally London has a vested interest in 'its' Japanese and American banks doing well. *Nexus II* is the interactions between business service sectors and the nation-states. The professionalization of knowledge-intensive services has been a national process involving the state in either legitimizing self-regulating (national) professional associations or else regulating directly. In turn, these professionals have manned the state apparatus to enable the state to function. This is the original private–public partnership. Traditionally it has been lawyers who have straddled the private–public boundary, followed by bankers, but today accountants, management consultants and, of course, advertisers with their PR skills are also becoming prominent in government circles. In sum, each nexus represents a binding together of agencies in a conjoint exercise. (p. 58, emphasis in original)

Elsewhere, Beaverstock et al. have argued that a new 'metageography' of inter-city flow can be identified and mapped. This entailed a categorization of cities based on their relative connectivity, measured in material terms by data on internet connections, airline passenger traffic and office location patterns, particularly in advanced producer services such as law, accountancy, advertising and finance. As they argue:

World cities are not eliminating the power of states, they are part of a global restructuring which is 'rescaling' power relations, in which states will change and adapt … The 'renegotiations' going on between London's world role and the nation's economy, between New York's world role and the U.S. economy, and with all world cities and their encompassing territorial 'home' economies, are part of a broader change affecting the balance between networks and territories in the global space-economy. (2000: 132)

Thus a sense emerges here that such cities are no longer articulated towards leading their national economies, that they are agents of themselves co-ordinating flows that will possibly bypass, and probably even 'leak' from, the national economy in a number of ways.

Taylor deploys the concept of 'embedded statism' to describe this situation. By this, he is referring to the widespread popular – and scholarly – assumption of territorial space and social, economic and cultural behaviour as being coterminous. Put another way, the state acts as a 'container' of social action: this mindset 'contains the remarkable geographical assumption that all the important human social activities share exactly the same spaces':

> This spatial congruence can be stated simply: the 'society' which sociologists study, the 'economy' which economists study, and the 'polity' which political scientists study all share a common geographical boundary, that of the state. However abstract the social theory, it is national societies that are described; however quantitative the economic models, it is national economies that are depicted; and however behavioural the political science, it is national governance at issue. (Taylor 2004: 189)

This search for a new spatial ontology with which to understand cities and urban economies has been developed by other theorists. Amin (2002), seeking to make sense of the distanciation of economic transactions (in other words, the stretching of social interaction over many miles and continents), poses two viewpoints as to how cities can be understood. First, they can be seen as 'a string of place-based economies' (p. 392), a set of bounded territories that can be literally measured, in square footage for example. In contrast, Amin sees cities 'as a site of network practices' by which he means that the city is a 'nexus of economic practices that does not return the urban as a place of localised transactions' (p. 393). In this view, 'the city thus conceptualised is no longer a bounded, but spatially stretched economic sphere' (p. 393). Amin's argument is thus based upon a finely grained distinction as to how we see cities: not, as he puts it, 'islands of economic competitiveness or knowledge formation', but rather as 'circulatory sites', restless and unstable (p. 395). Thus we cannot *assume* that cities are cohesive entities. It is the aggregate of practices that make networks between cities more or less durable.

GLOBAL RANKINGS

To tell stories of agency and organization is to tell stories about hierarchy and distribution. This much all the managerial modes of ordering have in common: that they are celebrations, performances and embodiments of ranking and reward; and, as I shall argue, of deletion. (Law 1994: 114)

Modern city government has become increasingly subjected to forms of performance measurement and 'benchmarking'. As John Law has suggested in *Organizing Modernity*, this involves a stripping, or deletion, of measures or metrics that don't correspond to the dominant organization paradigm. Generally speaking, there are two schools of thought on the nature of global cities. On the one hand, there is a model based upon scale, network and hierarchy. This has been seen as based upon a static, fixed notion of the world, where cities can be identified as a single entity,

(Continued)

CASE STUDY

(Continued)

then categorized, compared, contrasted and debated. The other school of thought sees globalization as a process, disputes an easy identification of cities as objects and emphasizes flows and movements between actors operating in the spatial formations that we know as cities. This division has been debated vigorously within geography and other disciplines, and the discussion that follows is an inevitably brief attempt to chart out some of its contours.

But when it comes down to it, the power of state discourse is such that these subtleties are often elided. For example, the use of various forms of global referencing and signification, including explicitly comparative techniques and metrically constructed global city 'standards', has been a central element of state strategy in Sydney and New South Wales for over thirty years (McNeill et al. 2005; Baker and Ruming 2015). The following is an excerpt from the New South Wales Trade and Investment strategy document *Progressing the NSW Economic Development Framework* (2014: 29):

> This section of the report presents a range of indicators, including the four macro-economic and external measures identified in 2012 for ongoing measurement, with the associated targets:
>
> **Labour Productivity** – Improvements in the rate of growth in labour productivity over the economic cycle (Industry Value Add / hours worked)
>
> *Target: The growth of NSW's IVA / hours worked to increase at a rate faster than the rest of Australia over the period to 2021.*
>
> **Industry Value Add** – NSW's share of national Industry Value Add (IVA) for priority sectors to indicate NSW's economic performance relative to the rest of Australia.
>
> *Target: The growth of NSW's IVA for priority sectors to be faster than those of the rest of Australia over the period to 2021.*
>
> **Exports** – NSW's share of the world exports in the priority sectors and growth rate of NSW relative to the rest of Australia.
>
> *Target: The rate of growth in NSW's priority sector exports to be faster than those of the rest of Australia.*
>
> **Sydney's Global Ranking** – Review of a range of global city ranking surveys to ensure that the perception and experience of international businesses dealing with Sydney remains globally competitive.

Target: Sydney to be consistently recognised as one of the top global business cities in a range of relevant global city ranking surveys.

How Sydney is ranked in global indexes is important – not just for Sydney but also NSW. The NSW *Economic Development Framework* includes a target for Sydney to be consistently recognized as one of the top global business cities in a range of global city rankings. Sydney's position on such rankings is important to ensure that the perception and experiences of international businesses engaging with Sydney remain globally competitive. (NSW Trade and Investment 2014: 40)

The report then goes on to list eleven separate global rankings systems that they consult, including: AT Kearney's Global City Index; Mori Foundation's Global Power City Index; Economist Intelligence Unit's Annual Global Liveability Ranking; PricewaterhouseCoopers' Cities of Opportunity; The Network's Mobility Survey; Global and World Cities Research Group (GaWC) (p. 48).

These ordering exercises thus become internalized within urban planning strategy. As Baker and Ruming put it:

As political spaces and objects of governance, cities reveal themselves amid spatial imaginaries comprised of perceived global city standards, comparative techniques and extra-local sources of 'best practice'. (2015: 63)

Sydney thus becomes reduced and defined by its ranked relationship with its proximate neighbour Melbourne, and regional competitors such as Singapore and Hong Kong.

THE 'ORDINARY CITY' DEBATES

The world cities metageography, while influential, has been challenged by various scholars. Some, such as Brenner and Schmid (2013, 2015), have tried to avoid engagement with specific cities or urban formations in an attempt to steer debate from the 'global' to the 'planetary', though this battle plan has received some sharp critique (Walker 2015). Others have argued that a relatively small number of cities are endowed with excessive scholarly significance, 'a hierarchy of attention' as Bunnell and Maringanti (2010: 417) put it. Ananya Roy has forcefully argued that a wider gathering of city experiences is crucial in building a convincing urban theory: 'the centre of theorymaking must move to the global South ... there has to be a recalibration of the geographies of authoritative knowledge':

> As the parochial experience of EuroAmerican cities has been found to be a useful theoretical model for all cities, so perhaps the distinctive experiences of the cities of the global South can generate productive and provocative theoretical frameworks for all cities ... It is time to blast open theoretical geographies, to produce a new set of concepts in the crucible of a new repertoire of cities. (2009: 820)

The ease with which 'EuroAmerican' is deployed in accounts that are otherwise admonitions of a lack of geographical sensitivity is itself quite ironic. Regardless, it is notable that there has been a burst of studies that have used less commonly studied cities as crucibles for the development of urban theory. In his review of this literature, Jamie Peck suggests that:

> The embrace of flatter ontologies in this first take on ordinary urbanism seemed to coincide, initially at least, with conceptions of a flatter earth, politically, materially and conceptually – not a world of North/South divides or global peaks and valleys, but one of relatively unruly complexity and geographically 'levelled' diversity. The call was to unshackle the study of the city from what were dubbed essentializing or structural theories of (inter)urban systems, forces and processes. Instead, and on the 'inside', ordinary cities were to be explored expansively, adventurously and in a non-essentialist fashion. In a sense, everywhere was now different (or ordinary), and nowhere was more different (or ordinary) than anywhere else. (2015: 165)

Alongside this flattening was a confluence of scholars working to write these cities, ordinary or otherwise, within a more expansive urban theory, escaping from the 'pigeon holing' of writing through development theory. Parnell and Oldfield's (2014) edited *Handbook on Cities of the Global South*, for example, set out to work 'towards a geographical realignment in urban studies, bringing into conversation a wide array of cities across the global South – the "ordinary", "mega", "global" and "peripheral"'. Roy and Ong's (2011) collection *Worlding Cities* possessed a similar ambition, though worked very much within an optic of highly mobile transnational or globally oriented movement.

The ordinary city approach has been set out through an influential set of papers by Jenny Robinson, who has argued strongly that the dominant traditions of Western social theory – which she traces back to the likes of the 'classical' urban theorists such as Simmel and Benjamin – have had the effect of over-valorizing certain key European cities, such as Paris and Berlin:

> Theories of urban modernity have bequeathed a complex inheritance to urban studies. They have operated to disqualify some cities from defining the realm of the urban; they also exemplify the wider and not insignificant methodological challenge of thinking cities in a world of cities – relating the specificity of individual cases of urbanity to any attempt to offer a wider theorisation of the urban. (2013: 660)

FIGURE 3.1 Mumbai, 2014: this type of photograph, with informal dwellings in the foreground, and modern skyscrapers in the backdrop, is a popular image composition in trying to capture rapid urban modernity.

Source: John A. Carroll / Shutterstock.com

The key element here is a sense of teleological progression towards an idealized, fully 'developed' city:

> In this analytical frame, where the urban is closely tied to the invention of the 'new', unexamined assumptions that some cities might be 'first' and others follow inform theoretical innovation. In the 20th-century version of this, western (advanced capitalist) societies and cities showed the way for poorer (underdeveloped or developing) countries and cities and therefore formed the basis for analytical interpretation of these cities, whether this was as catching up, deficient or incommensurable. (pp. 660–1)

For Robinson, the problem lies in the division between economic and urban geography and sociology as sub-disciplines that focus on advanced capitalist economies, and development geography as focusing on less developed countries: 'In the same way, then, that global and world city approaches ascribe the characteristics of only parts of cities to the whole city through the process of categorization, mega-city and developmentalist approaches extend to the entire city the imagination of those parts which are lacking in all sorts of facilities and services' (2002: 540). The effect of this, for Robinson, is to pathologize such cities as being poor, and requiring external help, ignoring the potential to redistribute wealth (which is concentrated in certain zones within African cities) internally within cities. More generally, a range of authors (Pieterse 2008; Parnell and Robinson 2012; Simone 2012) have argued that urban theory-building has glossed over the specific conditions of African cities, or – worse still – has even exoticized this urban experience. Working in a similar vein, Shatkin (2008) argued that seeing certain cities and nation-states as being irrelevant to global cities research due to very low levels of foreign direct investment is to ignore the increasing integration of cities such as Phnom Penh or Nairobi within the world economy.

This certainly has an element of truth. It is argued in some influential management consultancy literature that the failure to export or embed 'Western' modes of economic organization in the developing world context has been largely the result of weak or corrupt locals (see Frenkel and Shenhav 2012 on post-colonial perspectives on global management consultancies). However, in a carefully argued essay entitled 'The ordinary city trap', Richard Smith provides a robust critique of the 'ordinary cities' literature. His starting point, which he calls 'a critique of a critique', argues that a number of urban theorists use the 'ordinary city' term in a misguided manner, where:

> *evidence of absence* actually means an *absence of evidence*, and so [they] have merely invented a false problem to assert that the alleged failings of the neo-Marxist world city and global city concepts can be addressed through the solution of an ordinary cities approach that will now valorise all cities and therefore include and evidence that which has been overlooked or negated. (2013b: 2301, italics in original)

Adopting a 'critique of critique' is obviously a tricky endeavour, as it easily descends into accusations of misquoting and misrepresentation on both sides. Nonetheless, the basis of the debate is instructive as to what is at stake in this branch of urban theory. Smith's key argument is that the implications of the ordinary cities approach is

> politically conservative because rather than being taken as an inclusive call for urban studies to value all cities, they can be equally understood as an attempt to 'flatten' the diversity and difference of the urban world and consequently move away from the critical focus on the concentration of power, control, command, and the vested interests of neoliberal capitalism in and across a few strategic cities; a critique which has long been the essence of the world city and global city concepts. (p. 2301)

Leaving aside the political terms of this debate, it might be useful to consider how within particular regions, there are processes of 'mimicry' that see business models travelling relatively short distances between cities. Abaza (2011) describes the redevelopment of central Cairo in terms of the motif of nearby Dubai; Bedi (2016) provides a fascinating account of how Mumbai's taxi industry was to be remodelled along the lines of a Singaporean model of ownership.

ONTOLOGIES OF BIG CITIES

In scholarly terms, 'big cities' sounds commonsensical. The 'bright lights, big city' aphorism can sometimes be difficult to navigate past, with its tropes of loss of innocence, moral disorder, brash consumerism, and the anomie or ennui detected by the classical modern sociologists like Durkheim and Simmel. And yet, given that it is now very common to hear about the problems of the metropolis, it is quite important to think about all the different ways in which materiality affects urban theory, and to understand the visceral response that sheer size engenders in urban theorists. There are two big things which we might consider here in terms of the global cities literature: the big building, and especially the skyscraper or high-rise; and the big city, expressed through terms like megalopolis.

Tall buildings have for a long time taken on a representational role as a metonym or shorthand for modernity. However, their representational power can hide or forestall discussion of the intricacies of their internal social relations and material components. An important corrective, and contribution to debates on materiality, size and symbolism, is provided by Jane M. Jacobs in her essay 'A geography of big things'. Here, she elaborates on her approach to working with some of the most prevalent 'big things' of cities, high-rise buildings:

> I would like to investigate these themes by way of a specific type of architecture-building-house: the modernist, state-sponsored, residential highrise. This is the 'big thing' of this paper. Of course, I might have more accurately called it a 'tall thing', or even perhaps not worried about 'sizing' it or 'thing-ing' it at all, and simply called it a building, an urban form, a style of settlement, or housing. By using the term 'big thing' to describe the highrises I want to forestall the constructivist force of those more coherent terms like architecture, building or housing, a force that predetermines specific understandings as it precludes other kinds of knowing.

As Jacobs continues:

> By dubbing the highrise a 'big thing' I am establishing the preconditions for engaging in this exercise of 'surface accounting'. An interest in surface does not mean a disinterest in the wider systems in which a 'thing' is entangled (be they systems of production, inhabitation, valuation or dissolution). Rather, it is to bring into view how the coherent given-ness of this seemingly self-evident 'thing' is variously made or unmade. Further to that, I seek to demonstrate the part played by the constitution of scale in relation to stabilizing this 'big thing' called the highrise. At a very cursory level we might, by way of example, observe that it is not simply the physical size of the highrise that allows it to claim a status as a 'big thing'. The residential highrise has been variously drawn up into a range of indisputably big stories and organizational events: utopian visions for living, stellar architectural careers like that of Le Corbusier, bureaucratic machineries of mass housing

provision, national projects of modernization, the claims of critical social sciences and spectacular instances of failure, as well as popular and academic imaginaries about globalization. These stories and events are components in the networks of association that work to keep this form in place or to pull it apart – that is, they contribute as much to its thing-ness as they do to confirming something we might think we know about its scale. (2006: 3–4)

Jacobs continues to describe how such 'big things' are too easily cited as justification, or shorthand, of an otherwise elusive form of global power.

What about the other big thing, the megalopolis or megacity? Although there are some megacities in the global North, such as Tokyo, it is important to recognize that one of the drivers of the ordinary cities literature was that bigness is often seen as part of the 'pathology' of global South cities: their sheer size, lack of co-ordinated development and strained infrastructures, be this water, telecommunications or transport. On the one hand, this has been gathered within the institutions of global neo-liberalism such as the World Bank, which advocates market-based solutions for the problems of city government, such as structural adjustment and public sector austerity, along with the deregulation of markets. On the other, there is a discourse that posits an apparent hopelessness of cities of the global South can easily generate a dystopian response, as in the work of the Marxian scholar Mike Davis, whose *Planet of Slums* (2006b) provided a critique of global capitalism as being polarized between a class of super-rich, shaping urban space in a way that protects their lifestyles, and a global class of marginalized slum dwellers with a weak hold on both terrain and livelihood. Writing from a left perspective, some critics have argued that *Planet of Slums* is overly apocalyptic, effectively depoliticizing and homogenizing urban slum dwellers as lacking in political agency. Angotti presents a coruscating critique of this book, which he sees to be full of 'condemnation and moral outrage, not serious analysis' (2006: 962), containing a blend of anti-urban bias and simplistic dualisms regarding slum dwellers. Angotti contends that Davis's use of 'slum' as terminology is itself racialized; that he is excessively reliant on the economistic data of the World Bank in drawing his conclusions; and that he lapses too often into the apocalyptic tones that marked (or marred) much of his writing on Los Angeles (Angotti 2006).

Nonetheless, the materiality of bigness, and its connotation of disorder, has generated a significant literature seeking to understanding the urbanity of the cities of the global South. Chief among these has to be Mumbai. As McFarlane argues, there is an intrinsic, rambunctious materiality to the very make-up of the city itself:

> Mumbai's urban fabric is rarely hidden or taken-for-granted; rather, its ownership, regulation, production, distribution, maintenance and use are the most important feature of urban politics. In this process, a range of sociomaterialities matter, from land, pipes, wires, cables, drains, sewers, toilets, water taps, roads, flyovers and buildings, to political parties, civil society groups, builders, developers, protests, resources, expertise, legalities, policies and states. (2008: 353)

And the urban sensibilities of this are carried about within the subjectivities that constitute the city:

> As one Mumbai journalist recently reflected following the 2006 bombings on the city's suburban rail system, Mumbaikers do not worry so much about terror on infrastructure as the challenges of negotiating the terror of infrastructure on a daily basis – of trying to move through rail and roads, ensure clean water and reliable toilet and drainage facilities, and of maximising daily electricity loads to keep fridges, fans, radios, TVs, computers and businesses working. In addition, struggles over the distribution of infrastructure across cities as territorial and unequal as Mumbai or São Paulo means that infrastructure – seen or not – is rarely hidden from social life. (p. 351)

The use of inventories of material things, and their newly transparent importance for city life – often hidden away or take for granted in the Western city – is illustrative of the need to factor in size into these urban theories. This is a long way from Latour and Hermant's rather neatly circumscribed version of Paris – although there are interesting things said in *Paris, Invisible City* about bigness and smallness – and it has brought with it a rather different form of theoretical project.

There are several notions of bigness we can think through here. First, there is the idea of the statistical bigness of a city's population. Periodically, the media will publish lists and rankings of the population sizes of cities. Chongqing, for example, is believed to have a population approximating 30 million inhabitants. It is clearly huge, and is often mentioned in passing in media reports or urban commentaries to be the biggest city in the world. But it is not clear from this why this is an important observation in itself, to consider what it is about Chongqing's sheer massiveness that is of interest. This is a general problem for global cities work. Urbanists have tended to explore this from two different approaches. On the one hand, this can be the attempt to start with what we know as the globe, identify what we think of as its key cities, and then attempt to work out what relates them, as in the 'metageographies' of global cities described above (Beaverstock et al. 2000). On the other, there is a growing body of work which takes a set of key cities as singularities and considers them in their own right: their histories, economies, populations. One high-profile recent example was *The Endless City* (Burdett and Sudjic 2010; see also 2011), published by the Urban Age project located at the London School of Economics. This book mixed case studies of the likes of Berlin, London and New York, with those of the global South: Mexico City, Johannesburg and Shanghai. The book consists of striking full-page colour photographs, 'expert' essays and striking lay-out, design and typography of graphs and tables that enumerate each city's key properties. Yet some readers react with unease to the presentational apparatus of these books. As Reinhold Martin put it in his review of the book:

> I, for one, cannot help but feel that there is also a deeply aesthetic dimension to all of this, which emanates from the sincere and noble efforts to make

sense of what might otherwise seem senseless. By aesthetic, I do not mean a stylistic or even vaguely architectural perspective on the city … I mean an aesthetic of enumeration that dallies with the sublime. That is what is really at stake in this enigmatic volume: the management of the apparent endlessness and ungraspability of global and/or mega-cities, not so much spatially or territorially, but cognitively. After all, was that not Kant's great insight with his notion of the mathematical sublime? That the incalculability of a particular phenomenon, made manifest precisely in rational attempts to grasp its scope, produces a curious combination of pain and pleasure, and that this admixture is, in a very precise sense, aesthetic (but most definitely not beautiful) in character. (2009: 146–7)

As Martin concludes, 'Its rhetorical project, whether intentional or not, seems not so much to provide a tool-kit for managing growth in global or megacities, but to verify that what we call globalization actually exists in the first place' (p. 147).

It is interesting in this context to think about geometric – often called Euclidean – bigness. Cities can be measured by surface area, footprint, distance from the two most remote points on their circumference. Problems begin here because city government units rarely correspond to size: many of the problems of nomenclature in the global cities debate are because global cities – in a municipal or civic sense – may have very small city councils covering their very core, but may be driven by major employers on the city's peripheries. And so debates on global cities that don't account for size tend to become chaotic very quickly unless all parties have a stable delimitation of the object of discussion.

Moreover, it is impossible to freeze cities. They are always growing or shrinking. By the time data is gathered by census or survey it is often out of date, so analysis proceeds by a mixture of anecdote and selective evidence. Furthermore, as the spatial analyst Mike Batty has argued in his short essay called 'The 22nd-century city', 'much of what we now do does not relate to the place we inhabit which, in some senses, is becoming independent of the activities that support and sustain us both economically and globally' (2012: 973). This is often expressed through 'network' discourses. And yet,

> our sense of place is not really network based. Although most places and the activities and populations within them now depend on others, once we recognize that such networks are spatially disjoint, we lose the recognition that pertains to clusters that we have defined as cities for the last 5000 years. (p. 973)

Batty raises a key issue: to grasp what a city is, to make it meaningful, requires attention to its existential nature. This can either be through the use of 'big data' about cities. Indeed, tropes about global cities and big cities are often framed using numerical languages and presentational devices (usually statistical tables, sometimes graphs, and increasingly typographical and infographical big numbers). There are probably several different kinds of big data relevant here: population data, based on residence; employment and labour market data; transactional data – what is being bought and sold when and where, by whom and from whom; movement data – who is travelling where, when, why and how. Or it can be achieved through ethnographic approaches, often aligned with 'area studies' traditions. Or, through a narrative that teases out our Big Paris and small paris.

STANDARD CITIES

The study of standards, and their global spread, has become of increasing importance in globalization studies. Along with Bowker and Leigh Star's (1999) significant work in this field, scholars such as Easterling (2014), Larner (2014) and Zeiss (2014) have elaborated on the non-governmental transnational bodies, particularly the International Organization for Standardization (ISO), headquartered in Geneva, that set standards that allow technologies and products to be commensurable and comparable. This body develops standards in a wide range of fields: by 2015, the organization had produced over 20,500 standards. As ISO define it, 'A standard is a document that provides requirements, specifications, guidelines or characteristics that can be used consistently to ensure that materials, products, processes and services are fit for their purpose' (http://www.iso.org/iso/home/standards.htm, accessed 29 December 2015).

Larner describes one of these in detail, ISO 9000, a process which 'involves the use of standardized management tools that provide a methodology for documenting, adapting, and improving organizational processes' (2014: 272). There are three significant impacts that the process has. First, it provides a stable and reliable product for transnational corporations, 'a way for geographically remote organizations both to recognize each other and to imagine themselves in the shared economic space of a global supply chain' (p. 275). Second, it demonstrates the emergence of non-governmental forms of transnational authority, given that it demonstrates a degree of soft power: 'organizations opt for it because of the external perceptions it generates and the opportunities that subsequently ensue' (p. 275). Third, ISO 9000 'is an exemplar of the diverse range of calculative practices, including audit, benchmarking, and standards, through which the activities of organizations and individuals are now being governed' (pp. 274–5).

In a similar vein, Easterling uses the ISO as an exemplar of her discussion of 'extrastatecraft', which 'plots to bypass bureaucracies with an effective spatial practice at the global scale' (2014: 209). She argues that these standards percolate into the globalizing habits of businesspeople:

> Important as it is to understand what quality management does, it is equally important to understand what it does not do – indeed what it obstructs. Despite being treated as a seal of approval, it does not set technical performance standards for some of the world's most pressing issues related to labor and the environment. Only its non-specific, non-binding management standards inch toward these issues. (p. 173)

To attain the right to advertise its products as meeting a global standard, firms must seek accreditation from a quality engineer: 'An audit often consists of interviews, with a set questionnaire ... Small companies may spend tens of thousands of dollars and large companies may spend hundreds of thousands and several months on completing the initial accreditation' (p. 177). This has to be continually renewed, and has a cascading effect on the supply chain, where large firms 'encourage their suppliers to be certified' (p. 177).

So, if cities are held together by objects and organized systems of standards, it would be useful to audit how some of these types have emerged in the city historically, and how they have become established as norms by which capitalist urban economies are reproduced. The final sections of the chapter examine two of these cases: the role of hotels both as formats that promote and enshrine particular standards, as well as being held accountable to standards via reviews and audits; and the importance of air conditioning as a mode of standardizing the interior environments of cities.

GLOBAL STANDARDS I: HOTELS

> In post-World War II Europe and the Middle East, the Hilton hotel was quite literally 'a little America' ... American postwar wealth produced the uppermiddle-class travelers who staged their business or pleasure activities in the Hilton. The Hilton provided this elite with a familiar environment. From American suburbs and country clubs came the Hilton's lawns, swimming pools, and tennis courts. From American upper-middle-class social practices came its cocktail lounges and rooftop supper clubs. From American popular culture came its cheeseburgers, milkshakes and soda fountains. From American technology came its ice water tapped to individual guest rooms, its direct-line telephones, its radios, its air-conditioning, and, most fundamentally, the architectural form of the building itself. (Wharton, 2001: 1–2)

Hotels are important metronomes of the commercial rhythms of cities, but also have a paradoxical essence, both enabling intense, time-poor interaction as well as allowing spaces for relaxation and repose, exemplars of the 'malleability' of urban space. The late nineteenth and early twentieth centuries was an important period in the development of luxury hotels, both within the maturing industrial economies of North America and Europe, as well as in colonial economies. Hotels were key nodes in an emerging world system of cities, such as Raffles in Singapore, the Eastern and Oriental in Penang, and the Métropole in Hanoi (Peleggi 2005). They were often early adopters of the latest technologies in terms of building systems (lifts, plumbing, electric lighting and heating) and communications systems (telegrams and telephones), and showcased the latest architectural and interior styles. The construction of a luxury hotel was, therefore, an important element in the development of urban economies, and was driven as much by the building's use value for local business elites (for neutral meeting and banqueting spaces, for example, that hitherto had not been provided by the market), as by realizing

FIGURE 3.2 The façade of the now demolished Australia Hotel, Sydney. Hotel management was an early example of the active promotion of international standards.

Source: State Library of New South Wales [hall_25247]

the exchange value of the building itself (the immediate financial revenues and profits generated by the building). As such, shareholders in these hotels tended to come from existing local landowners and businesses who recognized the importance of hotels in engaging with extra-local markets, and were able to host banquets, celebrate society events such as weddings, trade fairs and suitable accommodation for travelling businesspeople (McNeill and McNamara 2009; Sandoval-Strausz 1999).

To illustrate this further, consider the case of the Australia Hotel, a now demolished 'palace' hotel that was built in the 1890s in the centre of Sydney, then a colonial city. At the time, Sydney was well established on world shipping routes:

> From London one could sail six weeks via Gibraltar, the Suez Canal and Ceylon (Sri Lanka) to Perth, Melbourne and Sydney; or seven weeks via South Africa … Another circuit – the Pacific Rim – began in California: three or four weeks by steamship from San Francisco via the Pacific Islands to Sydney, then returning, or island-hopping north through the East Indies, China and Japan and back to San Francisco or Vancouver. Travellers, performers, immigrants, machinery, commodities and ideas of all nationalities were picked up and dropped off at every point on these routes. (Matthews 2005: 105)

Many of the things being shipped on the trade routes included the reproducing machines that would transform entertainment and communication worldwide, the 'gramophone, wireless, cinematograph and the rotary press' (Matthews 2005: 103). The Australia thus made its appearance alongside a series of new buildings dedicated to social consumption: pubs, hotels, department stores and dance halls. Over its first decades, the hotel would house Sydney's most fashionable guests, both foreign and domestic, from Indian and English Test cricket teams to Viennese opera singers or French actresses. And yet, the hotel seemed to embody the vernacular culture of Australian commercial society at the time, as one tourist told a journalist for *The Home* magazine in September 1928:

> It was a Saturday midday, and the place was crowded with just the same smartly dressed people one sees in the lounge of any fashionable hotel any-where in the world. American horn-rimmed glasses, Paris model dresses, English tweeds, high heels, cosmetics, field glasses, actresses, page boys, young men-about-town – everyone very urbane and sophisticated. There were the usual glass showcases displaying diamond wrist watches and cigars and hot house flowers – the usual luxurious nick-nacks of ultra-civilised life. But in another showcase, between a display of Parisian perfumery and another of chocolate in gold caskets tied up with satin ribbons, was a case containing a specimen of sheep fodder. It was Australia to me, that, and an Australia I liked – the glittering spun-glass palace of city life, frankly and simply acknowledging the earth in which it was rooted. (In Rühen 1995: 46–7)

This image of The Australia as both a fashionable and cosmopolitan focus of Sydney social life, as well as residence of choice for its commercial agricultural elites when visiting the city, thus marked the hotel as an expression of the city's place both within circuits of tourism and entertainment, but also of international trading relationships.

The hotel's management was conscious of its role in the institutionalization of international traffic. By the 1930s, The Australia's eponymous in-house magazine, copies of which were distributed to guests, was focusing much of its content on international travel, with city profiles and features on other world-famous hotels. The hotel confidently announced its position within these circuits:

> To lure the traveller across 'wide seas,' two things are necessary – good steam-ship services and good hotels. The shipping companies are fully alive to their obligations, and they are playing their part in keeping their fleets up-to-date.

> 'The Australia' has ever borne in mind the standard demanded by the over-seas traveller, and it has attained its position as the premier hotel of the Commonwealth, and its reputation as one of the finest hotels south of the line, because of the progressive policy of its management. At different times members of the directorate and management have travelled abroad to glean latest ideas in the matter of equipment, etc., and these have been applied

wherever possible to 'The Australia'. As a hostel, it is known all over the world, and practically every distinguished visitor to Australia has been housed within its portals. (*The Australia Journal*, Christmas 1932, quote from inside back flap)

The journal also demonstrated management awareness of how American hotel entrepreneurs were adopting techniques and management styles from other manufacturing sectors, influenced by Fordism and Taylorization. These included E.M. Statler, whose use of modern design layouts, materials, construction principles, and franchised management set in train a novel way of thinking about hotels and their customers; and L.M. Boomer and Roy Carruthers, of the Waldorf-Astoria Group, who set forth some of the new principles in hotel design in influential publications in the 1920s, management techniques that were translated into built form by a small number of specialist architectural firms such as Holabird and Roche and Schultze and Weaver. Attention focused on the development of commercial architecture that systematically programmed the ideal location of each part of the money-making activities of the hotel, accompanied with new engineering techniques in plumbing, air conditioning, heating and elevator design (see Wharton 2001: 167).

These trends within American hotel management were certainly noted in Sydney. The Australia's magazine carried an interview with Boomer, one of a series on 'Notable Hotel Personalities', and eulogized his application of standardization to guest service. It made an interesting juxtaposition to narratives that celebrated the continuing ties between Australia and Britain, particularly as developments in communication and air travel improved existing colonial travel patterns. An issue in 1934 carried an interview with a Mr Edwards, chairman of the Grosvenor House hotel in London's Park Lane:

'The whole idea of travel is going to be revolutionised' stated Mr Edwards. 'Just as one thinks little to-day of running over to Paris by aeroplane and coming back the same day or the next, so people in Cape Town or Melbourne or other distant outposts of the Empire will soon be planning visits to London or to each other with as little idea of entering upon an adventure. It is not so many years ago that Australia was a three months' journey from England. It took six months to get a reply to a communication. To-day our pioneers of the air have brought Australia within a few days' physical journey from London, and I can pick up my telephone in Grosvenor House and within three minutes be talking to a friend in Melbourne. We hardly appreciate the fact that distances are disappearing.' (*The Australia Journal* 1932: 11)

The improvements brought by faster ships, early airlines and wireless communications were, as Edwards continued, a fundamental aspect of British imperialism:

Closely connected to the development of speedy communications and its relation to travel is the importance of the hotel as a centre of Empire life.

> Hotels serve as meeting places for visitors from all parts of the Empire, and as distances become less and less will be more and more potent factors in strengthening the ties between British citizens and in every corner of the globe. Just as the inn is at the centre of village life, so the super-hotel will become the centre of Empire life. (*The Australia Journal* 1932: 11)

In the immediate post-war period, The Australia was operating at high capacity, and was at the forefront of international communications. In the 1948–9 tax year, the hotel accommodated 142,153 guests with phone bills that totalled £12,000, 'Sydney's biggest phone bill' given the huge number of overseas calls (McNicoll 1949: 17). However, the first manager of the post-war period, Lex Rentoul, was well aware of the impending competitive threats arising from innovations in building technology and hotel management, and undertook a fact-finding trip of 13 leading American hotels in 1947 (along with one in Mexico City), including the St Francis in San Francisco, the Parker House in Boston, the Waldorf Astoria in New York and the Washington, DC Statler. Rentoul produced a detailed report and spreadsheet of his findings for each hotel. His comments on the Statler are telling, and are summarized in Table 3.1.

The Australia's decline mirrored trends in the United States, where the first wave of nineteenth-century downtown 'palace' hotels were beginning to suffer from physical deterioration and outdated management ideas, their passing unlamented by many tired of their increasingly shabby appearance and substandard plumbing. In Rufus Jarman's eulogy of the Statler hotels, *A Bed for the Night* (1952), the palace hotel is already seen as an anachronism: 'Regarded in a cold and unromantic light, these old palaces did more harm than good to the American hotel industry; they tended to be more confusing than constructive to Americans who wished to enter the hotel business' (p. 300). For Jarman, the (first) Waldorf was an example of hotels built 'because of loyalty, or pride, or passion' (p. 300) rather than on the basis of commercial efficiency. By contrast, new hotel formats such as the Los Angeles Statler (1950–1) incorporated a more 'logical' organization of space such as a single central kitchen for the different food and beverage outlets, and the ability to partition grand ballrooms into smaller meeting rooms, hitherto used for only a small number of days in a year. As described at more length elsewhere (McNeill and McNamara 2012), The Australia was demolished in the early 1970s to make way for a commercial skyscraper.

GLOBAL STANDARDS II: AIR CONDITIONING

> Today, the amount of networked, seamlessly cooled space is continuing to expand rapidly, meaning that, if desired, residents of Bangkok, Shanghai, Bangalore, and Singapore can now move between the office, classroom, home, restaurant, shopping mall, and other climate-controlled environments with minimal exposure to the 'outdoors'. In the region's less developed countries, public trains, buses, and taxis all signal their status and affordability through a classificatory system of 'non-AC' and 'AC'. (Winter 2013: 527)

TABLE 3.1 Visit to Statler Hotel, Washington, DC, by Lex Rentoul, Manager of The Australia Hotel, 1947

Accommodation: Adjoining rooms. K's a double, converting to daytime sitting room; ours twin-bedded, with combination writing-desk-dressing table. Inadequate drawer and cupboard space but layout good.

Bathroom: Bathroom with outside vent, but no window. Voices from lower floor came clearly through vent. No Kleenex fitment. Sanitized lavatory seat; glasses in sterilized cellophane; plugs in bath and basin. Excellent lighting for shaving cabinet; slot for razor blades. Shower with adjustable spray but no mixer. Toilet paper in wall but rail for curtain rusty.

Room Service: Fairly quick (20 mins) and accurate. Breakfast in bed encouraged – only 5 cents per portion extra charged. Printed cesarine tablecloths. Inventory of silver sent with table.

Service generally: Maid appeared in our room 3 mins after our arrival to turn down beds, check linen etc. Porters explained use of writing desk – d.t. Room done daily about 1pm. One maid to 14 rooms.

Food: Food excellent. New electronic cooking device in use. Wonderful sweets.

Atmosphere: Our arrival expected. Made welcome in atmosphere by suggesting modernity and efficiency. Lift boys most courteous and efficient. Flowers from management.

Linen etc: Plenty of towels and bed linen; 2 pillows for bed, 1 blanket to match carpet; spreads poor.

Laundry: wonderful 24 hour valet and laundry service available. Suits and laundry left before midnight returned by noon. Drycleaning and shoe repairs all well and briskly done.

Morning tea and papers: No tea but paper under door each morning.

Writing facilities: Combination dressing table and writing desk; quite efficient. Supply of paper not maintained.

Room telephone: Non-automatic, good service.

House rules and facilities: Excellent. Breakfast and beverage menus in room. Full instructions about laundry, valet etc. Hotel restaurants omitted, but these shown elsewhere.

Heating: Air conditioning controlled by guests.

Wireless: In bedroom. Free. Four stations available.

Source: Report to board on visit to United States by Lex Rentoul, General Manager. Mitchell Library Box 4351.

The next systemic form of standardization considered here is that of air-conditioning technology. Air con is an important back-story to the growth of modernity and global cities, part of the distribution and spread of a set of 'cool' technologies that have sought to improve the quality of everyday life, from fridges to industrial coolants. Many of these technologies have been most enthusiastically embraced in the cities of South Asia, with tropical and sub-tropical climates. As Tim Winter (2013) describes, these affordances are often geared at standardizing the space of cities, but not in a socially equitable manner necessarily: a resident of a high-income area of Shanghai will likely have more in common in terms of their access to domestic technology with a resident of Sydney or Los Angeles than with a low-income dweller in their own city. Indeed, their availability is often linked to the act of consumption, with cafes and hotels advertising the presence of air conditioning as a promise of comfort to potential customers. In *Keeping Cool in Southeast Asia*, for example, Sahakian (2014) provides a detailed study of the socio-economic nuances of thermal comfort in cities such as Manila, placed somewhere between the near universal provision of cooling in the likes of Singapore, and the condition of non-automated cooling.

FIGURE 3.3 Air-conditioning units in Singapore: thermal comfort standards have agency in reducing climatic difference between cities

Source: © Tim Winter / http://www.comfortfutures.com/

In her book *Comfort, Cleanliness and Convenience: the Social Organization of Normality*, Elizabeth Shove puts forward the following argument as to why the '3 Cs' of her title are so important:

> despite persistent and extensive variation, there is some evidence to support the view that comfort and cleanliness are subject to distinctive forms of escalation and standardization. Escalation here refers to the ratcheting up of demands, for instance for levels of comfort or for degrees of cleanliness. Standardization implies that the reach of what counts as normal is more and more encompassing. Conventions once confined to particular cultures seem to be extending (and eroding) in ways that suggest convergence in both technology and practice. Global acceptance of the business suit, the waning of the siesta and the expectation of always wearing freshly laundered clothing

give an indication of this kind of change. Such trends are neither simple nor inevitable: pockets of habit stick fast, old ways die hard and some are obdurately resistant to change. Even so, there is an arguably new and certainly niggling tension between the production, appropriation and maintenance of standardized and localized interpretations of normal practice. (2003: 3)

How does this apply to global cities? The first thing it does is to introduce something which is often 'flattened' out of the literature: the nature of climate and weather as experienced in cities. This is key to understanding the programmatic production of global cities, as the wealth accumulated in these places often allows for a high degree of atmospheric control, the existence of ready consumers and markets for products that enhance comfort, and a particular set of building and space types that are able to be structured and designed in such a way as to create atmospheres that are clean, convenient and comfortable.

> The invisibility and intangibility of air is a significant factor in its absence from public debates about climate change and sustainability. Air too often remains in the unconscious background, far beyond the robust, critical debates about the material world … Put simply, if we are to alter the current path of electronic conditioning we need to open up a new material imagination of air, and redefine how the air is imagined in material terms. Built environment sustainability is much more than the technical questions of design and engineering. (Winter 2013: 528, 529)

Such a 'technopolitics' of social and urban development, the way in which the state and other corporate actors use material technology to shape space quality, is often missing from political economy accounts. This might suggest a closer attention to the materiality of air, microclimate and comfort: the use of thermometers, observation and interlocution of users to assess and gather the thermal city.

It was noted above that luxury business hotels are often the forerunners in bringing new technologies to a particular place, including air conditioning. And the hotel is a good – perhaps unique – mechanism for global ordering:

> *Ego, hic, nunc* – identity, place, time – this is probably the most unsure starting point for an exploration of the social. *Ego*: identity cards, records of civil status, testimonies by neighbours; *hic*: cadastral plans, maps of Paris, guidebooks, signposts; *nunc*: sundials, watches, the electronic voice of the speaking clock. (Latour and Hermant 2006: 17)

Individuals identify themselves at check-in; the hotel location is often their primary concern in their choice; their stay is governed by a pure selling of time-space, framed by check-in and check-out. By contrast, the air-conditioning system sits in its mundane ducts, or else whirrs noisily on the wall, a standardized product sold worldwide by Carrier or Daikin or Panasonic.

★★★★

The intention of the chapter was to mix up various mechanisms of ordering: the ranking and categorization of things, but also the setting of standards for a global smoothness that renders urban life technically commensurable. They are all 'meta-geographies' that help to capture how world social life is organized. The set of representations and analytical methods adopted by the GaWC research teams over several years have served to shake up the sometimes static, nation-state-based notions of internationalism. As a set of metrics, and despite robust critique from different angles (Robinson 2006; Smith 2013a, 2013b) they set forth a 'relational' logic that explains why the state of cities and city-regions are as they are: in many ways, they can only be explained by forces emanating from far away. How far away is a tricky question, though, and as with Latour's discussion of the problem of the 'zoom', is often glossed over through the use of the unsatisfactory 'global–local' binary, an unhappy way of avoiding any reference to the nation-state, it seems.

The other key point is that of position. Hotels and air conditioning aren't everywhere, but their presence is an index in itself of global wealth. As Ananya Roy has written:

> Placing the 21st-century metropolis in its different world-areas runs the risk of reifying territorial jurisdictions and geopolitical stereotypes, of produc-ing a classificatory scheme that can obscure topologies and relationalities. However, when such world-areas are approached as 'process' rather than 'trait' geographies, and when the knowledge produced about these areas is seen as a 'strategic essentialism' rather than as a generalization, a more dynamic imagination and epistemology is possible. (2009: 828–9)

These views are important: at times they are in danger of replacing the focus on the iconic spaces of American or European urbanism with alternative 'celebrated' cities such as Singapore, Shenzhen or Mumbai. While these accounts are destabilizing the Western city hegemony, perhaps they often reinforce the 'primate city' phenomenon. Networked parts of these cities, whether linked through business, family or religion, may have more in common with cities of the global North than with their immediate, propinquitous, districts.

However, in the search for a suitable framing for the global, with all the work that has to be done in terms of clearing ground, there has been a notable tendency to ignore two of the other major categories of social analysis: gender and race. In a wide-ranging essay, Linda Peake draws attention to three different ways in which women are positioned within urban studies: first, that of gendered social relations, 'of women as productive/unproductive – referring to who works, who does not, what work and where work is counted or not – serving to give exposure to women in certain occupa-tions and workplaces while hiding others from view'; second, framings based around embodiment, and particularly the 'regulatory norms of gender, sexuality and morality [that] have dictated whether women are considered in or out of place'; third, perfor-mative framings based around 'identities and sensibilities that shape both a sense of self and of the urban fabric (the latter ranging from accommodating to hostile) have been explored. Although initially focusing on dichotomous emotions of fear and pleasure, this field is expanding to cover a range of women's affective and sensory experiences of the urban (from shackling to liberatory).' And it is driven in part by the disruption to the modernist project of ever expanding opportunities for all:

> Neoliberal developments highlight various debilitating concerns for feminist analyses. With the modern in disarray, contemporary urban forms continue to inspire modernist hopes for a better life, but no longer define a priori what this better life is and how it can be realized in the urban. Addressing these paradoxes constitutes the beginning of a feminist revisioning of urban geographies. Whereas the modern city has been closely characterized by positive associations of key tropes of European and North American nation states – people making, the public, freedom – contemporary neoliberal urban realities are marked by disintegration of family and community, the displacement of the poor, regulatory (and increasingly securitized) infrastructure and violence. (2015: 2)

In a similarly challenging vein, Simone asks about the role of blackness in the ongoing mutations of cities, aligned with the often brutal realities of policing, surveillance and segregation that continue to define black life in many global cities.

> How does one engage the very concrete efforts that constructed the city with all the layers of physical and cultural memory that new regimes usually attempt to cover up, and all that the city does not show, either because its inhabitants are prohibited from paying attention or because whatever is considered normative or spectacular in city life has to get rid of the messy labor and politics that brought it about. Simone (2016: 7)

The remaking of many cities built around black labour and modes of living, from Rio to Cape Town to Detroit, poses a massively disruptive challenge to global city theorizing.

LOGISTICAL TERRITORIES

CIRCUMFERENTIAL AND SURFACE GEOGRAPHIES

If a key element of the book has been that of mobility, then the spaces that are engineered to allow that mobility are a core interest. And so this chapter has an interest in setting out some of the geographies that relate to ports. It begins with a discussion of 'surface geographies', with a particular interest in the ways in which the apparently flat and lifeless maps of global cities are actually inter-related through practices of circumnavigation. An important task is to consider the spatial ontologies of ports, especially in terms of how they modulate the speed of globalization, and organize the surficial crossing of the globe. At first sight, this may have a maritime allusion, but it should also be opened up to think about railheads and airports. To be sure, we shouldn't allow the dramatic allure of Singapore, Dubai and Hong Kong to obscure the fact that many key port cities are organizing continental economies, be it the United States, China or Russia. And that this, as Deb Cowen (2014) has described, is a set of logistical practices that have emerged out of military supply and distribution chains. Circumnavigation and logistics are not just mundane technical practices of shifting crates of artificial Christmas trees and keyboards from manufacturing to consumption zones, but are also the core mechanism of resource exploitation and delivery.

Moreover, this also requires stepping back to think about the nature of fixity and flow, and to briefly cite the role of the classical Greek thinkers Ptolemy, Euclid and Heraclites. In his book *A History of the World in Twelve Maps* (2012), Jerry Brotton describes the different ways in which maps have come to define different social and political perceptions of the world at various times over the last 2500 or so years. One of his most striking discussions concerns the role of Ptolemy, whose *Geography* 'was the first book that, either by accident or design, showed the potential of transmitting geographical data *digitally*' (Brotton 2012: 32, italics in original):

> This first rudimentary digital geography created a world based on a series of interconnecting points, lines and arcs grounded in the Greek tradition of astronomical observation and mathematical speculation ... Ptolemy threw a net across the known world, defined by its enduring abstract principles of geometry and astronomy and the measurement of latitude and longitude. (Brotton 2012: 32)

Similarly, the Greek emphasis on measurement, codified by Euclid, has come to dominate many traditions of contemporary geography, and its influence still can be felt in the global cities literature, one that focuses on the bounding and delimiting of territory. And then there is the concept of 'flow' or 'flux', with its origins in the writings of Heraclitus, whose *Fragments* emphasized the nature of the existence as being of constant change.

There is thus a set of practices of organizing contemporary global capitalism which can be found in the field of logistics, which has a particular view of the material nature of the globe. For Martin, this can be defined as 'logistical surface', 'the type of surface envisioned by logistics and supply-chain management (SCM) practices, but more precisely by containerization, as one of global compatibility, where the previously disaggregated sectors of land and sea freight transport were combined' (2013: 1021). Thus world trade has been enabled by a set of international legal agreements as well as the development of a standardized measurement (the twenty-foot equivalent unit, or TEU) and container size. Martin draws parallels with the automated grain elevators that were a transformative technology in nineteenth-century Chicago:

> The determining factor in the grain elevator was the construction of an automated system (minus extensive human labour), resulting in the almost continuous flow of grain through the space; the organisation, temporal scheduling, and integration of operations; and finally, the designation of the system as a single functioning totality. This example serves to highlight the wider spatiotemporal logic of controlling movement within a systemic whole, but also the movement between the grain elevator and transport infrastructure. Fundamentally, the logic of the seam is that of two surfaces meeting, and the desire to move from an atomized notion of individual items of cargo towards the flow of cargo en masse (albeit in larger scaled units) produces a similar question with regard to the movement and transfer of containers across the various transport platforms and, in particular, how this moment of transfer within a wider logic of continuous movement was and is envisioned. (2013: 1032)

This apparently totalizing system is thus ripe for continuing monitoring and exploration.

These infrastructures make it easy to identify global flows, and flows of capital, of labour. Yet these can often be presented as mercurial, as completely voluntary, with modernity allowing vast distances to be traversed with ease. And yet this is clearly not likely to be the case: much work is done within the logistics industry to make sure this appears to be easy, whether this be with the software that optimizes movement (Rossiter 2016), or the insertion of modes of government that securitize port areas (Cowen 2014). Instead, it is going to be tense. Anna Tsing's *Friction* (2005; see also Tsing 2009a, 2009b) provides an immersive anthropologist's account of why and how deforestation is occurring in the rainforests of Kalimantan. It uses a layered discussion of the interaction of actors that would in simple accounts be called 'global' and 'local', but occupy a rather more complex set of spaces. Globalization as a process is therefore often very sticky (frictional), occasional and prone to disruption or blockage.

This is by no means new. John Law (1986) has applied actor-network theory to maritime imperialism, raising important questions about globalness and localness in the early Portuguese colonial trips:

> the problem for the Portuguese was not just one of social control, though this was important. It was rather, or in addition, one of how to manage long distance control *in all its aspects*. It was how to arrange matters so that a small number of people in Lisbon might influence events half-way round the world, and thereby reap a fabulous reward. And it is also my argument that if these attempts at long-distance control are to be understood then it is not only necessary to develop a form of analysis capable of handling the social, the technological, the natural and the rest with equal facility. (p. 235, italics in original)

And so it is important to consider the work that goes into the standardization of surface, circumference and other ways of conceiving the globe. A starting point is in the field of logistics.

FIGURE 4.1   Stacked shipping containers in port: technologies of both standardization and mobility

Source: © Sheila Fitzgerald / Shutterstock.com

LOGISTICAL TERRITORIES

> If the port is a privileged site of logistical operations, a space from which repatriation corridors can be established and maintained, it is also an important site in any genealogy of the free zones, enclaves, and 'lateral' spaces that dot the contemporary world. The emergence of free ports in antiquity and the Middle Ages marks the beginning of a global geography that assumes a very different shape than that pertaining to territorial states but plays no less a role in the establishment of trade circuits and the ascendance of capital. Exemptions from taxes and tariffs were a key feature of these particular thresholds of land and sea, some of which organized themselves into sophisticated alliances of commerce and politics, such as the Hanseatic League, even before the rise of the modern state. (Mezzadra and Neilson 2013: 206–7)

It may appear at first glance that logistical networks are neutral, technocratic ways of efficiently organizing space. Everyone wants their parcels delivered on time, their food supply to be predictable and secure, and so on. Yet those who benefit from this are not created equal. Instead, we have a globe constituted by 'logistical territories': in other words, sea routes, land corridors, flight paths that have their own internal political economies of predictability and disruption. This has historically been related to how nation-states have secured territory, usually through military force or economic power. And so the logistical routes tend to bear a close relation to geopolitical power.

There have been several significant elaborations of how these exemptions, or exceptions, are actively structuring globalization. There are premium networks of territorially defined zones based around infrastructure: Graham and Marvin's (2001) *Splintering Urbanism* addressed this in some depth, highlighting the widespread process of 'bundling and unbundling' of infrastructural assets, particularly in developing cities, which effectively marginalized the urban poor. In her book *Extrastatecraft*, Keller Easterling (2014) provides a taxonomy and imagined geography of some of the techniques by which nation-states and corporations collude and compete to organize economic territory. The current proliferation of free trade and special economic zones, technology parks and offshore enclaves finds one of its most important precedents in such borderscapes.

These spaces can be structured by a set of agreed standards that are 'zonal', in the formulation of Andrew Barry (2006). It is important to understand how the major global technology firms are, through their interventions in both software and the hard infrastructure of the city, operating in the definition and alteration of various networks and routes. These zones 'point to the existence of forms of space which are neither territorially bounded nor global in their extension … a space within which differences between technical practices, procedures or forms have been reduced' (p. 239). As Ned Rossiter argues in his book *Software, Infrastructure, Labor* (2016), this requires a deeper engagement with the nature of the protocols and algorithms that underpin the material global trade system of goods and less tangible things such as intellectual property. He highlights the material significance of software protocols and standards, and their impact on everyday life through the capacity of software to analyse how long, and how 'efficiently', it takes workers to complete particular tasks: 'The capacity of algorithmic architectures to organize and analyze data on labor productivity in real-time, for instance, means that they operate as key technologies for governing labor within logistical industries' (Rossiter 2016: 4). These automated landscapes, governed by 'enterprise resource planning' software and the algorithms within, relentlessly re-engineer space yet remain little understood. The global logistics industry uses specialist software applications 'to visualize and organize these mobilities, producing knowledge about the world in transit'. For Rossiter, then, a fundamental element of the globalization thesis would be the extent to which a set of standards and protocols within the software industry, marketed by global firms such as SAP and IBM, are adapted and implemented by global logistics firms. These would effectively flatten out the localized labour conditions in each place. The field known as 'software studies' thus becomes a fundamental element of understanding relational urban economies.

This might steer us back towards a focus on the mundane technologies that allow the existence of a global condition. To take one example, credit cards compress individual identities and financial liquidity into one small piece of plastic, used simultaneously as a marker of identity, a store of value, a tool of instant international transactional exchange and one element of a chain of material sites, which link the human user and owner to a wider banking credit system. In *A History of the World in 100 Objects*, Neil McGregor, the Director of the British Museum, nominates a credit card as one of his key motifs of world history, choosing one issued in the United Arab Emirates, as a way of illustrating this global circuitry:

> This particular Gold Card is issued by the London-based bank called HSBC, the Hong Kong and Shanghai Banking Corporation. It functions through the backing of the US-based credit association, VISA, and has on it writing in Arabic – it is in short connected to the whole world, part of a global financial system, backed by a complex electronic superstructure that many of us barely think about as we key in our PINs. All our credit card transactions are tracked and recorded, building a huge dossier of our movements, writing our economic biographies on the other side of the world. (2013: 549)

The properties of a credit card are interesting in themselves: they also embody a miniaturization of technology that can be seen in many other everyday items, from smartphones to cameras, based on complex data compression algorithms on the one hand, and chip and circuit technologies on the other.

The zoning of territories in this way is often associated with 'exceptional' labour contracts and conditions. In her book *Flexible Citizenship*, Aihwa Ong has argued that many nation-states are now structured around a 'graduated sovereignty', where territory is divided into a 'series of zones that are subjected to different kinds of governmentality and that vary in terms of the mix of disciplinary and civilizing regimes' (1999: 7). Working with a similar logic, Mezzadra and Neilson's *Border as Method* (2013) theorizes the multiple ways in which borders are political tools by which contemporary economies are striated, sorting out labour into different categories of job security. And as Katie Hepworth notes, the figure of labour is often hidden within supply chains:

> Whether understood as 'productive', 'efficient', or 'flexible' labour, workers are made to subsume the frictions in the supply chain, and smooth out the glitches and bottlenecks through the deregulation of their personal and familial temporal boundaries. Shifts are made flexible in order to use terminal and maritime infrastructure more efficiently and productively, to maintain regular schedules despite unforeseen circumstances, or to ensure the smooth flow of containers through the quay and landside of the terminal so as to ensure compliance with government regimes aimed at improving the performance of the port as a whole. These embodied temporalities associated with the port extend into the city through the 'extended gateways' and distribution centres discussed above. (2014: 1132)

So it is important to identify the changing role of labour in the reorganization of supply chains between air, sea, rail and road transport that has characterized the globalization of trade in manufactured goods in recent years. Whether it be cars, toys, coal or components, the key innovation has been the mastering of 'intermodalism' – the ability to shrink shipment times and distance through the shifting of containers between ship, road, air and rail. As Martin has identified, this has relied on various types of standardization:

> The decisive difference between the protoforms of containerisation and the intermodal shipping container we know today lies with standardisation. Without agreement on the design and dimensions of the container, a global system of compatibility in the form of intermodalism would not have been possible. Equally, without standardised container handling and, more fundamentally, without the standardisation of the entire freight-transport infrastructure, the logic of integration that we have seen emphasised numerous times by those advocating the economic imperative of containerised freight movement would not have been feasible. A key issue in the literature on standardisation is that of 'guarantee' … guaranteed standards that remain stable across space and time through a legislative framework, such as the ISO, to protect these agreements. (2013: 1028–9)

And so we can see that economic territories are being driven by global firms, some of which have a very tight relationship with major government actors in various countries. Having control of ports is thus a fundamental element in delivering, fulfilling and enacting these geographies.

PORT ONTOLOGIES

> Ports have been historical holding zones where a multiplicity of techniques
> for filtering and surveying movements of people and things have been
> invented and refined, from the migration processing systems that evolved
> at sites like Ellis Island to methods of quarantine inspection and isolation.
> (Mezzadra and Neilson 2013: 207)

For many centuries, the cities often thought of as global were characterized by their
rambunctious port scenes. Think of New York's Lower East Side or New Jersey's
waterfront or San Francisco's Embarcadero; the European ports of Amsterdam,
Marseilles and Venice; or Shanghai and Singapore, important colonial ports of Asia.
These were ports where merchandise was actually brought to market and stored
right next to the waterfront. Many contained auction areas, reflecting the fact that
the prices and markets of mercantile capitalism were made only when the scarcity of
a good was known. Then there were the processes of 'bulk-breaking' where a large
ship's load was manually brought to land by gangs of dockers, many of whom were
paid very poorly, part of a maritime proletariat that might move between working
on shipping lines and the logistics of dry land. In many cases, these workers provided
some of the earliest examples of a transnational working class, whose presence links
together cities as diverse as Liverpool and Kuala Lumpur (Bunnell 2016).

Ships have been key technologies in the construction of a particular set of global
power relations. Their use of oceans to dominate and organize land territory makes
them precarious, yet romanticized, agents of world-making (Law 1986). This is
perhaps why the pirate is such an important figure in Western popular culture,
especially children's literature, a haunting trace of the unsettled and fragmented
landscapes of power that constituted the pre-modern unregulated land–ocean
nexus. In US ports, the dreaded 'Shanghaiing' practice of forcibly indenturing
port workers into ships was a significant feature of the nineteenth-century capitalist organization of maritime cities such as San Francisco and Portland. Mezzadra
and Neilson:

> As enclaves for the harboring of ships, ports were also peculiar legal spaces
> where different juridical orders came into interaction. In the fifteenth and
> sixteenth centuries, when the first modern empires were emerging, the ship
> was organized around the legal authority of the captain, who assumed an
> absolute power analogous to that of a monarch. (2013: 207)

And so, ships became fundamental motors of globalization, despite the risks involved.
As a basis for global trade, they provided a parallel geography to the emergence of
imperial cities that centralized commodity trading (Driver and Gilbert 2003). They
also created a market for additional financial services such as insurance: the establishment of Lloyds of London, still a landmark in London's financial services centre, was

based substantially on covering the risks involved in shipping. Its famous bell, which chimed when a ship was lost at sea, heralded a loss in capital as much as a loss in life. And so, 'The discontinuous legal seascape resulting from the movements of these floating islands and from the projection of the territorial law of European monarchies across the oceans anticipated the peculiar relationship of modern empires with territory' (Mezzadra and Neilson 2013: 207).

How the port landscape has changed. The advent of containerization in the late 1960s, combined with the opening or widening of key trans-continental canals such as Panama and Suez, meant that global trade could now be conducted by larger and larger ships. Cargo was standardized into TEUs; crane technology made many of the manual dock jobs unnecessary. And as ports became more and more automated, so they became easier to privatize. And so, the maritime port now has a completely different set of geographies. Consider this discussion by Olivier and Slack:

> The internationalization of port management is premised on TNCs [transnational corporations] capitalizing on institutionally defined, terminal-level entry opportunities. We suggest that this has induced a *rescaling effect* that recognises the terminal as the relevant entity upon which to build a theoretical and empirical research agenda. This does not imply that we should ignore the port as a *politically cohesive entity* (as a stakeholders' consensual space), as in recent debates over the fate of port authorities, but that we recognize that intermodality, logistics, and institutional change have brought about a spatial fragmentation of the port based on commercial principles. As such, governance approaches have been most successful in challenging a diachronic monolithic view of the *port as a space*, a simple dot on a map, varying in size and shape: rather, presenting the *port as a place* where synchronic forces are played out among a pluralistic port community striving for common internal and external goals. We contend that this spatial 'deconstruction' of the port constitutes an epistemological condition for theorizing the port as an expanding nexus of terminals under corporate governance. (2006: 1417–18, italics in original)

The typical port is now an area characterized by three or four contiguous terminals, with a small number of global shippers operating them as part of a global supply chain. Hepworth provides an interesting example here:

> *We export air.* These words were spoken to us during a tour of the MSC yard for empty containers in Sydney, as we drove between stacks of empty containers, B-doubles queuing to be loaded, and straddle carriers organising the layout of the stacks and getting containers onto trucks. For the most part, the tour focused on local operations and regional logistical relationships; our tour guide described the operations of the yard, the introduction of new ICT to facilitate the tracking and loading of containers and significantly

> improve turnaround time, and explained the relationship between the port, the container yard, and local and regional distribution hubs. However, three words – we export air – subtly invoked the global context within which these local logistical operations took place. They transformed these stacks of empty containers into the material effect of Australia's asymmetrical relationship with its main trading partners, in which only one full container is exported for every two imported. (Hepworth 2014, 1123–4, emphasis in original)

Most of the cargo moved by ocean is not high value, but rather bulk. Airports offer a different time-space for higher value items, such as perishable food and flowers, making air cargo a major contributor to the globalization process:

> Moving large amounts of freight over great distances, as the air-cargo industry does on a daily basis, is a complex business that involves many firms and requires ongoing coordination between them, with respect both to the physical movement of goods and to the management and exchange of information. Moving freight internationally adds an additional layer of complexity because of the regulations involved, ranging from traffic lights and licensing requirements to customs and security regulations. International air cargo, by its very nature, involves companies that are located in different time zones, and have different languages, economic systems, and cultures, necessitating both in-depth local knowledge and the ability to bridge these gaps on a global level. This complexity has resulted in an industry with actors ranging from the very small and local to the fully integrated and global in reach. (Schwarz 2006: 1468)

And so, port spaces are technologies in themselves where border problems are overcome. Wang and Cheng (2010) highlight the ways in which Hong Kong has undergone a transformation from being 'a hub port city to a global supply chain management center', with port operators pursuing a 'gateway supply chain integration' (p. 111) which has included both air–land and air–land–air logistics. This has required modes of making border crossing between Hong Kong and China routinized: initiatives have included the introduction of bonded trucks, and a customs processing centre inside Hong Kong territory from where trucks can take a 'green lane' on the highway without stopping at the border.

Similarly, ports such as Amsterdam – central to the famed Dutch flower industry – are now configured as part of routinized 'cold chains', where perishable foods such as fish, flowers and fruit are flown long distances. An important literature – 'commodity chains' – has emerged that explains how this process creates 'added value', as non-seasonal or remotely sourced foods become staples in the households of advanced economies (Hughes and Reimer 2004). The cold-chain technology, though, demonstrates the time-specific nature of this element of globalization:

What emerges from the planes is not a loose stream of boxes but a sequence of aluminium canisters, abbreviated by the ramp workers as 'cans'. Pie-sliced and semi-circular, cans are to air cargo what the container is to shipping and tracking … If all goes well, each package inside will be touched only twice by a pair of hands – once exiting its can upon arrival, and then again as it's placed into a second can for departure. The progress of each parcel is guided by the 'smart label' affixed to it at pickup. The labels contain a zip code and … a tracking number. (Kasarda and Lindsay 2011: 65–6)

These cans are then internally sorted within complex sorting depots:

Every package entering the sort passes under a camera and infrared sensor capable of reading characters and correctly estimating dimensions and weight. In the future, even that won't be necessary once radio frequency identification chips are embedded in their sides, broadcasting the vital signs of what's within. (Kasarda and Lindsay 2011: 66–7)

And so, the 'fast' logistics industry, dominated by the likes of Fedex or UPS, is a key element in the production of the 'aerotropolis' model, which at best would strategically co-locate 'just in time' industries with air-based distribution. The rise of e-commerce has enhanced the viability of these 'shipping and handling' hubs.

A key spatial practice, then, is the co-ordination of these chains, which in turn is a perfect example of what Dodge and Kitchin (2004) term code/space: the constitution

FIGURE 4.2 Shipbreaking in Chittagong, Bangladesh, 2016: the often invisible end-point of global trade.

Source: © Katiekk / Shutterstock.com

of material territory by way of software. For example, Hepworth (2014) describes how two separate software systems, bridging the container vessel and the dock area, speak to each other to stitch together land and sea. The relationship between the container ship, and how it stows its containers, and the high-intensity, ultra-rational space of the terminal, provide the specific modes by which the grand notion of time-space compression is achieved:

> The interface between these different software systems – the terminal operating system and the ship stowage plan – determines and tracks the location of each container. It also determines how it moves through its various locations, aiming to optimise the time taken to move through space, and the intermediate positions between its start and end points on the quayside, landside, or ship. However, these ICT systems do not just determine where each of these containers goes, they actively reconfigure that 'where'. (Hepworth 2014: 1125)

A SHIP-CENTRIC ONTOLOGY OF THE URBAN?

Of all the spatial motifs concerning the globalization of cities, few can match the shipping container. The mysterious names on their sides – Maersk, South China Shipping, DPO – provide a glimpse of their geographical origins. Yet not far from the stacks of containers that might betray the existence of a container port, many cities possess maritime museums, which emerged as a standard spatial format on deindustrialized, devalorized docklands, no longer organized around bulk-breaking, far too small to enable the unrolling of the oceanic supply chain into national and continental territories. These are some of the few visual reminders of the importance that ships once had within the texture of cities, especially trading cities. Woodcuts and lithographs of cities such as Venice and Oslo show ships prominently in the foreground. But, with the advent of containerization, has the figure of the ship been lost? Do we need to reconnect the motif of the ship with framings of the urban? As Hasty and Peters (2012: 662–3) point out, ships are still key in the production of knowledge about the globe:

> We need only think of the icebreaking floating laboratories that chart the effects of climate change at either pole, or those that are mapping changes in levels of biodiversity in the coral reefs of the southern Pacific, or indeed the sonar-mounted ships seeking untapped submarine deposits of oil or gas around the world. The ship has ever been entangled in the production of knowledge, a site of thought and accumulation of thought, a place wherein the facts and theories about which curious minds wonder or hold dear are both crafted and contested. The ship then has a place within geography, in the making of geographical knowledge.

A ship-centred ontology is not one that springs to mind when thinking of global cities, but perhaps it should be:

> The material construction of the ship, its voyages and the finance that underpin them, the people that form its crew and the exchanges they have with others, and the cargo it traffics, all highlight the connected and entangled nature of the globalised world ... This is because the ship is a moving technology, traversing a moving surface; in a space of fluid legal boundaries. It is also so intricately bound-up with the everyday lives of much of the world's population, indeed approximately 95% of trade is still carried by ship. A whole range of sea-going cargo vessels traverse vast ocean spaces and littoral zones. Thus it is important to explore the mobilities of vessels which carry with them cargo which shapes our daily lives. ... Questions too about the mobilities of human subjects arise with the subject, about the conditions of labour and transit, about the actual freedom of movement experienced by seemingly mobile subjects, for example. (Hasty and Peters 2012: 669)

Maritime transport is core to the formation of an urbanized world. This is not to say that ships be considered alone, but rather as part of a necessary apparatus of connections and infrastructures that allow trade to happen. John Law's (1986) account of Portuguese imperial expansion is a classic actor-network tale:

> I want to argue that it is not possible to understand this expansion unless the technological, the economic, the political, the social, and the natural are all seen as being interrelated. My argument is that the Portuguese effort involved the mobilisation and combination of elements from each of these categories. Of course kings and merchants appear in the story. But so too do sailors and astronomers, navigators and soldiers of fortune, astrolabes and astronomical tables, vessels and ports of call, and last but not least, the winds and currents that lay between Lisbon and Calicut. (p. 235)

The notorious flat ontology is on display here: kings and astrolabes, sailors and currents. But it is a persuasive account of how the global is not simply large, as Law later put it (2004).

This mix of the mundane and glorious opens up a vast terrain of enquiry which allows the stripping back of the process of globalization. Consider Crang's (2010: 1084) discussion of the dismantling of ships and the treatment of waste, captured in art and documentary, which requires us to take account of

(Continued)

(Continued)

the temporal dimension of commodities through their wasting and disposal comprising the abject material of capitalism, which we seek to expel from our view and consciousness, yet is an intrinsic part of consumption. Rendering waste invisible to its producers is now made all the easier by flows that take used commodities from consumers and break them into various constituent parts elsewhere around the globe.

While many of the geographies of surface described in this chapter concern the constitution of cities, there remains an 'abject' element to complete the commodity life cycle: shipbreaking, which has its own specific geographies. Much of the global distribution of waste ends up in South Asia, in cities such as Chittagong in Bangladesh.

AIRPORT TERRITORIES

The aviopolis, the networked and dispersed city of the air, operates rather differently than a metropolis. This city has a different command over space than the city of skylines. The aviopolis turns mobility and connection into a productive force that produces value and in the process reshapes a city and its infrastructure. (Fuller and Harley 2004: 140)

The development of air travel as the dominant mode of global networking and travel has had a profound effect on the territorial logics of port cities. With an increasingly diverse range of commercial activities, a large and complex workforce, and a potentially integrative role in the construction of new regional economies, major global city airports are emerging as a novel and vitally important aspect of contemporary urban life. While they certainly possess an internal logic of organization and governance, given the need for careful co-ordination of plane movements, security and surface access, their impact on the existing metropolis can be very significant. Airport management, which was in many places dominated by military or state bureaucratic leadership, is becoming more commercialized and sensitive to the growing waves of financialization of state assets. These management corporations are increasingly aware of value adding in areas such as terminal retailing, business tourism (with hotel and convention centres), and logistics, cargo and aeronautical engineering functions.

This is particularly pronounced within globalizing city-regions, especially in emerging regional economies such as Southeast Asia and the Gulf, where airports have been increasingly used as a motor for rescaling the existing urban structure (e.g. Bunnell 2004a; McNeill 2010, 2014). The wave of new airports being built across

Asia, from the Gulf in the West to Japan in the Northeast, has escalated air-passenger numbers in the region, meeting underlying demand for travel. States have taken the opportunity to implement major city-regional spatial strategies around their airports, evident in the huge developments in the likes of Osaka, Incheon, Guangzhou, Kuala Lumpur, Shanghai, Bangkok and Dubai.

The concept of the airport city or aerotropolis has been popular for some years (Kasarda and Lindsay 2011). Instead of being seen as noisy, polluted, and boring, advocates suggest that airports can be planned around well-paid logistics industries, high quality housing, and mixed use education and entertainment hubs. This debate has included the use of international airline passenger data as a key indicator of international – indeed, global – connectivity (Smith and Timberlake 2001). At first sight, therefore, airports are fairly stable, taken for granted prerequisites for global city status. City-states such as Hong Kong, Dubai, Taiwan and Singapore seem particularly apposite for interpretation in this way, and have been built up on the basis of a competitive advantage in trade, both of tangible and intangible goods. Singapore particularly, is widely recognized as having maximized its logistical influence despite having a small territorial footprint. As Olds and Yeung ask:

> How can a city no larger than Surabaya in Indonesia, Ankara in Turkey, Cologne in Germany, Monterrey in Mexico, Montreal in Canada, or Boston in the United States ensure that economic and social development proceeds when there are *no* natural resources within the boundaries of the city, and *no* sources of intergovernmental transfer payments (or multilateral aid)? It does so by using the powers and capacities of the nation-state (in material and discursive senses) to transform society and space within the city, all in the aim of embedding Singapore within the evolving lattice of network relations that propel the world economy. (2004: 491, italics in original)

Such developmental states (those that have emerged from colonialism and adopt globally competitive economic sectors as a central plank of all policy) generate

> a plethora of state-directed institutions, policies, programs, and projects … to spur on the outward investment process. This is in part because the historical underdevelopment of indigenous entrepreneurship in the private sector has convinced the state that regionalization drives cannot effectively be taken up by private sector initiatives alone. (Olds and Yeung 2004: 512)

The facilitation of trade thus becomes a key element of state policy, which in turn places infrastructural development in an elevated position within state policy priorities.

Airports and container ports, alongside utilities and telecommunications infrastructure, are thus fundamental aspects of such economies. There are key mechanisms whereby extra-territorial power relations can be designed, regulated and managed by state authorities, and where

> people, organisations, institutions and firms are able to extend their influence in time and space beyond the 'here' and 'now' … This applies whether users are 'visiting' websites across the planet, telephoning a far-off friend or call centre, using distantly sourced energy or water resources, shifting their waste through pipes to far-off places, or physically moving their bodies across space on highways, streets or transport systems. (Graham and Marvin 2001: 11)

However, developing these extra-territorial links involves a substantial investment in terms of sunk costs, and such mechanisms 'represent long-term accumulations of finance, technology, know-how, and organisational and geopolitical power' (p. 12).

Given this, the airport has a powerful role in increasing the connectivity of national territories, both internally and internationally. While often associated as a facilitator of globalization, it is still often conceived in geopolitical terms both as a means of uniting large dispersed national territories. In Malaysia, for example, the new Kuala Lumpur International Airport was sited in Sepang, at the centre of an emerging high-technology corridor anchored at both ends by the new city centre dominated by the Petronas Towers, and a planned information technology hub, which together sought to form a '"backbone" controlling the national geo-body' (Bunnell 2004a: 109). In China, new terminals (such as in Beijing) and airports (such as at Shanghai's Pudong, or Guangzhou) act as important hubs for pulling together the hugely dispersed urban centres of the national territory.

For city-states such as Singapore, Hong Kong and the smaller Gulf states such as Dubai or Abu Dhabi, the airport and its territory can play a dual function in terms of extra-territorial relationships. Airport authorities can act in partnership with state airlines, such as Singapore Airlines, Cathay Pacific, Emirates or Etihad, in order to address issues of curfews, slot availability and gate-service quality. In these cases, the strong performance of both airport and airlines will be mutually supportive, and can collectively add to the brand power of each territory. This can have important benefits in terms of positioning the city-state as a global business space, such as in the hosting of trade fairs (Beaverstock et al. 2009; Jones 2009), or else in augmenting the city's tourist industry. As importantly, however, it allows a closer integration of globally operative logistics firms with the physical spaces of cargo transportation, as Schwarz notes:

> In effect, the virtual space of information flows has become just as important in determining the industrial structure of this transport sector as the physical space of transportation. Many air-cargo firms are never directly involved in the transport of commodities and are, instead, dedicated exclusively to coordinating and information-processing functions. All types of air-cargo company now compete on the basis of their IT and management. It is this virtual dimension of air cargo that is the center of growth and economic dynamism during the present phase of industrial restructuring. (2006: 1481)

FIGURE 4.3   Hong Kong International Airport: the programming of terminal space is now a specialist management practice

Source: © Sorbis / Shutterstock.com

For Schwarz, the air-cargo industry highlights the tight relationship between virtual and physical space.

In order to smooth the path of goods and people into the city, state authorities are paying increasing attention to the nature of the airport platform, the totality of the aeronautical and non-aeronautical activities that take place within the airport's footprint (Güller and Güller 2003), and in turn how this platform is integrated with the surrounding metropolis. Many of the sunk costs associated with new airport development tends to be expended on improved surface accessibility, given the growing preference for dedicated high-speed public rail access, along with the usual increases in road capacity. In states with highly centralized powers, new airports can be planned methodically and with the minimum of opposition.

Airport development cannot be understood using a singular logic, or indeed by conceptualizing the airport as a singularity in itself. It may be better to speak of airport territories, a more expansive term that includes the following components: (1) an awkwardly scaled jurisdictional space, under the management of an airport authority, which operates within a complex web of state bodies, and could be variously governed by acts of parliament, regional or metropolitan governments, private equity groups, aviation authorities, competition watchdogs and local councils (e.g. Güller and Güller 2003); (2) an aggregate of sub-divided spaces, each with their own sub-jurisdictional operational autonomy, from a terminal cafe to a maintenance hangar, and each with specific labour contracts; (3) a space of public mobility, bound up with a temporality of arrival, dwell-time and departure (e.g. Adey 2003, 2008); (4) a topographical positioning, mapped within larger territorial spaces (e.g. Cosgrove 1999); (5) airspace, as in the corridors of approach and take-off that are required for the airport to function safely, but which are in many case hotly contested by those 'on the ground' (e.g. Cidell 2008). Consequently, we should seek ways of narrating the airport's ontology in ways that acknowledge these more extensive territorial entanglements, and which position the airport as polity and urban spatial formation.

THE PRODUCTION OF HONG KONG INTERNATIONAL AIRPORT

Hong Kong is often described as a bridge or a gateway, but neither metaphor conveys the extent to which Hong Kong and its firms actively set up, direct, and manage activities for the local, regional and global economies ... A Hong Kong company, for example, might help a United States apparel company design its autumn collection and then organise purchasing, manufacturing and logistics to get the product onto retail shelves on time, meeting the right quality and product specifications, and on budget. (Enright et al. 2005: 20)

The development of Hong Kong International Airport (HKIA) took place at the juncture of two important economic and political moments in the territory. The 1980s were marked by a striking shift in perspective from colonial ties to the UK, to a more global perspective. The territory's largest corporations, such as Hong Kong and Shanghai Bank, Jardine Matheson, Swire Pacific, Hong Kong Telecom, and China Light and Power, began to alter their terrain of operation (Sum 1995). Politically, the lease of Hong Kong and its surrounding territories to Britain was due to expire in 1997, and given the impending arrival of a suspicious Chinese government, there was concern as to how far the city-state would be allowed to develop economically. The existing airport, Kai Tak, was rapidly approaching full capacity, constrained by its notorious inner-city location, where planes landed in between high-rise apartment blocks and the harbour. Most importantly, its single runway meant that there was little room for increasing flight numbers at the very moment when Southeast Asia was developing rapidly, and with a rapid increase in passenger and cargo numbers projected.

As a result, the development of a new airport was fast-tracked by the British government, through Governor-General Chris Patten, and the ruling council of the Hong Kong government. As Dimbleby (2002) shows, the negotiations over the airport were one of the key agenda items in the negotiations between Patten's team and the Chinese government. Sunk costs and project finance became a very serious discussion point during the formation of the Sino-Anglo Agreement, with the Chinese concerned about the scale of the project, and the size of debt that they would incur when accession took place. Ultimately, the resolution of the dispute in 1995 was one of the most significant post-war political territorial moments in Southern China (*New York Times* 1995).

The Chinese concerns were well founded, given the huge scale of the proposed project, which achieved worldwide attention for its size and complexity. The site chosen for the new airport was on the small island of Chek Lap Kok, which sat close to the large island of Lantau, approximately 34 kilometres to the west of the existing downtown. This had potential for a very large airport platform to be developed which allowed for future growth. However, the site was remote from the existing business hubs of Kowloon and Central on Hong Kong Island. To address these issues, the entire airport development was embedded within a framework known as the Airport Core Program (ACP). This entailed ten separate, but interdependent, projects: the airport itself, which included very significant earthworks to create a platform for the developments; a new 34 kilometre rail system consisting of both a dedicated express airport link and a new commuter line linking the airport to Hong Kong Island and Kowloon; a new suspension bridge capable of carrying both car and rail traffic (the Lantau fixed crossing); three new highways; a 1 mile tunnel beneath the harbour (the Western Harbour Crossing); a new town adjacent to the airport, known as Tung Chung; and two large tracts of reclaimed land to allow for new port and industrial facilities, one in West Kowloon, and the other in Central/Wanchai. Taken together with Hong Kong's other major development projects, the government was engaged in a conscious process of 'world-city formation' (Ng 2006).

The completion of these projects has had a significant effect on the Hong Kong economy, in three separate ways. First, it has provided a major boost for the old trading conglomerates as they sought to navigate closer integration with China. Some of these were directly related to the airport. The major tenant of HKIA is Cathay Pacific, whose major shareholder is Swire Pacific, a company with its roots in the Hong Kong–British colonial relationship. Cathay has a large headquarter area, Cathay Pacific City, within the airport platform, close to Tung Chung new town. Second, it has allowed for a multi-modal port facility to develop which has given Hong Kong leverage within global trade. This has allowed for a significant expansion of cargo processing, especially of high value added products. Third, it has facilitated the emergence of a new Hong Kong transnational subjectivity. As Ley (2010) describes, the end of British colonialism coincided with the creation of new visa regimes in several countries, most notably Canada, Australia, New Zealand and the UK. These often allowed favourable tax treatment for Hong Kong entrepreneurs who became 'astronauts', frequently shuttling between Hong Kong and their adopted homes.

(Continued)

(Continued)

The presence of an inter-locking set of corporate leaders in key sectors such as finance, property and manufacturing is evidence of how Hong Kong's economy is underpinned by arbitrage, but also its often uneasy interplay between state and private enterprise (Studwell 2007; Goodstadt 2009). The airport and associated logistics systems are central to attempts to increase the intensity and value-adding capabilities of this process. As is described in Kasarda and Lindsay's *Aerotropolis* (2011), the Pearl River Delta is world-leading in terms of manufacturing due to the size of its labour pool, the availability of credit, and the existence of firms that are able to marshal these resources to meet the demand of global operators. Firms such as the now notorious Foxconn in Shenzhen, or the logistics firm PCH International, are some of the key motors of the Delta. The latter is particularly attuned to arbitrage, as Lindsay finds when he interviews the CEO:

> We had barely crossed the border before he opened his laptop and began walking me through the true costs of these shipments. He'd built a widget calculating every conceivable variable: the weight, volume, value, and quantity of the products in question; the lead times for sourcing and building them; time spent in transit; their shelf life; the spread between paying his vendors and being paid himself; the cost of money in the meantime; and the cost of returns. An entire calculus, in other words, underlies the pivotal question of our era: *What is the price of speed?* (Kasarda and Lindsay 2011: 361, emphasis in original)

This price was central to the new wave of airport operators who were increasingly being appointed with backgrounds in business rather than civil or military aviation, as had often been the case in airport authorities around the world.

★★★★

This chapter has focused on the development of various technologies and practices that have organized movement across the surface of the globe, with a focus on both moving technologies, such as ships, and the organization of urban spaces in ports. They themselves require a new ontology, as port studies as a field of enquiry has followed a parallel route to that of the global cities debate, their paths rarely crossing (Olivier and Slack 2006). They are now fully implicated in the geopolitical organization of economies. As Mezzadra and Neilson point out:

A crucial question in this regard concerns the changing intersections between jurisdiction and territory and their relevance for understanding the political, economic, and legal constitution of such indeterminate and ambiguous spaces. All of the spaces that we have evoked here, from the free trade zone to offshore enclaves, appear as anomalous from the point of view of the modern state and its legal and political standards. Despite the fact that states still lay claim to the whole of the Earth's surface, including the submarine depths and ocean tops, there has been a proliferation of such spaces. (2013: 208)

An important interpretive task here is to consider the nature of fixity and flow. In some ways this is a mirror of the local and global, and has the same problematic binary properties. It also hints at material properties which I see as important: with fixity comes a sense of heaviness, a difficulty of moving, like rock – which brings forth metaphors of sedimentation, for example. It is an important corrective to the sense – often exaggerated – of global elites flying around the world at will. Here, contemporary corporate titans such as Amazon would affirm, it is 'fulfilment' of transactions, as much as the volume of transactions themselves, which are key. Allen, in his book *Lost Geographies of Power*, makes exactly this point:

One of the prime difficulties with the 'authoritative' centre view of power is that it tends to be judged by its *intended* rather than its *actual* effects. Because various agencies within global cities have the skills and resources 'to run' the global economy, it is somehow assumed that this is indeed what happens. (2003: 157, italics in original)

We can find fixity even in things that move. For example, using ideas such as inventory or contracts such as leasing, we can see that even things that move (such as container vessels) are stuck into certain patterns. Perhaps they are as fixed as the multiple interpretive fields of the contemporary city are fluid. And it is clear from the work of scholars such as Ong (2006) and Mezzadra and Neilson (2013) that global cities are in fact borderlands themselves, as well as 'arrival cities' in many cases.

There is also a sense in which the links between labour and logistics is ignored, and the end life of ships as objects. Crang (2010) draws attention to vivid representations of shipbreaking by the photographers Edward Burtynsky and Allan Sekula, advocating a closes focus on the life cycle of ships as material objects, and in particular shipping and 'wastes': 'products at the end of their lives, dumped, discarded, and being dismantled'. Crang argues that this is an important focus for three reasons.

First, thinking through waste creates a time-image that discloses the instability of things. An image that goes beyond a focus on being, and even one seeing things as always becoming, with its sense of positive vitality, to one that stresses their undoing and unbecoming. The second reason is that waste highlights unbecoming things in the adjectival sense where synonyms include discreditable, indecorous, and unflattering. Those connotations make waste amenable to being used politically to highlight the negative outcomes of globalization ... Third, if the materiality of commodity flows is too easily forgotten, then the large global flows of wastes which have emerged in tandem with them restates their materiality. It is the ultimately abject material – denied, concealed, and distanced from the body social yet irrevocably connected to it. (p. 1085)

A core task of many of these photographers is to ensure that these processes are exhibited in the places of their consumption, particularly the cities of advanced capitalism. Salgado's *Workers: an Archaeology of the Industrial Age* (2005), for example, continues that photographer's 'preoccupation with enabling workers who produce goods to become visible and also to return the gaze of the consumers' (Crang 2010: 1090). The images are 'a restatement of the presence of labour, and the pictures are an assertion of these worlds of manual toil in an age that often claims to be postindustrial; they are images out of time that depict labour conditions that many in the West have consigned to history' (Crang 2010: 1090).

Finally, it is important to consider how the materiality of the container or vessel is determinant in the type of flow, and its predictability. Certainly, an interest in how cities are 'chained' would be useful as Hasty and Peters (2012: 669) propose:

Rather than simply focusing on trade routes themselves, or the connections between places, or broader globalising processes of ships, we might also ask what governs the watery mobilities of ships engaged in trade. How, for example, does the size of the ship, the flag under which it sails, the company whom owns it, the cargo it holds, the insurance underwriting the vessel, the security level of the ship, determine where it might travel and dock?

Another important process which we can borrow from the logistics industry – tracking – might be helpful in providing evidence of all this, but at the same time giving it a firm epistemological basis. And we must also be aware, of course, that the growing sophistication of software coded spaces is itself creating a series of digitized corridors where the supply chains of the contemporary world are organized and interconnected.

CENTRES OF CALCULATION

> Desks, filing cabinets, mimeographs, adding-machines, card indexes, desk calendars, telephone extensions, adjustable desk lights. Wire correspondence baskets, erasers, carbon paper, type-brushes, dust rages, waste paper baskets. Pencils, hard and soft, black and blue and red. Pens, nibs, backing sheets, notebooks, paper clips. Gum, paste, stationery: the half dozen sorts of envelopes and letter heads. Tools were these, as important in trade as the masthead and black flag … As important and perhaps to be deemed as romantic some day; witness the rhapsodic advertisements for filing cabinets that are built like battle ships. (Sinclair Lewis, *The Job*, 1917, in Haigh 2012: 90)

For many years, the 'central business district' (CBD) was a key term in explaining urban structure. However, as part of a wider critique on positivist urban and economic geography, it has dropped out of usage, despite the growth in work on – particularly global – cities more generally. This has left a vacuum: it is now widely accepted that the centres of many cities are as important as ever to national and global economies, but there has been little development of the epistemological and ontological frames needed to analyse these claims. This chapter employs several, loosely conversant, conceptual tools as a means of helping to re-specify the condition of centrality in cities.

Recent work on the historiography of geographical concepts, associated particularly with the work of Trevor Barnes, has queried the geopolitical basis for many of the key concepts of positivist spatial theory. In particular, the central place theory of Walter Christaller, a mainstay of urban theory for many decades, has now been called into question as evidence of Christaller's participation in Nazi governance has come to light (Barnes and Minca 2013). Its ease of application to the analysis of post-war urban economies belied its importance to a more sinister political history. As Barnes puts it, central place theory was fundamentally about spatial relations, speaking to key aspects of the Nazi project. It was seemingly modernist (rational, law-seeking, scientific), but made overtures also to tradition and the past. Theoretically, its beginning point were individual farmers surrounding the smallest urban unit, the village (*dorf*), emphasizing rural community, people and soil, *Volksgemeinschaft*. But the culmination of the hierarchy was über modernity, industrial urban behemoths like Dortmund, Essen, Bochum, and the ultimate, Berlin. (2015: 196)

And so the apparently innocent technique followed by students of geography for many years was, in its cold, rigorous detachment, a technique of the systematization of terror. And in turn, the emptying out of territory through genocide, to allow its subsequent repopulation.

Despite the growing sophistication of urban theory and research, there have been few attempts to specify, or write a specification of, what the central business district is now within urban theory, and especially urban economic theory. I argue that this is important, not least because we have seen a rush of new 'popular' urban theory books that speak of cities in an undifferentiated way (e.g. Glaeser 2011). Through their apparently thoughtless ascription of 'city' to their object of study, they wilfully misrepresent the complex work done within CBDs to structure territory. In other words, we must be aware that the CBD is an actant; that its calculative agents often seek to conceal themselves; that its territories, down to the metre, are increasingly subject to constant valuation and revaluation; and that a set of 'ethnoaccountancy' techniques are constantly deployed to reshape urban territories both near and far. Big cities are the site of big numbers: this is what makes them important and, arguably, makes some cities more worthy of study than others. The chapter highlights the way in which numbers, counting and accounting are incorporated in spatial discourse and practice, particularly in terms of how particular territories or sites are subjected to calculations of value.

To address this, the chapter proceeds as follows. The first section considers attempts to chart centrality, and contrasts the positivist modes of identifying central space to the possibilities offered by territorial governmentality (Hannah 2002, 2009; Elden 2007, 2010). This foreshadows the importance of calculative techniques in organizing office space, and the second section reviews how recent work on critical accountancy (Vollmer 2003; Mennicken and Miller 2012) might be squared with the presence of advertising, law and accountancy corporations in many city centres. The fall-out of the global financial crisis re-opened concerns about the importance of monitoring the activities of global corporations, particularly in terms of how much tax they pay, and I briefly consider how forensic fieldwork practices might augment other forms of corporate analysis and activism (as in the work of UK Uncut, for example) in tracing financial impropriety. I consider how the importance of 'business talk' is actually central to understanding the practice-based nature of the global city, a territorial–conversational complex!

CBD: THE CENTRAL BUSINESS DISTRICT AS A 'CENTRE OF CALCULATION'

> Traditionally, the CBD has been thought of as a somewhat indefinite region of the city that nevertheless has certain distinctive characteristics. It is central, at least in terms of accessibility. It has a greater concentration of tall buildings than any other region of the city, since it normally includes most of the city's offices and largest retail stores. It is the area where vehicular and pedestrian traffic are likely to be most concentrated. It averages higher assessed land values and taxes paid than any other part of the city, and it draws its business from the whole urban area and from all ethnic groups and classes of people. (Murphy (1971/2008: 2)

Once upon a time, urban geographers and sociologists were preoccupied by cities and their centres (Barnes 2004). The Chicago School, based around Robert Park and Ernest Burgess, played a fundamental part in shaping how cities were studied. Interestingly, qualitative ethnographic study of street life was combined with attempts to model and abstract this texture within diagrams and statistical tables. There developed a tradition of field trips, undertaken by school and university students alike studying urban planning, geography, and sociology, which adopted survey techniques: counting cars, noting down building storeys, categorizing space uses and retail mixes.

As such, the theorization of location, urban structure and central place theory was a core concern of, in particular, human geographers, often working within the tradition of Christaller. Texts such as Murphy's *The Central Business District: a Study in Urban Geography* (1971), Haggett's *Locational Analysis in Human Geography* (1966) and Bourne's *Internal Structure of the City* (1971) remain as evidence of how geographers 'did' cities. Certainly, a reading of some of the key papers that appeared during the period of the 1950s, 1960s and 1970s revealed a rather limited engagement with anything other than an unreflective collection of quantities – of hierarchies of functions, of a linear transition in space use, and of an analysis of land and space rents in key buildings, and their intersection within the downtown area (Murphy 1971/2008). While a wider locational analysis has remained a core skill of positivist geography, now enhanced by geographical information systems and spatial modelling, this has not been accompanied by a critical epistemology in the context of the city (Barnes 2003, 2012). In the positivist tradition, the central business district of cities was often regarded as the peak of an urban hierarchy and these scholars took advantage of the growing spatial data-processing capabilities of their universities to begin to map out the key determinants of centrality.

However, paradoxically, the more significant the post-structural critique of cities as concentrations of corporate activity, the greater the need for the numerical precision that the positivist work brought to the scholarship. Conceiving of these cities as territories which have a concentration of calculative agents within them requires at least a provisional understanding of numerical, statistical and quantifying practices in making these places real. For example, in a series of important papers based on interviews with City of London financiers, Sarah Hall (2006, 2007, 2008, 2009) describes how financial knowledge is produced within a spatially defined milieu by a cadre of research analysts, who effectively drive corporate restructuring via investment advice, and mergers and acquisitions. And a core part of this work is the construction of a quantitative, numerical analysis of economies:

> in response to the resulting rethinking of what counted as acceptable research amongst both corporate financiers and their clients, London's corporate finance community constructed a rhetoric around the numbers and formulae that lie at the heart of quantitative financial narratives that valued them as more objective, accountable and accurate than words. This rhetoric of 'scientific rigour' was then used to sell quantitative research not only to clients but also to more senior colleagues who analysts and associates were eager to impress as they sought to remain employed. (Hall 2006: 675)

It is important for critical political economy scholars to have the ability to provide an *accounting* of the city that explains the power of centrality not as something notional or metaphorical, but as a gathering of a great and diverse quantity of things that are then analysed. This extends to the significance of business media, such as Bloomberg, in the generation of financial knowledge. But it also requires an understanding of formalization of meetings as part of the 'calculative regime' of the financial industries, staged in physical meeting spaces within financial centres. Meetings are held in the bars and restaurants of the financial districts, but also in 'formal meeting rooms within banks that can be booked by all bank employees … client offices and designated business meeting rooms in "non-bank" spaces such as hotels and airports' (Hall 2006: 669). This occurs alongside new, virtual financial technologies, occurring with a parallel process of the 'professionalization of face-to-face meetings, in a more formalized setting and with different personnel' (Hall 2006: 669).

So, rather than seeing the CBD as a delimited space of pure spatial analysis, and recalling the introductory discussion in Chapter 2, we might see it as a centre of calculation. As Jöns (2011), drawing on Latour's (1987) introduction of the term, puts it: 'An emerging "centre of calculation" is both place of departure and destination of "cycles of accumulation" … when all the assembled human and nonhuman allies successfully control one another and thus act as a unified whole' (2011: 160). So even for sceptics, actor-network theory might provide a language and framing to help explain the complex arrangements of power within CBDs. As Bender asks:

> Is a *weak* ANT, used analogically, more useful in urban studies than the orthodox version? Perhaps what ANT offers is an unusually rich heuristic device rather than a formal method for studying cities. It is a metaphoric

approach that encourages a highly developed sense of urban complexity, of the unities and disunities, of the stabilities and instabilities, and especially the complex and heterogeneous networks of connection and association out of which the city as a social and as a physical entity is formed and sustained. (2010: 317, italics in original)

Interestingly, many of the answers to this question can be found in Cronon's (1991) 530-page history of the establishment of Chicago, *Nature's Metropolis*. This account of the city's key industries was notable in its integration of the agency of technical innovation, resource metabolism, and the restructuring of urban form. A core element of Cronon's analysis is the rise of the 'boosters', the group of landowners, industrialists and politicians who sought nothing other than 'to be the central city'. Cronon's narrative of how Chigagou, the 'wild garlic place' (1991: 23) became an established centre of commerce within the American continent, provides an important insight into how location, often premised upon 'natural' features such as rivers or harbours, is incorporated into everyday life through various practices, including that of naming:

> By using the landscape, giving names to it, and calling it home, people selected the features that mattered most to them, and drew their mental maps accordingly. Once they had labelled these maps in a particular way – identifying the muddy river flowing through the prairie grasses as a place where long-leaved plants with sweet bulbous roots might be gathered for food – natural and cultural landscapes began to shade into and reshape one another. (p. 25)

Cronon describes how crops became increasingly grown with an eye to market prices, and how the ability to fill the huge grain silos that dotted the city's landscapes could only be achieved through the invention of an institution: the Chicago Board of Trade which soon became a centre of calculation and measurement:

> In the beginning, it had no special focus on the grain trade. Its principal goals were to monitor and promote the city's commercial activity, and to resolve any disputes that might arise among its members ... The Board's earliest activities in the grain trade ... focused on improving Chicago's inspection and measurement systems, since all legitimate traders had an interest in agreeing upon uniform weights and measures as a way of suppressing fraud. (pp. 114–15)

This metrological emphasis on the establishment of Chicago as a central place is further developed by Caitlin Zaloom (2006, 2010). In her study of the historical development of the Chicago Board of Trade, *Out of the Pits* (2006), she attempts to explain the often elusive relationship between material city space and the development of markets. Zaloom accords significant agency to the layout and architecture of the buildings used by the Board of Trade through the many decades of its existence. She emphasizes the way in which technologies are incorporated into the spatial programme of the building, tracing its evolution from the 'pit' (where traders have historically used hand signals to communicate trades across the open sight lines of the trading floor) through to the contemporary screen-based trading rooms. As she puts it elsewhere: 'Such infrastructure, architecture and digital projects do more than just bring markets to life. They establish the city as a value locus, a place where physical structures, expertise and dense trading networks combine to make prices that act as general symbols of worth' (Zaloom 2010: 266).

This points to a need for an urban theory that allows that some places are more important than others: 'Before online technologies, the centrality of time and the centrality of space came together neatly in Chicago's trading space ... [However] ... Online value loci rely on temporal centralization indexed to their place of origin' (Zaloom 2010: 264). A key process is the way in which numbers are turned into prices, and stabilized: the city as a 'value locus' is about the agreement over the abstraction of numbers:

> Numbers acquire the status of definitive statements through a process of 'firming up,' becoming, in their ideal form, stable in time and meaning and adding to a transparent presentation of knowledge. These 'firm' numbers that scholars point to as a foundation for accounting and scientific knowledge contrast with the fluid numbers of the pit and screen. Firm numbers work in the service of accountability and objectivity as tools of standardization and commensuration, establishing expertise and authority, making knowledge impersonal, portraying certainty and universality, and contributing to resolving situations of doubt, conflict, and mistrust. (Zaloom 2006: 142)

This is a very important insight: it is the indexization that is important, and a 'temporal' centralization rather than a Euclidean spatial one:

> Something else orders and locates, gathers and situates, binds and distinguishes, sets the pace and the rhythm, but that something no longer has the shape of a Society and must be followed, step by step, by other methods – through photography, perhaps, or rather through series of photographs that we would need to learn to read continuously – even if our ways of thinking interrupt and disperse them. (Latour and Hermant 2006: 5)

This might be a controversial view, but it approximates I think the only coherent analytical construct by which the global city actually makes sense. Agents are not pure economic actors working on simple locational decisions; instead, they can be seen as drawing commercial space together, a Latourian compact of departments within firms drawing together very sector specific markets. For example, marketing departments will enrol local advertising agencies, financial departments will draw in accountancy firms, executives will see value in there being high-quality hotels in close proximity to their office location, and so on.

OFFICE GEOGRAPHIES

In his book *The Office: a Hardworking History* (2012), Gideon Haigh provides a captivating overview of the development of the cultural significance of workplaces as a key device of contemporary capitalism. This is geographically variable, and related to differing cultures of work in different places. For example, Haigh points out that the stereotypical agent of Tokyo's power has often been seen as the 'salaryman', who drove the huge, consolidated corporations that formed the core of Japan's economy:

> The salaryman was the mediator of Japan's future and past. He was generally as skilled as his foreign counterpart, and perhaps more worldly: the *zaibatsu's* [financial elite's] core trading activities demanded an adaptability to new activities, commodities and cultures. For even to the assimilative Japanese, the notion of equal pay for equal work was too alien: they calibrated salaries according to longevity, or by some other social factor unrelated to performance, such as the number of children a man had to support, so that it was broadly commensurate with a household's needs. (2012: 200–1)

While Haigh is partly providing a caricature for effect, the apparently homogeneous – and paternalist – nature of the Japanese corporation links the micro-practices of office districts with national economic cultures. It is notable when considering Sassen's work, for example, the importance accorded to Tokyo as a key node in the world economy, though her study doesn't delve into the cultural particularities of its rise. Within American popular culture, the elevation of this wartime enemy that had been 'sedulously and ceremonially demilitarised at the end of World War II, then successfully rebuilt as a democratic bulwark against communist despotism' (Haigh 2012: 198), had begun to assume a threatening profile through its commercial vitality.

The popular television show *Mad Men* may have also been a caricature of American office life in the 1960s, but supports the view that the corporation, and its materialization in the office block, is a socio-territorial complex with profound power effects. One of its most striking depictions is the nature of gender politics within the workplace, a defining feature of the contemporary CBD in terms of cultures of harassment, pay differentials and structural discrimination.

As a site, the office has often been regarded as boring and mundane, or captivating in the worst possible way. Over the years it has developed a set of devices – telex, fax, computer, laptop – that have changed the ways in which people work within it. At the same time, various 'sciences' of organization have tied the internal

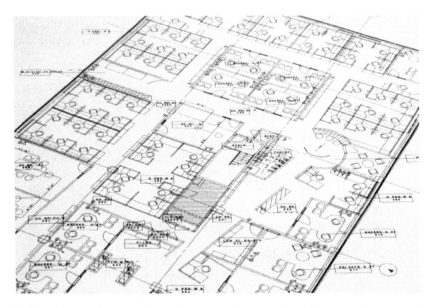

FIGURE 5.1 A typical office floorplan: the calculated distribution of an aggregate of labouring bodies within the central business district of cities.

Source: Ryan R. Fox / Shutterstock.com

geographies of office space to the innovative power of the corporation. Haigh's far-reaching discussion illustrates how the material organization of economic space is a calculated, monitored element of corporate life. Social scientists have stressed how face-to-face contact, a 'compulsion of proximity' (Boden and Molotch 1994; Urry 2003), prioritizes the understanding of context and co-presence for meaningful conversation and communication. This has been an important feature of contemporary capitalism, evidenced in debates about telepresence, part of the new temporal and spatial design of office structures, interiors and communications technologies (Duffy 2008). Many offices are now designed to maximize casual interaction, where the face-to-face contact that arises on a random daily basis is seen as having greater social interactional power than that of email. Where once offices were organized around closed doors lining internal corridors, most new buildings have, for some time, been open plan, with maximal vision within a single floorplate. Leading corporations, especially those in advanced producer services like law, accountancy, and advertising, see high design, comfortable offices as a way of retaining skilled staff.

Taken in aggregate, these office buildings together congeal to form a massive gravitational pull on the structure of the city. So an important task would be to see, thinking back to Latour's intricate observations on the institutional structuring of Paris, how CBDs are composed as territories. There is much more to be said about delimitation, practices of naming, of governmentality and political technologies, which might shed light on contemporary CBDs. We might consider business improvement districts, for example, as key elements where maps, names and bollards help to actively constitute space and aggregate office territories into a recognizable neighbourhood (Briffault 1999; Ward 2010).

BODIES AND WORK

> The city is a constant cacophony of talk. But talk has to be seen in a particular way, as a means of doing something, rather than as a means of representation … Cities, then, hum with talk which is based on shared conversational contexts in which categories and identities can be constantly articulated: local understandings which often very elegantly exploit the possibilities of ordinary talk.
> (Amin and Thrift 2002: 86–7)

The practice of talk is a core element of the constitution of the urban, as Amin and Thrift see it, which is more akin to sense-making or problem solving than anything else: 'successive speculations on states of affairs that are about making those states of affairs both intelligible and legitimate to those around us' (p. 86).

In her book *Capital Culture: Gender at Work in the City* (1997), Linda McDowell provides an important examination of the human geographies of two investment banks in the City of London. Her choice of research sites were notable in themselves, often seen as being off-limits, secretive and elitist, requiring her to adopt various tactics and strategies to gain access (see her discussion of 'elite interviewing' in McDowell 1998). She notes that: 'Despite working in a compressed global space made possible by new means of communication, and frequently moving between global cities, these new professionals spend their daily lives in more geographically restricted sets of spaces' (1997: 4). McDowell's focus is thus on the 'workplace', which should be understood by 'link[ing] together the analysis of material structures of power and the subjective constitution of the self' (p. 205). By doing this, she argues that individual workplaces can, in aggregate, help to explain the ongoing dominance of white masculinity in the UK: in other words, she shows 'how a materialist/semiotic analysis of the workplace as a physical artefact and as an organizational structure, combined with an investigation of gendered performances, helps to explain the persistence of gender and class divisions in a "new" City' (p. 205).

McDowell draws attention to the particular problems faced by female workers in her study:

> women are marked as 'Other' and made to feel out of place by the inappropriate ways men refer to them as sexualized bodies and by all sorts of puns, jokes and other forms of verbal harassment. It is also clear that women are often made to feel out of place in the workplace not only because of the disjunction between their bodies and the commonly accepted ideal of a professional employee but also because of the ways they talk.

There is thus an embodied politics of workplace performance.

> Conversation, like clothes, is an important social clue: gender, class, geo-
> graphic region, ethnicity, sexual orientation, age, religion and occupation all
> have an effect on how we speak and interact with others at work, be they
> colleagues, subordinates, or superiors. Many of these interactions become
> part of the ritualized nature of daily life. The vast majority of decisions about
> how to speak become automatic. These behaviours are not only class-based
> but also gender-linked. There are gendered patterns of behavioural practices
> to which many men and women, although not all, conform. (p. 147)

As she continues, the gendering of workplaces extends through almost every area of
the firm, from hiring, to career trajectories and promotion, to informally differentiated pay scales, to the performance of job roles in the workplace.

And so, it is important to consider the idea that global cities are defined by
standardized modes of relating to clients and customers (customer relation management). In McDowell's later book *Working Bodies* (2009), she focuses on the nature of
'interactive service exchanges with physically present clients', which she sees as key
to the contemporary consumer economy:

> Here the physical production of a particular appearance and the deferential
> performance of an often-scripted exchange are an essential part of embod-
> ied social relations and the construction of identity in the workplace. In
> retail sales, in leisure industries and in hospitality, both employers and cus-
> tomers have expectations of appropriate forms of servicing their needs by
> bodies that are present during the exchange. A range of expectations of
> and attitudes about 'good service' by appropriately embodied workers thus
> affects recruitment and employment practices. Customers' expectations and
> evaluations of the service provision influence their propensity to return and
> repurchase the service and so materially affect profit levels. As these types
> of services typically are used up in the exchange, there is an almost infinite
> possibility for reprovision if the service is deemed acceptable. (2009: 191)

It could be argued that the predictability encased in these institutional envelopes,
such as the global corporation (which in theory has to iron out internal difference
as far as possible), allow for the alignment and co-ordination of complex practices.

For example, as discussed in Chapter 3, hotel work is organized with clear divid-
ing lines between workers who interact directly with the public, and those who work
'invisibly', in maintenance and cleaning roles. The division between the visible and the
invisible can be carried over into the office economy more broadly. Invisible workers
are sometimes audible workers, considering the role of offshore call-centre operators
who allow many of the global firms headquartered in major cities to exploit national
differentials in labour. In *Global Cities at Work: New Migrant Divisions of Labour*, Wills
et al. (2010) set out a Marxian class analysis of the different types of labour that make
London work as a global city. Similarly, Allen and Pryke (1994) describe how three

cohorts of central city service industry around cleaners, security guards and catering staff work with the banks and financial services firms of the City of London. The routinized practices that these workers carry out on a daily basis are driven by the materiality of the objects that the corporation has gathered to reproduce itself. For example:

> The floors of finance within the new buildings ... are lived by cleaners as a variety of desk tops, terminals, chrome panels, and floor coverings – whether marble, wood, tile, nonslip, or a particular type of carpet. Each surface requires a technique of cleaning: computer screens and their casings can be dusted down but keyboards require an intricate clean using small wipes; computer rooms may require high-quality buffing or burnishing; whereas kitchens require 'deep cleaning' with specialist equipment and acid preparations; dust-free computer rooms may be adjacent to areas complete with antique furnishings redolent of a previous era; and so forth. (p. 467)

These sub-contracted workers, while being encouraged to identify with the firm that they clean, guard or cook for, and who interact with full-time staff members as part of their job, are effectively invisible, their work remaining 'unacknowledged unless the work is either not performed or not performed to a standard that reveals their past presence. Even in the daytime, cleaners will often be requested to take their lunch break at a different time from that of the "core staff"' (p. 468). As such, we can see that there is an 'ergonomics' of globalization, where the standards of comfort and cleanliness which are a social expectation within corporate space have a profound effect on the bodies of the workers that maintain them (Seifert and Messing 2006).

FIGURE 5.2   Traders in the wheat pit, Chicago Board of Trade, 1920

Source: © Everett Historical / Shutterstock.com

This can be mapped onto the structure of the office building itself. Parker (2014: 12) highlights how skyscraper office form was oriented around an intensely calculated floorplate based on deployment of capital:

> Starting from plot size, shape and location … calculations about floor space, ceiling height, distance from natural light, costs of heating, number and positioning of elevators and so on are necessarily calculations about return on capital invested. The application of scientific management and time-and-motion techniques to office space was not only a question of the rationalization of the worker, but also an attempt to rationalize the space that each worker would use. The more people, the more offices, the more return. Typical early office plans, with demarcations for window access, secretarial cubicles, typing pools and so on embedded gender and class hierarchies in terms of an economy of space.

As organizational cultures and work expectations have changed, so the floorplate layout and spatial organization of workers within a building is a core calculative technique in organizing networks of both co-presence and distance.

SASKIA SASSEN'S FINANCIAL CENTRES

> Key concepts in the dominant account – globalization, information economy, and telematics – all suggest that place no longer matters and that the only type of workers that matters is the highly educated professional. This account privileges the capability for transmission over the concentration of built infrastructure that make transmission possible; information outputs over the workers producing those outputs, from specialists to secretaries; and the new transnational corporate culture over the multiplicity of cultural environments, including reterritorialized immigrant cultures, within which many of the 'other' jobs of the global information economy take place. (Sassen 2012: 64)

The work of Saskia Sassen has been foundational in shaping 'global cities' as an object of analysis. Yet in many ways the naming of her book *The Global City* (1991) was somewhat misleading in terms of the analytical precision of her work which was less concerned with cities as polities, but more as concentrations of knowledge specialists – particularly in share trading and other practices of financialization – who crammed into the offices of CBDs to solve 'the problem of incomplete knowledge' (Sassen 2012). It is interesting that although Sassen's work on global cities is known for her identification of hierarchies of cities (the alpha, the beta, and so on), she was at pains to emphasize the specific set of interactions which constitute international financial centres (a more precise term than that of global cities). As Sassen argues, these spaces should be seen as a 'production complex', because many hands from several different firms are required to put together a saleable product. Just as the 'global car' may source its windscreen from one country, its wheels from another, and its electronic systems from a third, while being assembled in a fourth, it requires a skilled logistical process of data and cost management, labour contracts and market knowledge to ensure the car makes it 'to market'. Similarly, for Sassen: 'The production of a financial instrument, for example, requires inputs from accounting, advertising, legal expertise, economic consulting, public relations, designers, and printers' (p. 68). Sassen identifies three 'constraints that keep today's global and mostly electronic financial system from being the placeless electronically distributed system one might have expected' (p. 23).

A key issue is the 'problem of incomplete knowledge': when a firm becomes global, 'the more speculative, digitized, subject to speed, and globalized a firm's operations are, the more acute is its incomplete knowledge problem, and hence the more dependent on the financial business center as a strategic site' (p. 24). By this, Sassen means the following:

> Firms have always confronted incomplete knowledge in market economies. When such firms go global, this problem becomes acute. The specific contribution of the financial center vis-à-vis the incomplete knowledge problem, especially for global actors, is that its diverse networks, information loops, professionals coming from diverse parts of the world, together produce a particular type of knowledge capital. I refer to it as urban knowledge capital – a capital that is more than the sum of the knowledge of the professionals and the firms in a city … the more speculative, digitized, subject to speed, and globalized arm's operations are, the more acute is its incomplete knowledge problem, and hence the more dependent on the financial/business center as a strategic site. (pp. 23–4)

As a result of this, Sassen argues, financial centres become a lot more specialized in a way that undermines the erstwhile logic of the national regulation of economies in capital cities:

> The global financial system thrives both on standardized products and technical infrastructures, and on specialized differentiation in much of high finance. Each of the leading financial centers has developed its specialized advantages over the last two decades. No two of them are the same. Globalization homogenizes standards, a fact that has led many to interpret this as homogenization of markets and of urban economies. But the homogenizing of standards can coexist with growing specialization. In contrast, in the recent past, each 'closed' national economy duplicated all functions necessary for international transactions, and specialization was a somewhat secondary aspect. (p. 24)

Further, the global financial centres are about, precisely, 'finance', and 'financializing the nonfinancial' (p. 24). By this Sassen means that the new ways of organizing the ownership of almost every asset in the economy, from buildings to workers, is being explored as a mode of profit extraction:

> Today's global financial firms are largely geared toward entering the thick specificities of non-financial sectors and of national economies not yet fully articulated with the global economy. Financial centers, and even more so global cities, are a bridge, an intermediate space between the globalized part of finance and the thick national and local cultures of investment of a country or a region. (p. 24)

It is for these reasons that financial centres have emerged in a small number of places in the world. It is driven largely by global firms, but supported by often national specialists in the fields of law, lobbying, design and advertising.

The key point is that many of these products are so complex that the knowledge inputs required are either: (a) too detailed to put on paper in an email; (b) too confidential, either for reasons of intellectual property or for reasons of market influence, or even of pure illegality; (c) too time-consuming to be committed to paper; (d) too contentious to be resolved without face-to-face performances of the 'cloak and dagger' of negotiation. Or, better put by Sassen, 'what is thought of as face-to-face communication is actually a production process that requires multiple simultaneous inputs and feedbacks' (p. 783).

This is why CBDs now have such overwhelmingly packed and heavily occupied office complexes; why city streets are busy with workers during the day and not only during rush-hour; and why – given long, stressful hours of product completion and deal-making – there are so many gyms, bars and restaurants tucked in close proximity to the office floors where the primary work is taking place. These cities are *centres*: they are *central* to the functioning of the global economy in a very material sense.

METROLOGIES OF CENTRALITY: CRITICAL ACCOUNTING

So, what are the theoretical tools that can allow a closer penetration of these office industrial complexes? One important innovation is the field of critical accountancy, derived from the work of Michel Foucault:

> Accounting numbers have a distinctive capacity for acting on the actions of others, one that goes far beyond the abstract injunctions of economic theory. Through their ability to produce certain forms of visibility and transparency, accounting numbers both create and constrain subjectivity. This can be achieved at the level of the individual worker, manager, patient,

schoolteacher, social worker, surgeon, and so on. By linking decisions to the supposedly impersonal logic of quantification rather than to subjective judgement, accounting numbers configure persons, domains, and actions as objective and comparable. This, in turn, renders them governable. For the objects and subjects of economic calculation, once standardized through accounting, are accorded a very particular form of visibility. (Mennicken and Miller 2012: 7)

This is coupled to the notion of territorialization, which is an important element in understanding the global city. This concept is used to identify the point when some kind of summing up of an object – such as territory – is made. Foundational examples would be a statistics or census office (to count population), or a surveyor's office (to map and value land). Territorialization is often linked to governmentality, and very helpfully unpacked in the work of Matt Hannah (2009: 68), who has set out what he calls a simple heuristic model of modern calculable territory, consisting of six 'layers': 'basic geodesic grids and other coordinate systems'; 'nominal state or jurisdictional boundaries'; 'Built (or at least parcelled) human environments'; 'Basic socio-economic or demographic information tied to units of the human environ-ment'; 'Additional data tied to demographic and economic units, such as criminal records, consumption habits, income brackets; cultural preferences more generally'; 'More fleeting, "transactional" or "event-based" knowledge' which could include minor traffic infractions or credit card purchases. Hannah's schema allows an appre-ciation of the 'metrology' of urban development. Perhaps unsurprisingly, the ability to value, monetize and trade territory has become a highly specialized trade.

However, as important as counting populations, and surveying and mapping ter-ritory, are the processes of accounting that ascribe value (and future potential value) to different 'bits' of city. And a fundamental element of accounting, as discussed by Mennicken and Miller, is the way in which it links numbers to territory:

There are two principal ways in which accounting territorializes. First, it does so by making *physical* spaces calculable. This could mean a factory floor, a hospital ward, an office, a shop, or even a sub-area of a shop, and much else besides. Second, it does so by making *abstract* spaces calculable. Examples here could be a 'division' of a firm, a 'profit centre' or a 'cost centre' of an organization, or even an idea such as failure, public service, or personal identity. These are of course not mutually exclusive aspects or processes, and there is often reciprocity between the making of calculable physical spaces and calculable abstract spaces. (2012: 20, italics in original)

Within such a framework, there is important work to be done tracking the influence and practices of the 'Big Four' global accountancy firms: Deloitte, PwC, Ernst & Young and KPMG. These firms are co-located with other global firms that are subject to complex auditing practice to fulfil taxation and share market requirements.

Yet while they are best known for their role as auditors, they also work in the field of management consulting, legal services, financial services and strategic tax advice. Their role, for example, in allowing client companies to bypass national corporate regulation structures using legal methods (but in ways that are likely to be 'ahead' of regulators) is a key element of their growth strategies. The use of accountancy is now a key role of economic governance more generally.

For these reasons, it is important to consider the role of accountancy as a calculative practice that drives – indeed, partly defines – global cities. Accountancy has been closely associated with the rise of capitalism and its governing practices over many centuries: early twentieth-century sociologists such as Sombart (1915) and Weber (1922/1978) paid close attention to both the emergence of processes such as double-entry bookkeeping which developed among the textile magnates of Renaissance Florence, and argued for its centrality to the growth of capitalism. While the actual causality of accountancy is disputed, its role as an organizing device has been widely discussed and developed (Power 1995; Vollmer 2003). There are several ways in which it can drive debate on global cities. It has been suggested that business practice has been progressively 'captured' by finance in various areas, where the specialisms, technical expertise and – if it is not too strong a word – passions of a hotel, university, restaurant or railway corporation manager have long been replaced by a 'finance conception of control' that has 'restructured corporations into spaces rendered calculable by practices of financial accounting' (Vollmer 2003: 367).

Moreover, we might see these financial accounting practices as being at the forefront of urban politics in various areas. Muellerleile (2009) provides a fascinating account of the machinations behind the relocation of Boeing's corporate headquarters from near its Seattle production plant to the investment markets of downtown Chicago. Engelen et al. identified the student and faculty disquiet over the 'penetration' of financialization into the government of the University of Amsterdam, which exploded in a series of protests in early 2015:

> In our judgment, the combination of (over) ambitious real estate development, increasing indebtedness and the concomitant dabbling in financial engineering through interest rate swaps makes for a highly toxic mix that could easily blow up in the face of the highly paid financial professionals occupying the *Maagdenhuis*, with huge consequences for teaching and research. We can imagine a number of nightmarish scenarios: ongoing negative market sentiment and/or continued low interest rates; a book loss and/or depreciation on property values; changes in accounting conventions resulting in a downward revaluation of real estate and a weakening of the crucial solvency ratio. (2014: 1087)

Elsewhere, we can see the role of sub-contracting practices, for example, as being a key element in the breakdown of airport management in London's Heathrow

Airport for a period in the 2000s (McNeill 2010). These brief references to how some of the iconic, defining institutions of global cities – global firm HQ, university, airport – suggests that there are many of these stories of financialization that lie partially submerged within the smoother accounts of global-city development. It highlights that centres of calculation are indeed plural, and usually hotly disputed or in competition within organizations.

It is important to consider how firms and professions utilize their own set of metrics to understand performance. In her study of the British outdoor advertising industry, Anne Cronin describes how advertising professionals understand and employ calculative practices. She

> observed many times ... that formal quantitative calculation and measurement can be unduly restrictive. On one level, this corresponds to Callon and Muniesa's (2005) observation that there is no longer a strict division in calculative practices between (qualitative) judgment and quantitative (or numeric) calculation. But the practices I observed suggest something more – an awareness among practitioners that the referentiality of their classifications and calculation to 'the real world' is mutable and flexible, and that the commercial energy or vitalism which is performed in these market practices and relationships can be tapped for their benefit. (2008a: 2746)

In other words, firms and professionals don't hold to a singular view of statistical reality, but rather something more proprietorial: *their own* arrangements of metrics, combined with their own desk-top intuitions and shared interpretations. Cronin also draws on MacKenzie's (1996: 59) concept of 'ethnoaccountancy' as 'the study of how people do their financial reckoning, irrespective of our perceptions of the adequacy of that reckoning and of the occupational labels attached to those involved'.

While there is a broader issue for national governments in 'knowing the governed', this is also a challenge – and possibility – for businesses that can make money from the control of very small territories within cities. The emergence and application of tools of cartography and statistics that helped build national economies are also employed by property developers, advertising agencies, retailers and the entertainment industry. Both involved

> producing a version of the city that was amenable to governance, the map shared in the epistemic characteristics of statistics. The cognitive nature of both turned on a particular version of space, 'abstract space' ... Fundamental to the transportation of the idea of space into the social sciences was the idea of functional equivalence, the notion that space was reducible to schemata or grids. (Joyce 2003: 35)

What the CBD scholars were most interested in, it seems, was an attempt to develop the metrology of the city. Yet this was shorn of a critical element, and more recently metrology has been linked to concepts of the control and seizure of territory as a basis of power (Elden 2010). CBDs can be seen as territories where 'territory is more than merely land, but a rendering of the emergent concept of "space" as a political category: owned, distributed, mapped, calculated, bordered, and controlled' (Elden 2007: 578).

CALCULABLE CITY SPACE

> Since the CBD is an area, it would seem reasonable, as a first step in studying the CBD of any city, to outline it on a map. But where does it start? There is a critical point downtown that is likely to be well-known to the policeman on the beat and to the downtown businessman. This is the peak land-value intersection, or PLVI. (Murphy 1971/2008: 9)

The rise of global cities can be understood through the general penetration of the financialization of many elements of commercial activity (French et al. 2011; Engelen et al. 2014). Large financial institutions, particularly investment banks, use a number of different types of quantitative analysis to guide, or perhaps determine, their operations (Hall 2006). In terms of commercial property such as skyscrapers, major global cities are now dominated by increasingly influential property fund managers, using approaches such as discounted cash flow modelling to assess their strategic options. Tenants use this methodology to assess future space requirements and anticipated future rent liabilities; property owners to assess when the optimal time is to invest in capital expenditure on assets; financiers use it to work out risk assessments and lending criteria (Bill 2013). Such methods have grown in importance as the property industry grows in sophistication, and particularly as its leading firms are traded regularly and publicly.

Furthermore, as Beauregard points out, CBD property markets are 'textured': that is, they rely on various forms of 'functional interdependence' to be successful (2005: 2432). Major property sectors – residential, office, hotel, retail – are held to stimulate each other. This operates by practices of valuation, such as the key management ratios that constitute the curriculum of MBA courses. Contrary to neo-classical economic framings of the market as an abstraction, they are driven by strategic, calculative practices. The markets are 'made':

> Investors in each of these property sectors track demand by monitoring the shortfall in supply. Through attention to vacancy rates, asking rents and property sales prices and an understanding of the quality of the supply – for example the age of hotels, the proportion of class A office space in a business district – they make decisions as to when and how much to invest. In short, they follow a market logic: pay attention when supply falls below demand, consider the costs of new construction of renovation against future revenue streams and invest when the profits to be made (more precisely, the rate of return) exceed alternative investments and match the goals of the firm. (2005: 2432)

Furthermore, the commercial sectors are often 'timed' very efficiently in terms of leases, which – just as they fix revenues for owners and costs for tenants, thus creating security – also preclude the kind of free movement within the marketplace that the 'thin' market logic would suggest. For Sassen, the key issue is time: 'where time is of the essence, as it is today in many of the leading sectors of these industries, the benefits of agglomeration are still extremely high – to the point where it is not simply a cost advantage, but an indispensable arrangement' (1995: 783). And this will drive the locational decisions and real-estate requirements of firms.

However, the 'city' does not have an ontological significance in many industries and sectors, as Cronin shows in her study of the outdoor advertising industry:

> Despite the nature of their product – outdoor advertising sites that are almost exclusively situated in or on key approaches to cities – 'the city' as a conceptual zone does not exist in the industry's repertoire of understandings. As one industry spokesman explained to me, 'there is no interest in [the city as an] environment whatsoever. They're interested in the numbers of people.' (anon.) Cronin (2008a: 2737)

Instead, Cronin found that her respondents understood urban space in a more complex way, 'not as a fixed arrangement of specific locations but as spaces and times of density – that is, densities of people which could be translated by market research's classificatory practices into "target markets"' (Cronin 2008a: 2737).

These are all defined by an ongoing set of metrological practices:

> framed and quantified as time-spaces through a standard industry taxonomy which includes the metrics of 'opportunity to see' and 'visibility adjusted contacts'. This taxonomy frames the classification of each advertising site according to the number of people who may see it (the density of visual contacts). The field of orientation used by the industry focuses on core themes: 'centrality' (the density of flows of people in and around a city centre will generate an intensity of 'hits'); positioning in relation to flows of people (busy commuter routes will deliver large numbers of hits); scale (size is understood to translate into 'impactful' advertising and generates a range of its own classifications such as 'super-sides' and 'mega-rears' in advertising on buses); contingent proximities (high-street shops often advertise on the sides of buses, which operate as mobile billboards travelling through commercial centres). (Cronin 2008a: 2737)

This very different language of understanding urban space provides an insight into how just one industry works not with 'the city', but with more specific modes of understanding *sites*. Moreover, this is not a passive set of practices:

> It is clear that the outdoor advertising industry has a range of appreciable effects on urban space. Advertising on panels, billboards, buses, and taxis, etc directly impacts on the making of spaces, not merely by adding its semantic content to the rich textual mix of city space but in helping to shape the

affective geographies of urban space, introducing new visual technologies into public space (moving image billboards, interactive bus shelters etc.), constantly reiterating the commercial nature of supposedly public urban space in a hypervisible way, and financing urban infrastructures such as the London Underground through the large contract fee required from the media owner of tube advertising sites. (p. 2747)

It is important to be clear that these calculative practices are not necessarily seen as being a singular, pristine truth. Rather, they are part of a wider set of knowledges used in acting in space. As Cronin puts it:

> To promote their assets, media owners commission market research companies to produce data on the benefits of the types of sites they hold and the people or 'target markets' likely to view those sites as they move around urban spaces. These data are then selectively edited into PowerPoint presentations which the media owners use as a form of promotion to persuade clients to advertise with them. Indeed, all project findings are presented by the industry in ways which integrate a pitch – they are all oriented towards persuading media agencies and clients of the value of using a particular company's services. The data produced by the research projects of the industry are not necessarily viewed by its practitioners as accurate or 'true', but they function efficiently as a currency for the industry in their everyday practices of producing and maintaining commercial relationships between media owners, media agencies and clients. (2008b: 99)

And so, by contrast with the positivist take on the city, quantitative data can be used in multiple ways. For Cronin, these include 'as a decision-support technology, a post-rationalisation, or an alibi for commercial decisions, and as all parties in the industry agree to the system, this use of data "stitches together" these market relationships enabling them to function smoothly' (p. 99).

GLOBAL CITIES AND THE 'SUPER-RICH'

It is increasingly obvious that the over-heated housing markets of many global cities are being swollen with surplus investment capital, much of it individually owned as opposed to corporate. There has always been a latent 'geography of the super-rich', but it is only recently that there has been a critical social science that attempts to theorize how this plays out through spatial practices. An important insight is offered by Beaverstock and Faulconbridge (2014) who identify the concept of the 'socio-technical systems of the super-rich', driven primarily by consultancies such as Capgemini. The establishment of the classification known as the 'high net worth individual' has been followed through with 'retail private wealth management' markets. In other words, individuals with a minimum of US$1 million to invest will qualify for such a service. These individuals will have an interest in elite modes of travel, be this private jets or luxury cars. And there exists an infrastructure that will enable their global mobility:

> a practice perspective draws our attention to the importance of the ecology of corporate actors who reproduce super-rich mobilities. The private wealth management companies, yacht and private jet operating/chartering groups and other providers of services to the super-rich all play a crucial role in defining and reproducing the meanings and competencies that render certain forms of mobility taken for granted, normal and needed. Not only do the companies devise and maintain the material technologies needed to uphold the mobile lives of the super-rich, but they also imbue the products with meaning and set the terms of reference for their competent use. (Beaverstock and Faulconbridge 2014: 52)

Leaving aside those who gathered wealth through inheritance, the super-rich are typically the beneficiaries of major corporate strategies that have a global footprint. They may include hedge-fund owners, who have had a significant influence on global stock markets; the leading executives of major corporations; or the founders of companies that have been acquired by corporations.

The concentration of investment by the super-rich into property has been the cause of much controversy in major cities such as London, Sydney and New York. Webber and Burrows (2015) describes the situation in the leafy London suburb of Highgate, which has been the site of a series of clashes between the conservative tastes of existing wealthy elites and with the mansion-building vim of super-rich investors; the media frequently comment on the 'buy to leave' approach by wealthy overseas investors who may buy high-quality property such as condominiums (usually built precisely for this purpose) and leave them unoccupied, as a pure financial asset.

MORAL GEOGRAPHIES

It is now abundantly clear that a scepticism towards the assumptions and actions of most of the main players in the field of finance is necessary. The growth of hostility to corporate tax avoidance gathered momentum in the 2010s, with the rise of the Occupy movement in many cities, and nationally specific activist movements such as UK Uncut. This group took direct action by boycotting high-profile locations of major firms, drawing public attention to their negotiations with government tax departments to reduce debt. In turn, these corporations relied upon the use of assertive accountancy strategies that – purchased by corporations from other global service firms – were able to by-pass government treasuries and tax offices.

In a high-profile UK case, Starbucks were targeted and ultimately paid a more sizeable tax bill than they had originally intended.

This is particularly important in the context of the CBD as a space with its own 'moral geography'. In other words, rather than seeing the banks and financial services companies as being faceless corporations, a closer – indeed forensic – attention to the activities of CEOs, fund managers and, importantly, non-executive board members is an important element of a renewed political economy. The ways of doing this, from examining the narrative strategies of firm executives (Schoenberger 2001) to tracing corporate governance moves, is a crucial element in creating a sense of how 'the big end of town' engages in its own self-governmentality.

A key area here is the nature of investment banking, one of the major examples of advanced producer services in leading global cities. Hall describes the two key roles of investment banks:

> First, it involves advisory work in which corporate financiers suggest ways of maximising shareholder returns to clients, typically through corporate restructuring such as mergers and acquisitions (M&A). Second, banks make loans to clients to facilitate M&A. In advisory work, research is used to identify potential takeover targets and to suggest prices that might be paid for them ... Corporate Finance and securities trading departments come together when a corporate finance client needs to issue securities. When this situation arises, the brokers in securities trading use their contacts with investors to distribute or sell the securities. A conflict of interest arises in this situation because research produced by the investment bank is being used by the two departments simultaneously to advise buyers and sellers in the same transaction. (2007: 711)

This has led to conflict of interest clampdowns in New York, giving an apparent competitive advantage to London's 'light touch' regulation. It also offered a new field of advanced producer services for management consultants, in terms of corporate regulation and advising on adherence to legislation such as the Sarbanes–Oxley Act of 2002. New York's regulatory outcomes included the physical separation of research departments not only being required to be 'physically separated within investment bank offices, but also to have separate reporting lines, budgets and legal and compliance staff' (Hall 2007: 711).

The large accountancy firms are also important players in the normative definition of corporate moral geographies. The regularity of their workforce – suits, conservative appearance – and the orderliness of their workspace – the office – can mask the more than occasional forays beyond the boundaries of corporate law (and, for many, common decency). For example, KPMG LLP (the American arm of KPMG International) came under detailed investigation in the mid-2000s for their role in 'tax shelter fraud', and were fined $456 million by the US Department of Justice. However, the global firm dissociated themselves from their American division:

> KPMG International is a Swiss firm that serves as a coordinating entity for a network of independent member firms. KPMG International provides no audit or other client services. Such services are provided solely by member firms in their respective geographical areas. KPMG International and its member firms are legally distinct and separate entities. (KPMG 2014)

And so it is clear that charting corporate geographies is in itself a challenging methodological task. In some places, these landscapes – often given a somewhat neutral, if spectacular, role as the visual mnemonic for corporate cities – become material sites of corrupt practices. Consider the high-profile raid of the offices of Enron, one of the most famous corruption cases of the 1990s:

> FBI agents swooped on Enron's Houston headquarters yesterday to investigate allegations of document shredding. The raid followed fresh claims that employees were still disposing of potentially awkward paperwork last week, despite court orders to keep everything … Security guards now police the 19th floor of Enron's building, where the accounting operations were based and where some of the shredding is said to have occurred. (English 2002)

There is also a link between offshore tax-exempt 'havens' and the corporate head offices that cluster in global cities (Roberts 1995; Clark et al. 2015). CBDs are plugged into a logistical system based on the movement of financial flows that are largely virtual in terms of the materiality and durability of their volume (though they are by no means immaterial). As confirmed by the leaking of the 'Panama papers' in 2016, tax havens such as the Cayman Islands, or even developed cities such as Dublin, have become important reference points in the offices of major financial centres. During the global financial crisis, there was much discussion of Ireland's role in harbouring various entities that were channelling financial flows in ways that eluded regulators. The UK's *Guardian* newspaper sent a journalist to Dublin's office lands, including its International Financial Services Centre on the Liffey, to track down various companies involved in shadow banking and found that many were merely letterboxes and signboards, the entity territorialized offshore (O'Toole 2010).

And so an important task for a renewed CBD ontology is to theorize how cities are production sites for global taxation regimes, corporate reporting activities and shareholder activism. For example, an interesting story could be told using a forensic study of Google's international locational choices, using their headquarter development strategies as a means of auditing their influence within national policy-making. To do so requires a 'corporate nano-geography': an attempt to understand the corporation through careful readings of their stock-market filings, press releases and the careful consideration of corporate employee sharing sites such as Glass Ceiling (www.glassceiling.com).

FIGURE 5.3   Spreadsheets: General Motors managers, 1941, co-ordinating materials used for wartime production

Source: © Everett Historical / Shutterstock.com

CASE STUDY

FORENSIC URBAN GEOGRAPHY

Much has been made of the power of the financial corporations that dominate global city discourse. But what about the moments when the apparently settled order of the corporate office tower is disrupted? Here we see the importance of offices as stages for the negotiation of major, law-defying, corporate practices, especially when unearthed and agonizingly recounted in court cases or by investigative journalists. Corporate law trials at some point usually revolve around the presence or misplacement of transcripts of conversations – emails such as Barclays Bank's manipulation of LIBOR.

I want to link this sense of a corporate forensics to the exciting research projects led by Eyal Weizman in the Centre for Forensic Architecture at Goldsmiths College in London. This is primarily focused on providing an evidence base for human rights trials in the Middle East, and especially between Israel and Palestine. He explains his approach as fitting within a wider moment of thing-agency:

I am interested in forensics because it embodies a shift from the speech of humans to the communicative capacity and 'agency' of things. Several legal and cultural scholars have labelled the third part of the 20th century, with its attention to testimonies, truth commissions, and interviews, as 'the era of the witness.' It seems to me that in the field of international law, but also in general political culture, we might have entered a stage when we have become more attuned to the communicative capacity of things, of things speaking, if you like, between themselves and to us. This material approach is simultaneously evident in a number of areas and disciplines. Today's legal and political decisions are based upon the capacity to read and present DNA samples, 3D scans, nanotechnology, and the 'enhanced vision' of electromagnetic microscopes and satellite surveillance, which extends from the topography of the seabed to the remnants of destroyed or bombed out buildings. This is not just science, but its associated rhetoric. (Weizman 2010)

How might this be carried over into the field of global cities research? Gerard Nestler, a contributor to the wider Forensic Architecture project, has provided a discussion of how an understanding of financial forensics is a fundamental task for critical theory, as in the examination of stock-market 'flash crashes':

As collateral damage, the epitome of territorialised capitalism, Wall Street, had become a mere symbol. While the crowded trading floor of the New York Stock Exchange (NYSE) is still the undisputed televisual icon of the 'market,' the media presence obfuscates, more than reveals, what the market has actually become, as a result of what I term the *quantitative turn* in finance … The new pivotal architectural nodes of what has turned into a deterritorialized, informational capitalism are now the nondescript and non-representative warehouse buildings, filled to the brim with computer servers and fiber optics, in suburban areas such as Mahwah, New Jersey. *Forensis: the Architecture of Public Truth*

What each of these studies also demonstrate is an interest in reading behind the corporate structure of the firms that shape urban space. This is not easy for reasons of commercial confidentiality, but various 'ways in' are usefully discussed

(Continued)

(Continued)

in *Show me the Money* (Roush 2010), which is primarily aimed at journalists, but which has a good application to an urban accountancy of the type I am describing. Near the start of his book, Roush makes the point that 'higher education and mass communication have failed miserably in effectively training journalists for careers in business reporting' (2010: ix). He explains some of the key methods for doing this work, from analysing stock-exchange filings to unpacking the 'celebrity' of the CEO. As a starting point, studies of board memberships of government quangos, chambers of commerce, transport authorities and even arts organizations will likely reveal a preliminary map of the interacting agents who form the power structures of global cities.

The range of opportunities offered to those pursuing a forensic methodology are immense. The work is painstaking, detailed and time-consuming, but it will offer a new urban geography of great radical possibility.

★★★★★

This chapter advocates a reinvigorated CBD study as an important adjunct to a wider analysis of the spatial platforms of corporate activity worldwide (though not to the exclusion of the gated suburban campuses of technology, arms and oil companies, which are intertwined). Doing so involves taking a post–quantitative view on numbers, calculation and statistics, and an understanding of the CBD as a complex assemblage of different quantification techniques and representations and their interpretation. The insights of the critical accountancy literature (e.g. Mennicken and Miller 2012) are important here, as are attempts to understand both the synoptic and forensic features of any urban economy (Hall 2006, 2007, 2008, 2009). Office territories gather a range of business knowledges that can rarely be contained within singular professional boundaries: the interplay of producer service firms and capital managers interact to such a degree that the CBD becomes some kind of calculating space in its own right (Faulconbridge and Hall 2011).

This is significant because global city research has tended to underemphasize the importance of territorial sites and has tended to hold the 'global city' stable as an object of analysis the better to consider how relations and flows operate. Handled insensitively, this can have an important effect: it renders the embedded, sunk, locally dependent actors as being static, while global actors flow around them. In other words, the geography of global cities might require a closer attention to the way in which they are organized as sequences of spaces, in the process indigenizing the 'global'.

So how might the work of economic geographers and sociologists be applied to CBDs as a means of understanding the objects and practices that organize the spatial formation of the wider city, and other, distant cities? How important are the technologies of office districts – boardrooms, elevators, restaurants, gyms and so on in the active reproduction of the corporate city? And what is the moral geography of the calculative practices that are hidden within the 'corporate citadels'? Does it make sense to speak of a 'milieu effect' through the co-presence of trusting actors in a small space that enables behaviours and conduct that would otherwise be less reliable in a more distanciated business space? The core technical practices undertaken in offices, such as auditing, accounting, trading and marketing, are in themselves constitutive of ontological worlds. This is the work that offices do, and why I suggest that they can be seen as political territories. Methodologically, research into the nano-geography of the corporation would help to recompose the global city: a forensic study, starting with its headquarters and drilling down into the networks of agents, products and technologies that hold it together.

WORLD-MAKING

MODELS, EXPERTS AND CONSULTANTS

This chapter deals with how economic practices are engaged in 'world-making' with specific reference to cities. It ties in with an important 'performative turn' that has taken place in understanding economies, inspired by the likes of Michel Callon, Donald MacKenzie and other economic sociologists. In an influential book, MacKenzie (2006) argues that economics is 'an active force transforming its environment, not a camera passively recording it'. Rather than viewing it as a 'pure' science with a closed and unassailable episteme, economic knowledge is understood more specifically as 'the economic techniques, models and calculations embedded in the wider world of business, finance, consulting, policy and regulation' (Christophers 2014: 81).

Much of this work has sought to define the formulation, transmission and consumption of knowledge as a spatialized social practice. This is partly because the way in which knowledge is understood can be split into two types, the codified and the tacit:

> Codified knowledge is necessarily explicit, formal, or systematic, and can be expressed in words and numbers, scientific procedures or universal principles. This codified category of knowledge is easy to transfer, store, recall and valorize. On the other hand, tacit knowledge is extremely difficult to transfer. The main forms of tacit knowledge are know-how (gathered from the accumulation of practice), mastery of a language (gathered from the accumulation of the ability to communicate), and 'representations of the world' (gathered from the accumulation of wisdom). All these forms result from complex learning processes that require considerable amounts of time to be translated from an 'emitter' to a 'receiver'. (Amin and Cohendet 2004: 23)

As we have seen, these various accumulative practices are central to global city formation. And this analysis aligns with a growing scholarly interest in what has been termed 'relational urbanism' (McCann 2011a; McCann and Ward 2011; McCann and Temenos 2015) where city policies are clearly constituted through a close reference to other cities. On the one hand, this can appear on the surface to be a naïve acceptance and copying of successful models from elsewhere. In practice, their deployment is not as clean-cut as would appear, but rather they are incorporated within the growth coalitions, vested interests and party machines of urban politics-as-usual. McCann and Ward argue that it is most accurate to frame 'mobile' policy as 'assemblages of parts of the near and far, of fixed and mobile pieces of expertise, regulation, institutional capacities, etc. that are brought together in particular ways and for particular interests and purposes' (2012: 328).

This means that policy-making, learning and transfer may be actualized in places 'that are fleeting or mobile, such as conferences, seminars, workshops, guest lectures, fact-finding field trips, site visits, walking tours, informal dinners, among many others' (McCann and Ward 2012: 329). Scholars thus need to identify how cities and their problems are objectified and acted upon, often using an amalgam of 'ingredients' that have been observed in several distinct socio-economic milieux. And so this chapter discusses the agents that have been active in circulating these ingredients. It explores the nature of management consultancy as an organized global industry of considerable size in its own right; the role of celebrity management 'gurus' whose inspirational talks and 'manual' style airport bookstand bestsellers encourage change (Thrift 2005); and the growing sense of the city as a site of experimentation (Bulkeley and Broto 2013; Halpern et al. 2013; Evans and Karvonen 2014; Karvonen and van Heur 2014; McGuirk et al. 2014).

The chapter outlines three concurrent trends in global-city practice that follow these distributed knowledges. First, there is a popular discourse, embodied in books such as Florida's *The Rise of the Creative Class* (2002), Glaeser's *Triumph of the City* (2011) or Moretti's *New Geography of Jobs* (2012), that 'cities' have been rediscovered and, moreover, are now major contributors to the future economy. This American-centred discourse is really code for addressing the observable shift 'back to the city' from the suburbanized office parks and edge cities that characterized much of the American spatial economy from the 1960s to the 1990s. These works, each written by scholars who have published a significant amount of fairly sober, evidence-based work, represent a representational shift to a pamphleteering style of argument. Taken together, they form something approaching a discursive field that Gleeson (2014) refers to as 'urbanology', or alternatively a form of urban critique that could be labelled as 'guru' theory.

Second, city (re)management is big business. The most recent evidence of this is the boom in 'smart cities', based largely on the rapid adoption of mobile devices from smartphones and tablets to simpler mobile phones by urban dwellers, and the easier availability of sensors of various types (Townsend 2013; Marvin et al. 2015; Luque-Ayala and Marvin 2016). Major technology and utilities providers and information corporations, from Hitachi to Siemens to Google to IBM, are at the forefront of this trend. But global management consultancies, such as McKinsey and Deloitte, have for several decades been developing formats and spreading standardized policy models and methodologies to build economies of scale across different national markets.

Third, there is a sense in which urban-oriented practitioners are becoming increasingly self-aware of different ways of running cities, models and products, and are more inclined to undertake practices of experimentation (Karvonen and van Heur 2014). There is an increasing use of urban pilot projects, for example, whether in the field of smart grids, eco-cities, and so on. This, combined with the rise of the so-called 'sharing economy' which bypasses existing retail structures, is arguably redefining the ways in which cities are understood and acted upon.

ACTUALIZATION

From previous chapters, we can recall the importance placed within actor-network theory on the associations between humans and objects that either settle, or are forcibly brought, into relations. And the core message of this is that there is no simple causal mechanism by which a powerful 'global' actor exerts itself on another weaker actor. There is force and structure, but it may be difficult to sustain: the path to global influence may indeed be relatively simple to achieve; in others, it is likely to involve a significant material change in the thing being distributed.

The actor-network theorist Michel Callon has developed an influential framework that is helpful in explaining this (Callon 1998; Callon and Muniesa 2005). Summarizing his approach, Müller stresses the importance of processes of *translation*:

> According to Callon, it proceeds in four moments: problematization defines the problem and the set of relevant actants that relate to it; *interessement* is the group of actions through which a primary actant recruits other actants to assume roles in the actor-network and defines their identities; enrolment is the outcome of problematization and *interessement* and describes the successful alignment of actants' interests in the actor-network; during mobilization, finally, the primary actant becomes able to speak for the other actants in the network, making them act towards a common goal. As this description suggests, the process of translation is akin to creating agency: it makes action possible through aligning interests and leads to the emergence of an actor. (2015: 70)

So, while ultimately the primary actant may appear to be all-powerful, they have only achieved this through several preparatory stages which have involved processes of selection, networking, the magic moment of enrolment, and then the completion of the task.

We can see that from an ANT standpoint any notion of a simple global–local transfer does not stack up. In a key passage in his advocacy of ANT, Latour has argued that

> the solution explored by ANT ... has nothing to do with offering still another compromise between micro and macro, actor and system – and even less with pushing the swing so forcefully that it circles through some dialectic circles. To follow our argument, it's essential, on the contrary, not to try to be clever by striking an even more sophisticated balance between

the two clichés of social science. We do not claim that interactions do not really exist because they have to be 'put into' a context, not that any context never really exists because it is always 'instantiated' through individual practice. Instead, we claim that another movement, entirely different from the one usually followed, reveals itself most clearly through the very difficulty of sticking either to a place considered as local or a place taken as the context for the former one. Our solution is to take seriously the *impossibility* of staying in one of the two sites for a long period ... If there is no way to stay in either place, it simply means that those places are not to be reached – either because they don't exist at all or because they exist but cannot be reached with the vehicle offered by sociology. (2005: 170, emphasis in original)

So in many ways, ANT can be seen as a method for locating global cities. The agonizing work of defining them, and researching them, is *supposed to be* painful and never to be completed. We saw earlier how Latour's own application to the problem of the city was undertaken in what could be called a single site: what we know as 'Paris'. Within urban theory, the long-standing focus on studying single cities has long been overtaken by a desire to understand how cities influence each other, whether in a language of dominance and submission (as in some of the earlier imperial cities literature), or through a more recursive or circulatory geography of borrowing and learning.

These processes are illustrated in the work of Colin McFarlane (2011a, 2011b), who traces the emergence of alternative policy models within the global South, led by activist movements that have emerged from informal settlements, whose leaders work tactically to attempt to improve the provision of sanitation infrastructure in Mumbai; or the Porto Alegre social forum which, drawing on an already established sense of leftist and eco-socialist internationalism, debated and educated activists on techniques such as participatory budgeting. As a milieu, cities can for McFarlane be seen as 'machines for learning', acting as crucibles for the actualization process, through translation, which 'focuses on travel as the product of what different actors do in and through distributions with objects (statements, orders, artefacts, products, goods, etc.)' (2011b: 363). As opposed to 'diffusionist' models, which see ideas and practices spreading worldwide in a somewhat frictionless manner, this approach is far more contingent on different points along networks, as well as specific human–technological interactions. For this reason, the role of 'intermediaries' is given more value. Embedded within this are

> two inseparable relational perspectives: first, the importance of relationships between the 'near' and 'far' in producing knowledge, for instance in the ways in which the internet or a policy exchange may make distant actors proximate; and second, the agentic capacities of materials in producing knowledge and learning, for example the differential and contingent role of urban plans, documents, maps, databases or models in producing, shaping and contesting urban learning. (p. 363)

By contrast with the formal modes of policy transfer undertaken by consultancies, McFarlane discusses the improvised form of learning that takes place through urban forums, 'particular kinds of education of attention that urban improvisation entails, not as a field of informatics but as getting a "feel" for dwelling the city through the senses in relation to fear, hope, fantasy, solidarity and so on' (p. 373). And so rather than automatically positioning marginal communities as beyond help, instead there should be an attempt to understand the often concealed or submerged modes of adaptation that is going on in particular places.

However, and here is an interesting conundrum, perhaps we would then expect to see cities of the global North as having less need for such experimental modes of learning. Not so. Perhaps it is as a result of the constantly unstable nature of capitalism (Thrift 2005) or perhaps the desire of profit-seeking firms to create new knowledge products. But the development of new urban policy models in Northern cities has a similarly dramatic mode of production. Brett Christophers provides an exemplary study of how to approach this methodologically. He describes the process by which a UK consultancy known as Three Dragons produced a model that met British city government's need to calculate how many 'affordable' housing units should be provided by property developers within an overall development of market-rate dwellings:

> In the 1990s there was no such thing as a formal, discrete, publically-visible and commercially-marketed model for assessing the economic viability of providing affordable housing within new residential property development projects – no model, in the terms favoured in this article, according to which the world could, yet, act. (2014: 85)

And so, the consultancy set out to identify the key variables that determined affordability, settling on – or 'discovering' – that they were density and house prices. As Christophers continues:

> The team's discovery would format the structure of the model and would thus necessarily come to shape, in turn, the world in which the model became actualized … the model allowed its user to 'flex' different variables to construct different scenarios under which affordable housing viability could be appraised. But which variables could be flexed, and which were inflexible? This is always a conundrum for a model builder; not everything can be variable, at the user's discretion. (p. 86)

So to bring this into material existence, to have a 'world-making effect', involves actualization:

> This has occurred through a complex, iterative set of processes. On the one hand, the model and its authors have – again, after Callon – 'progressively discover[ed]' the world that the model refers to; this world

is not known at the outset; it is discovered through empirical observation, conceptual incorporation, and analytical experimentation. On the other hand and simultaneously, the model's release, utilization and incorporation into society's decision-making fabric literally 'put[s] into motion' the world described in the model. In short, by the time of the model's maturity, 'the world it supposes has become actual'; its assumptions about the world have become more, not less, accurate. The implication of such actualization is that we cannot understand that world except in relation to the model and the work it has performed. The world and the model are not exactly equivalent, so much as being two sides of same coin. They are, most importantly, not separate, although ironically the appearance of the model's separability from the world is most powerful 'when the world (finally) acts according to it'. (p. 80)

This set of practice-based approaches offers quite a radical view as to how globalization occurs. As a tool for action, they provide an escape from the passivity often associated with the 'bigness' and 'powerfulness' of global forces (see also Allen 2003, 2010).

However, a spatial perspective on this is important, particularly because the scholarly literatures in political science, political sociology and comparative institutionalism often tend to take for granted how policies move in a material, or networked, sense. As Peck puts it:

Contemporary policy-making processes have promiscuously spilled over jurisdictional boundaries, both 'horizontally' (between national and local political entities) and 'vertically' (between hierarchically scaled institutions and domains). They also seem to be accelerating, as measured by the shortening of policy development cycles and the intensity of cross-jurisdictional exchanges. Today's 'fast-policy' regimes are characterized by the pragmatic borrowing of 'policies that work', by compressed reform horizons, by iterative constructions of best practice, by enlarged roles for intermediaries as 'pushers' of policy routines and technologies, and by a growing reliance on prescriptively coded forms of front-loaded advice and evaluation science. On the face of it, policy ideas and techniques have become mobile in entirely new ways – exhibiting an extended reach as well as a diversity of registers. (2011: 773–4)

For Peck, this is part of a shift in how the policy-maker is conceived: 'Orthodox conceptions of policy transfer typically invoke a rational universe in which decision-makers more or less freely choose between policy models–cum–options, albeit in terms of varying degrees of knowledge and uncertainty' (p. 776). However, Peck argues that it would be more fruitful to explore the interaction of mobile policy influence with grounded, embedded policy restructuring. As he concludes:

These intensely contested and deeply constitutive contexts, which have their own histories and geographies, shape what is seen, and what counts, in terms of policy innovations, preferred models, and best practices. They also frame those narratives of 'policy failure' that establish the premises and preconditions for policy experimentation, and which variously animate and constrain the search for new institutional fixes. (pp. 791–2)

For this reason, he argues that it is important to approach policy transfer as a form of 'mobility-mutation' rather than the more voluntaristic – or optimistic – prevailing ideas of 'transfer-diffusion'.

THE SELLING OF THE SILICON VALLEY MODEL

Since the mid-2000s, a highly visible new form of economic organization has emerged in the leading cities of the internet industry. The digital 'scene', the 'hub' and the 'ecosystem' have been deployed to identify the presence of start-up technology firms, which are often named in familiar, if slightly ironic, terms as Silicon Roundabout (London), Silicon Beach (Sydney/LA) and Silicon Wadi (Tel Aviv). The rapid expansion of the internet, the adoption of smartphones and tablets, and the corresponding rise in social networking apps, e-commerce and enterprise software have generated a whole new set of economic agents that are leaving their imprint on cities.

The 'Silicon' reference is to one iconic place of economic development that has been copied again and again throughout the world: Silicon Valley. This small spit of land lying to the South of San Francisco is renowned as being the location for the development of various waves of computing technology: the invention of the microprocessor at Hewlett Packard, the development of semiconductors, and more recently the establishment of the various industries that coalesce around the internet, from social media (Facebook) to cybersecurity (Palantir). It has been subject to considerable mythologizing:

> Like all of today's successful cities, its [Silicon Valley's] strength lies in its human capital, which is nurtured by Stanford University and attracted by economic opportunity and a pleasant climate ... Innovations cluster in places like Silicon Valley because ideas cross corridors and streets more easily than continents and seas. (Glaeser 2011: 31, 36)

The Valley is often promoted as an illustration of the intensely localized effects of economic development, where ideas are seen to be generated – and funded – by close proximity and face to face interaction. This was not accidental: Frederick Terman, the Stanford professor who invested in Hewlett-Packard as a start-up, actively promoted the Valley and its approach to technology innovation.

Given its success, the Valley has been subject to a process of 'mimicry', copied by governments around the world as a way of stimulating high-technology, high skill jobs. Harvard Professor Michael Porter's high-profile advocacy of the benefits of spatially proximate inter-firm networking has further underpinned this model, as has Saxenian's (2007) study of the benefits of international immigration for the Valley's rates of innovation. However, this is not new: as Leslie and Kargon described at length in their paper 'Selling Silicon Valley: Frederick Terman's model for regional advantage', there are huge problems involved in even assuming that the complex social-material relations that underpin any urban economy can be identified and transferred.

> In the fall of 1963, Colorado's public universities co-sponsored a national conference on 'the new technological revolution' and its implications for state economic development. How could emerging states like Colorado, Governor John A. Love asked in his keynote address, compete in the high stakes world of high technology? What could they learn from the experiences of the 'great electronics industrial complexes that have grown up and down the peninsula from San Francisco, or around MIT'? What should they do to encourage closer cooperation between industry and higher education in the pursuit of regional growth? ... State officials, daring to hope that the massive federal investment in space and atmospheric research flowing into the state following Sputnik might make Colorado the next major high technology growth region, thought Terman and Packard could spell out for them the 'ingredients' that 'have contributed to the growth of industrial-scientific complexes' in other parts of the country. Armed with this information, the state would be assured of success. (1996: 436–7)

The active identification of the secret 'ingredients' of successful urban economies has become a big business. Yet this is by no means a straightforward process of observation and reproduction. Identifying what makes the Silicon Valley 'model' (and we should be wary about even using this term) something worth copying is an important exercise in its own right. Gordon Moore, a key player in the establishment of the Valley as founder of semiconductor and chip firm Intel, himself made a jocular reference to the 'ingredient' metaphor in one presentation:

> Combine liberal amounts of
>
> technology
>
> entrepreneurs
>
> capital, and

(Continued)

(Continued)

   sunshine.

   Add one (I)

   University.

   Stir vigorously. (Moore and Davis 2004: 7)

Charting this success story has been a fascinating element of globalization discourse in itself. However, the real story behind Silicon Valley's success is a story of capital, and venture capital in particular. On the one hand, the Valley's venture capitalists act as an entrepôt for institutional funds raised elsewhere which are being invested with hopes of stratospheric returns; on the other, they are now increasingly part of globalized funds, especially in terms of Chinese investment. The major Chinese social media and ecommerce firms Alibaba and Tencent have taken out strategic positions in the Valley not as part of a generalized investment strategy, but rather as part of the specific geography of transnationally spread capital investment.

In many ways, what we see with the ongoing citation of a small number of places such as Silicon Valley is the latest manifestation of what Gieryn, reviewing the influence of the early twentieth-century Chicago School of urban social science, calls 'truth-spots':

> An interesting rhetorical trope emerges: authors of the Chicago School oscillate between making Chicago (the city) into a laboratory and a field-site. On some occasions, the city assumes the qualities of a lab: a restricting and controlling environment, whose placelessness enables generalizations to 'anywhere', and which demands from analysts an unfeeling detachment. On other occasions, the same city becomes a field-site, and assumes different qualities: a pre-existing reality discovered by intrepid ethnographers who develop keen personal sensitivities to the uniquely revealing features of this particular place. (2006: 7)

This 'modern epistemics of place' (p. 7) thus involves a 'hardening' of the social sites of the city into something that can be objectified, and thence open to manipulation (be it copying, alteration, or re-engineering).

MANAGEMENT CONSULTANCY AS WORLDING PRACTICE

The growth of management consultancy as a business in its own right has been a characteristic feature of post-war economic globalization. The major firms that have dominated this field, such as McKinsey, PricewaterhouseCoopers, and so on have built on their initial strengths in accountancy and tax advice with a wider search for market share based on analysis of the performance of firms, the productivity of their employees, the ideal location of offices and factories, and so on. This is interesting for two reasons: on the one hand, certain key cities have become known as attracting or retaining pools of skilled labour; on the other, these cities – as hosts of particular firms – are responsible for disseminating knowledge products. In other words, there is a global division of expertise in advanced producer services, be it law, advertising, architecture, accountancy or management consulting (Faulconbridge and Jones 2012). This includes the rise of global executive search firms who orchestrate the movement of specialists and executives to various points of the world, by maintaining databases of specialists, and taking commission in moving and placing them in different jobs in different cities (Beaverstock and Hall 2012).

This has had clear effects on the ways in which global corporations have shaped their management models. However, it is also clear that these consultants – when operating in the global South – have been key agents in the development of neo-colonial business models that perpetuate existing relationships of dependency. Frenkel and Shenhav, working from a post-colonial perspective, argue that there is a strong 'continuity between the "civilizing mission" that characterized the colonial regimes and the modern consulting process in formerly colonized societies' (2012: 515):

> the bearers of this knowledge rarely make do with the implementation of technical models, aiming instead at the moral and cultural improvement of the 'under-developed' subject … the encounter between the global expert and the rest-of-the-world client is often loaded with a sense of supremacy and, in many cases, soft racism … the unsuccessful implementation of imported know-how is often attributed to the clients' lack of development and their inferior capabilities, rather than to their active and conscious resistance to the people bringing that knowledge to them. (p. 515)

So, it is important to understand how this knowledge is embedded, particularly within the 'small local elites at the client end [that] are instrumental in promoting and legitimizing the transferred knowledge and techniques' (p. 515).

In this context, Goldman writes about the role of management consultancies in shaping models for fast growing Asian cities, particularly in terms of selling 'eco-city' solutions. She argues that such a 'speculative urbanism' has four characteristics: 'a new architecture of investment capital'; 'a new architecture of urban governance'; an 'intensification of inter-urban competitiveness and inter-referencing'; 'a global architecture of expertise on cities' (2011: 231–3). This latter is not only driven by global consultants, but also by United Nations agencies such as UN Habitat and the UN Development Programme, international finance institutions such as the World Bank and the Asian Development Bank, and policy forums such as the World Bank's Cities Alliance (Goldman 2011: 232).

This could be termed 'consortium urbanism', where cities are being targeted by a coalitions of firms and state development agencies, which bundle together investment finance with engineering and construction knowledge. And so: 'the *worlding of cities* is not a phenomenon derived, or trickling down, from the European experience; world-city projects throughout Asia and the Middle East exhibit new dynamics across and within cities' (Goldman 2011: 234, emphasis in original). What is fascinating, though, is that investors will carry their own analysis of country by country variation:

> an Asia-based North American pension-fund manager explained at this Delhi summit that her clients require a much higher rate of return if they are to invest in India: If they get 12 percent in the United States, why should they expect anything less than 20 or 25 percent in India, to offset what she called the volatile 'India risk' of doing business in the subcontinent? (Goldman 2011: 234)

Older forms of 'bureaucratic' urban government are being 'provincialized' in place of new autonomous state agencies capable of responding rapidly to overseas investment interest.

CASE STUDY

CO-PRESENCE AND BUSINESS TRAVEL

[B]usiness travel remains an important mode of production within firms with, amongst other things, travel being used to: attend firm meetings or training sessions; visit clients to close deals, pitch for business or provide product support; attend trade fairs/conferences; and visit sub-contractors and suppliers to monitor quality control or negotiate new business. For many workers, business travel is now a normal everyday reality of the working day or night, involving what can best be described as persistent or mundane travel. (Beaverstock et al. 2010: 1)

The nature of co-presence – actually being in the same physical space as colleagues or contacts – is a key element in the constitution of contemporary societies, and how this is configured is often dependent on structures of business travel (Urry 2003).

The early approaches to world city networks drew much of their evidence from 'pairing' data sets, such as office headquarter location data or the airline connectivity between cities. However, the qualitative nature of this data – what was actually going on at these offices and firms, and who was actually travelling between these points – was not clear. So, despite the metageographical importance of work in this area, it tended to ascribe 'globality' to things which for phenomenological, ontological or even epistemological reasons are far more provisional than might appear. Subsequent research began to explore these issues in more detail. Beaverstock et al. (2010) identify three distinct theoretical approaches that converge around business travel, which include transport geographies of particular industries, such as the importance of airports and airlines; the role of face to face contact (as opposed to, or complementary to, teleconferencing) in the economic sociology of inter-firm networking; and the nature and organization of workspace itself, understood as a complex mix of sedentary office work and mobile work.

It is important to break this down into the different constituent parts identified above. For example, although a significant percentage of business travel is conducted in business class, including seats 'at the front of the plane' and dedicated lounges in airports, there are many business travellers who are regulated by cost (Bowen 2010). At the elite or specialist level, however, global firms deliberately set out to 'create a cadre of executives and technicians who are able to think and act both globally and locally and also to develop the management mechanisms and resources available to mediate the transfer and assimilation of expertise' (Salt 2010: 109).

FIGURE 6.1   Trade fair: these temporary events are evidence of the importance of co-presence, and justify business travel

Source: Adrian Castelli / Shutterstock.com

(Continued)

(Continued)

While the rise of the mobilities approach in social science has been notable (Sheller and Urry 2006), there is a need to differentiate it. For Jones, there are four key issues to consider when assessing the nature of business travel:

> First, a distinction needs to be made between intra- and inter-firm mobility – that is employees moving within their firm as opposed to between their firm and another (or multiple others). This relates to a second issue – the distinction between mobility associated with clients (the market for services), and that with suppliers to professional business service firms. Third, there is the issue of which employees are mobile in professional business services. Existing research suggests that mobility is differential between employees in different roles and at different positions in the hierarchy within professional service firms ... Fourth is the issue of the temporal form (i.e. the frequency and duration) of business travel and mobility. The existing research clearly points to the fact that there is signifi-cant variation in the length of business trips, from short-term travel of one or two days to long term secondments of months or years. (2010: 201)

Alongside these subtle differentiations of the types of mobility, the frequency, substance and atmosphere of meetings are significant in understanding how networks function. As John Urry has argued:

> what is important is not the absolute number of links that people possess; this is a rather abstract issue. Rather what I will call the degree of *meeting-ness* is crucial to the nature of networks. Such meetingness varies as to how often the network or some sub-network meets up, the exchanges of information, gossip and informal pleasure that occur, the significance of meetings in producing outcomes and generalizing trust, and the degree to which weak ties extend through such intermittent but selective meetings. (2003: 161, emphasis in original)

Urry groups the need for meetings, and hence the need for travel, into five different categories: legal, familial and economic obligations, social obligations, object obliga-tions, obligations to place and event obligations (see also Boden and Molotch 1994).

Against this, of course, is the argument that contemporary videoconferencing will obviate the need to travel, given the range of new communication options that it offers:

> data display, group and project collaboration, the possibility of video display of both physical object and 'information objects' alike, chat among partici-pants, etc. Some systems also allow archiving the entire video conference.

This makes the video conference available for later use by employees that did not attend, for instance by making the sessions available as downloads on the corporate intranet. (Denstadli and Gripsrud 2010: 232)

What is important is the systematization of travelling knowledge through objects, and how it has transformed how corporations in turn organize their internal space within cities, their locational decisions, and so on.

FIGURE 6.2   Boardroom videoconference: the growth in 'virtual' communication between distanciated project teams is an important innovation in the materiality of firm organization and business networking.

Source: wavebreakmedia / Shutterstock.com

GURUS AND URBANOLOGISTS

A specific form of management studies has focused on 'guru theory', who is typically an academic or management consultant who has 'broken out' from their firm or university with the publication of a carefully and expensively publicized trade book. These books tend to follow the same format:

> a focus on a single factor; the contrasting of old ideas with the new such that the latter are presented as qualitatively better and superior; the creation of a sense of urgency such that the introduction of the ideas is presented as

pressing and unavoidable; an emphasis on the need for readers to reflect and change their practice; an individualistic focus in that readers are portrayed as having a moral responsibility and capacity for the improvement of them-selves and/or their organizations; the linkage of the ideas to highly treasured management values; case studies of outstanding success; and a stress on the universal applicability of ideas. (Clark et al. 2012: 355)

Many of these gurus are highly mobile themselves. Importantly, though, it is their material devices – often books – which carry their ideas. The individual guru may then follow and cross-promote the book through speaking tours or private meetings with urban officials. Methodologically, this has spawned a series of studies of how influential ideas are materially communicated, which requires careful excavation which may entail researchers tracking the experts as they give keynote addresses at trade fairs or public events, and/or an examination of how 'local' officials and media have received them (e.g. McCann 2011a, 2011b):

An approach that starts from the notion of policy mobility as a social process enacted through the apparently banal practices of bureaucrats, consultants, and activists, will entail an attention to the representational and compara-tive practices of these actors and to related questions of commensurability. It takes, after all, a particular type of persuasive storytelling, involving stra-tegic namings and framings, inserted into a specific context where actors are predisposed to a certain range of policy options, to convince actors in one city that their place is commensurate with another to the extent that policies formulated and implemented elsewhere might also work at home. (McCann 2011b: 115–16)

The policy impact of Richard Florida, the creative-city advocate, has been described in depth by Peck (2012) in terms of how new policies and business models are tested and generated in a small number of exemplar cities. Here it is important to explore 'the interior spaces and constitutive networks' (Peck 2012: 464) that underpin new ideas, such as the creative cities meme. As Peck argues using Amsterdam as an example:

Motivational homilies of new 'ideas that work', ground-truthed in (named) places of invention, therefore have the potential to be especially potent car-riers of fast-policy innovation, even if conditions on the ground in these and other places continue to diverge from ideal–typical formulations. In this way, the creativity fix typifies the rising generation of urban 'models' that have been purposefully disembedded and unmoored from local conditions of possibility, after which they can be prescriptively abstracted as ostensibly pan-urban solutions. As such, the models themselves are effectively con-structed within an interurban space of policy circulation, across which they continue to mutate. (2012: 479)

Some cities exist as a 'translation space' for the development and implementation of a set of business models that will be rapidly copied worldwide.

However, this does not mean that there is a wholesale 'diffusion' of the model, copied fully formed into city-government policy. Rather, the model is strategically adopted within existing practices and power blocks in the city government; as Peck suggests, 'Creativity discourses, as they touched down in Amsterdam, seemed to have carried with them the allure of apparently governing in fundamentally new ways, with new stakeholders and new strategic objectives … while at the same time changing very little' (p. 472).

In other words, they were incorporated within established policy manifestos and agendas:

> They facilitated a makeover of the discursive representation and political rationale of a loose cluster of urban-development policies (with a social-inclusion accent), without necessitating any substantial reorganization of the policies themselves. At their most candid, some officials would concede that the effort had degraded into a 'do nothing' policy, but one that happened to resonate with the pre-existing bundle of competitive strengths, governmental capacities, programming lines, cultural traditions and received images on which Amsterdam could credibly trade. In private, many officials distanced themselves from the Florida thesis; some evidently took pleasure in ridiculing it. Few were taken in by its exaggerated claims and many were slightly embarrassed at its flashy presentation. Savvy and worldly, these were by no means credulous consumers of the Florida tonic. They knew that the model was questionable and overstated, if not fundamentally flawed. But they also knew that its very elasticity provided an expedient means of achieving a range of other goals, while productively repackaging local policies under the sign of creativity, as a positive and trendy urban-development metanarrative that at least appeared to 'fit'. (p. 472)

So, while gurus may be a significant agent in shaping the general discourse on social change, it is more likely that it is local officials, politicians and consultants who work out which elements of the approach to adopt, and how they relate to pre-existing policies.

Following down a similar path as that of Florida, though bearing firmly to the right as a 'microeconomically rationalized cousin to the creative-class thesis' (Peck 2016: 6), the academic economist Ed Glaeser has become a highly publicized figure whose *Triumph of the City* (2011) gained wide distribution and media exposure. Again, Peck (2016) has made a detailed critique of Glaeser's contribution, arguing that the outward narrative of the pop-economist has a ready ear in government and mainstream media:

> Here, the figure of the economist-savant – who can see what others cannot, the invisible matrix of economic incentives, giving voice to the hard truths of market rationality – has been granted a new kind of public authority. At its most potent, this approach combines presentational accessibility with

flashes of statistical wizardry (along with a measure of feigned interpretive innocence), disclosing sometimes uncomfortable truths as way-of-the-world facts of competitive life. (p. 7)

What is troubling, for Peck, is that the underlying programmatic element of Glaeser's prose is a basic rehash of neo-liberal urban economics, repackaged within a homely, straightforward and open conversation about city policy. In turn, his narrative is carried by an association with 'success stories':

In the practiced style of the guru urbanologist, Glaeser reaches well beyond statistical proofs for positive examples of metropolitan vitality, cherry-picking from Paris and Bangalore, Vancouver and Houston, Tokyo and (of course) New York City. This rigorously systematic economist is liberally selective when it comes to best-practice policy prescription: the secrets of urban success are effortlessly harvested from the sites of that success. (p. 9)

In other words, contra to theoretical positions that argue for an uneven development of the world where resources are concentrated in several places at the expense of others, if only 'failing' places were more like Bangalore and Vancouver, then cities everywhere would be better. There are many problems with this, not least that skilled labour markets are agglomerative and seductive: they are successful because they can attract the most highly skilled workers away from the places in which they have grown up or received formative education and training.

Stylistically, this involves a tactical mode of public discourse: on the one hand, 'convictions-based policy advice, presented as economically justified pragmatism; its rather more playful side involves unrestrained (over)extensions of rational-choice logic, to just about any everyday problem or social puzzle, *freakonomics*-style' (p. 16, emphasis in original). The point of this, Peck argues, is to present a neo-classical interpretation of severe structural interventions in a light-hearted, casual mode, 'combining uplifting celebrations of urban life, as the pinnacle of human achievement, with the dispensation of sober(ing) advice on the economically conditioned – if not preordained – policy options available to cities today' (p. 2). This allows him to pursue the dogmatic ideological project of the Manhattan Institute, a right-wing think-tank that Glaeser aligns with, and which promoted his book, as a means of 'effectively colonizing the city as a projected space of economic rationality … a normative project for the rationalization and normalization of neoliberal restructuring, not only in United States but also beyond' (p. 1).

Taken together, the celebrity urbanologists have tended to either project or surf a neo-liberal flow, offering policy interventions using a narrow range of urban success stories to advocate policy reforms in particular areas. Their books, importantly, become influential not in a vacuum, but through a strategy of media placement, free copies sent to opinion formers, social media campaigns, and orchestrated speaking tours and media appearances. To recall Latour, these books are popular because they are synoptic: they offer a stable vantage point to capture the whole city, objectifying it to make it ready for intervention.

SAN FRANCISCO AND THE GLOBAL EXPANSION OF UBER

San Francisco became a key site during the 2000s in the monetization of what is often called 'collaborative consumption' or the 'sharing economy' (Botsman and Rogers 2010) in which individuals save costs by engaging in 'peer to peer sharing' in areas such as accommodation, car-pooling and the renting or bartering of equipment and services. These new areas of sharing – as with Napster some years previously – opened up all sorts of complex regulatory, rights and financial issues that were entirely new to state regulators. The Bay Area became home to a number of start-up firms that rapidly gained a global reach and reputation through the locally channelled venture capital system.

A popular sector was taxi and ride-sharing apps, and the city was the location of start-ups such as Uber and Lyft, who employed smartphones to allow potential riders to bypass traditional modes of dispatch. The case of Uber was particularly controversial. Under the aggressive leadership of CEO Travis Kalanick, Uber linked with 'town car' limo services; competitors such as Lyft linked potential riders with non-professional drivers directly; in both cases the riders and drivers used the app's GPS technology to find each other. Payment was handled by a secure credit-card-based portal, thus removing cash transactions. Unsurprisingly, existing taxi fleet and dispatch operators were hostile at what they saw as an unregulated competitor entering their field. Uber, notable in that it didn't possess a fleet of cars, argued that it was acting as a referral service rather than a taxi company. There were three particular criticisms raised by opponents, both from city hall and the taxi industry itself. First, while existing taxi licence holders had to accept rides across the city within a regulated tariff, Uber was able to set its own prices (through a time-based supply formula it called 'surge pricing'). Critics argued that this allowed the cannibalization of the richest passengers and routes. Second, critics argued that it had fewer checks on its drivers than the safety of their vehicles, and noted the absence of effective insurance policies should they get into accidents. Third, Uber made no contribution to city coffers, not having to pay the medallion fees paid by existing licensed fleets (Swan 2013).

Uber, with successive rounds of venture-capital funding, used its success in San Francisco to 'scale' to cities around the world. Although it quickly ran into regulatory problems in some key cities such as New York, Los Angeles and Paris, it was swiftly legalized in other jurisdictions. Yet despite the simplicity of its business model, it had to modify its approach to enter various cities. In Bangkok, it opened a motorbike service; in Mumbai, it had to deal with the specific structure of the existing taxi-industry market. One major problem was to sustain a secure

(Continued)

(Continued)

level of driver screening, and also to navigate the relatively low rates of smart-phone ownership. But perhaps the major challenge was regulatory:

> Smartphone application-based Uber taxis could be seen as another competing 'model' that has travelled via aggressive marketing and corporate expansion from Silicon Valley to cities in Asia ... In India, the running of 'private' cars as taxis (Uber's business-model) is against the law. Therefore, Uber has had to shift its model to entice both fleet-drivers and independent, permit-holding and car-owning drivers to get on board. (Bedi 2016: 14)

In China, a huge potential market, rival venture capitalists ploughing funds into the competing Chinese market leader Didi Kuaidi prompted Uber to pour huge amounts of cash into subsiding its expansion. While its global longevity remains to be proven, the business model has been widely copied and adopted, and a cliché in start-up circles is to aspire to be the 'Uber of pet food', the 'Uber of home decorating', and so on.

FIGURE 6.3 Italian taxidrivers protest against Uber, 2015, showing solidarity with French colleagues

Source: Mike Dotta / Shutterstock.com

TESTBEDS AND EXPERIMENTATION

The popularity of policy gurus and guidebooks has been driven by seemingly unending demand from politicians and policy-makers for ideas to either fix urban problems, or else valorize underperforming urban assets. Furthermore, there has been a search for approaches that will help them insert their cities as part of a global commons. For example, the Rockefeller Institution's 100 Resilient Cities programme, or the C40 group of cities that have sought to share best practice in climate change mitigation, are evidence of the discourse and practice of experimentation, testing and analysis. This has become central to city government for several reasons.

First, it suggests that cities are at the forefront of new technology markets. And as with other new economy sectors such as cleantech (Caprotti and Romanowicz 2013), these are markets that are in the process of construction, and so are 'shaking out'. In future years we may look back to this stage in urban history and reinterpret it with a sense of order. In their study of the historical stabilization of the US electricity industry, Granovetter and McGuire (1998) argue that business histories tend to smooth out the process of invention and innovation: the success of Edison and his collaborators in dominating the early years of electricity infrastructure *appeared* to be driven by protagonists who were 'uniformly insightful, proactively exercising initiative, pursuing efficiency, and achieving rational outcomes', but were in reality 'reactive', 'backing into the future as much as or more than striding into it' (Granovetter and McGuire 1998: 166). They conclude that more attention should be paid to the formation and reconfiguration of 'particular industries' especially at times of rapid technological change, where new markets may open.

Second, there is no doubt that social problems can be 'urbanized' and thus technologized. For some scholars, this provides evidence of a 'solutionism'. This term, coined by media theorist Evgeny Morozov (2013), refers to a technologically determined process of problem definition, quantified data analysis, and heavily marketed software solution. In other words, urban diagnosis has become a growth industry, where management consultants observe a problem, formulate and frame it, before providing the tools to solve it via software programs, for example.

Third, solutions can be achieved on a defined project by project basis, thus limiting risk. Through the establishment of goal-oriented, fixed-term urban projects, governments partner with private corporations to put into practice exploratory schemes, such as smart-water-meter installation or new transport management systems. What tends to mark out such schemes is the way in which they are configured as closed systems, where their success is measured against self-generated criteria, rather than the overall response of urban dwellers. And so:

> From a traditional perspective, conceptualizing the city as a laboratory is nonsensical. Cities are messy, multivariate, open systems – the very opposite of the scientific laboratories that are valued for being hermetically sealed off

from the world ... Laboratorization is about setting boundaries within which controlled experiments can take place and be recorded. The purpose of these spaces is to allow the staging of experiments that can be repeated dependably anywhere, transforming events (experiments) into facts (knowledge). (Evans and Karvonen 2014: 416)

This also presents methodological difficulties, and in particular the issue of coping with cultural variability and comparability.

Fourth, this means that smart cities firms are also experimenting as to how best to leverage and transfer existing knowledge within their spatially extensive organizations and markets. These firms take quite a narrow 'zonal' focus (Barry 2006) in order to valorize their assets. As Kitchin points out: 'companies such as IBM, Cisco, Siemens, Intel and SAP do not fully share a conception of smart cities, in part due to different corporate ethos, but also because they are competing oligopolists selling different products (for example, consultancy, networks, hardware and devices, chips, software, system solutions)' (2015: 133–4). Furthermore, the nature of spatio-temporal competition within a global economic marketplace means that the sheer size of firms can make them vulnerable to failure. They may 'even fail to act in their own best interest, even when they have good information about what to do' (Schoenberger 1997: 113). This is often blamed by commentators on the 'culture' of the firm in question but, as Schoenberger argues, it is 'misleading to speak of a single culture, for even within the firm there are many sites of cultural production' (p. 121). As such, the creation of smart cities markets might be seen as part of the ongoing 'cultural crisis of the firm', where the possibilities offered by innovation are geared against shareholder expectations of short-term dividends, and the strategies of competitors, new and old.

CASE STUDY

URBAN LABORATORIES: NEW SONGDO AND MASDAR CITY

The concept of the urban laboratory is odd because it implies that the real world can function as a laboratory. Studies taking place in the real world (or 'the field', as natural scientists call it) are generally understood to be situated in particular places at particular times, and thus incapable of producing generally valid knowledge. They tend to be descriptive and specific in their applicability owing to the inability to manipulate variables and isolate cause-and-effect mechanisms. In claiming to be a laboratory in the field, the very notion of an urban laboratory violates this distinction. (Evans and Karvonen 2014: 416)

Recent years have seen attempts by global technology firms to present demonstration cases of how a large-scale urban 'tech' fit-out might work. The 2000s also saw the development of numerous eco-city projects (Rapoport 2014), promoted by governments as evidence of a commitment to climate change adaptation, through the establishment of sites with a focus on innovation in sustainability technology (Caprotti 2014). Masdar City, in Abu Dhabi, was perhaps the most ambitious model.

> The idea was to build, for the first time in history, a zero-waste, zero-carbon settlement, having no adverse environmental impact. In order to accomplish this, Abu Dhabi bet on architecture and technology. Foster and Partners (F + P), the renowned global architectural firm, planned a 6 km^2 city whose design would facilitate the reduction of energy consumption and possess a smart resources management system. This, along with the employment of cutting-edge green technology, such as smart utility grids, concentrated solar power (CSP) and electric personal rapid transport (PRT), was to be the recipe for the ultimate completely sustainable city. The Masdar City project quickly gained great visibility and attracted high-profile companies eager to obtain a spot in what promised to be a leading centre for the development of green technologies. General Electric, Schneider and Siemens were among the first to join the Masdarian enterprise, seeing in the new city a perfect place to test, implement and promote their new products. (Cugurullo 2013: 28)

On the one hand, this is an interesting example of what could be called 'consortia urbanism' where a coalition of sector specialists are co-contracted to deliver specialist systems. They are attractive for city governments that lack the scope and resources to innovate in a comprehensive manner:

> Urban laboratories offer a potential silver bullet for cities aiming to make the transition to a low-carbon economy, producing knowledge that will help them reduce their environmental impacts and resource consumption, generate new economic growth and develop reputations as leaders in sustainable development. There is an assumption that by producing knowledge 'in the real world' and 'for the real world', urban laboratories can catalyze rapid technical and economic transformation. (Evans and Karvonen 2014: 415)

Such eco-cities are difficult to assess and, given their near-instant construction as a whole, are often eerily disproportionate in terms of buildings to people (see, for example, Caprotti's (2014) observations on walking through Tianjin eco-city). As a postscript, it was announced in 2015 that Masdar had stepped back from its

(Continued)

(Continued)

zero-energy ambitions, and would proceed towards a more conventional form of urban development.

Another notable example of the experimental city was provided in New Songdo, a large-scale development site close to Seoul. Here, infrastructure firm Cisco played a key part in the development of a 'smart' city:

> Songdo is, arguably, the most extreme instantiation of a far more prevalent and genuinely ubiquitous faith in the place of big data and interactive feedback to monitor and sustain daily life. The technologies tested in Songdo are beta versions for similar systems put in place by many cities and rolled out regularly by high-tech and telecommunication corporations to service the now naturalized faith that human beings require ever-more information and bandwidth for social life. If many technologists and planners view these massive greenfield spatial products as banal and uninspired, it is at the cost of failing to realize that the array of conduits and cell phone towers of IFEZ are practice spaces for corporations to perfect the design of data collection and management infrastructures for any network – urban or otherwise. (Halpern et al. 2013: 290)

Songdo is a high profile example of the 'corporate story-telling' that accompanies many 'smart' urban development projects (Soderström et al. 2014). The danger that many critics identify is that a small number of global corporations will come to consolidate and monopolize data holdings, creating captive markets that can be used to distribute more and more products, removing the privacy of contemporary life. For Halpern et al., we are at something of a watershed in the development of urban life:

> Never before in history have cities been subjected in such scale to the technocratic visions and trials of a few anonymized global companies. But never before have there also been so many new agents and agencies – human, machine, and other – networked in new arrangements and intelligences. (2013: 300)

A core element of these experiments is the gathering of data via sensors, either of how objects and infrastructures operate in terms of technical efficiency, but also of how humans occupy the spaces, giving evidence of behavioural patterns.

Such 'big data' is now central to urban governmental best practice. In her essay on the 'methodolatry' of big data's application to urban problems, Shannon Mattern (2012) comments on how the formerly drab world of positivist urban science has been opened up in all sorts of politically dangerous ways:

> The default recourse to data-fication, the presumption that all meaningful flows and activity can be sensed and measured, is taking us toward a future in which the people shaping our cities and their policies rarely have the opportunity to consider the nature of our stickiest urban problems and the kind of questions they raise. Often they do not even stop to wonder if the blips – which 'the system' flags as 'snafus' or 'clogs' – are really problems at all. Are all 'inefficiencies' – having parent–teacher conferences, for example, rather than standardized electronic evaluations posted to a government website – necessarily obstacles to be overcome?
>
> The computational power offered by the new technologies allowed the human element of urban policy to be neglected in a 'normative' mode of good government.

There is a danger, which needs to be acknowledged and confronted at all points, that the performativity of economics can end up being a rather empty truism unless the wider social and political materiality of such performativity is explored and conceptualized. Or, put bluntly: economics is performative, but so what? Recognizing that economic models make and mould markets and other socioeconomies may be interesting, but should it not be more than that? (Christophers 2014: 83)

This chapter has discussed different modes by which certain urban development models, policy programmes and business models have been formatted, packaged, transmitted, translated and distributed worldwide. Having already considered some of the devices by which Rome became established as a global city in Chapter 1, it should be obvious that this is not a new idea. Cities have always had a role in co-ordinating resource economies, faith communities, and population movements. That said, it must be noted that a key element of global-cities theory in this area has been about both an increasing speed and intensity by which knowledge is recognized, turned over and absorbed.

Each of the authors discussed here are at pains to demonstrate that ideas, discourses and models tend to become adopted or actualized only as part of a wider process of governmentality, or state restructuring. If city government is seen not as powerfully dynamic but rather as powerfully sclerotic then we can get a sense of why gurus and consultants are accorded influence. As Barbara Czarniawska has described in her comparative study of European city management, city managers are constantly exposed to composite pictures of models of practice that have – apparently – worked elsewhere. The introduction of new policy ideas to long-established organizational fields of city management must also take account of embedded local norms in, for example, accountancy or engineering. Getting beyond this lacunae in general terms is important, though difficult: 'Management might be worth condemning, but it isn't worth studying … it is assumed that managers *have* power, and therefore there is no need to know more about them, as a knowledge of the nuances might hamper their demonization or hagiography' (2002: 143, emphasis in original).

This raises questions about the globalization of expertise, and the performance of knowledge that occurs when inexpert city councils are procuring services. The power and technique of the marketing departments of global corporations is striking, as in the wave of ill-advised investments made by municipalities prior to the global financial crisis of 2007–8, which was driven largely by aggressive marketing by the likes of Goldman Sachs, and which bring techniques of seduction into the process of city management (Weber 2010; Hendrikse and Sidaway 2013).

Throughout this we can see the importance of various practices of travel. Whether through the 'live' presence of a guru in a city, or the development of trusting business relations through out-of-office socializing, the embodied movement of individuals is a core element of the composition of global cities. And as Gieryn states, knowledge formation occurs in a complex dialectical process of immersion and detachment:

> Place is normative: certain behavior patterns and dispositions are expected from people in part because of where they happen to be … In science, field-sites and laboratories have each developed their own demeanor, as analysts are differently positioned with respect to their research materials – and this has given rise to two distinctive geographies of credibility. Researchers in field-sites trade on being near to the objects of study, deeply among them; by contrast, scientists in laboratories draw on the validating virtues of distance – being far from nature (or society) in the raw, remote from its immediate distractions and potential compromises. Paradoxically, near and far can coexist as simultaneous registers of epistemic legitimacy. (2006: 21)

World-making is thus a complex mix of citation, mimicry and truth claims, a performance of knowledge. And yet it is also more than that: world-making is a commodity, and the management consultancy is a proof of that.

CONCLUSIONS

The aim of this book was to bring together the set of literatures linking materiality and practices, with that of the political and cultural economy of global cities. The starting point was that the term 'global city' has become something of a fetish, over-determined to the point of being meaningless. I have had considerable sympathy for the motivations behind the 'ordinary city' literature and approach, which has become established in the field. However, the problem facing global-cities studies is only partly caused by locational overstretch; as important, I suggest, is that all sorts of city- and world-making practices have to be made banal and everyday. The pendulum has swung so far in the opposite direction that the key global cities of the North, so to speak, are arguably being omitted from study and left out of key urban theory debates at a point in time when their role in the composition of global power is perhaps as important as it ever has been. So, the book has stuck fast to the belief that there are very important concentrations of wealth, brainpower, office infrastructure, air and logistics routes, which come together to both compete and collaborate in the making of a global capitalist vernacular. In other words, it defends the study of major global cities such as London, New York, and Los Angeles, and regional economies such as Silicon Valley, despite claims that their world-making importance is overplayed, or else aggressively concealing difference in their absorption into an apparently universal urban theory.

Global cities are definitely big things (recalling the discussion of Jacobs in Chapter 3). We can think of bigness in terms of power and knowledge. Bigness in this context tends to be applied to relational bigness, as larger economic units are often held by neo-classical economists to mean larger internal markets, and hence an ever-growing prosperity. Within the 'big thing' there are many micro practices involved, of pricing, praying, packing and processing, to name but a tiny number, which are not necessarily 'global' in their ability but are part of a world-making set of practices. Or they might be reified, ascribing more power to them than is analytically sound. As Peter Taylor has put it:

> Often a city name is used as shorthand for describing all the processes with their agents that are operating through a city. During the Cold War, the contending parties were sometimes recoded as 'Washington' dealing with 'Moscow'. This need not be a problem when it is clearly understood what the use of the city name implies; what its referents are … 'St Petersburg' was identified as having a 'parasitic' role in the tsarist Russian economy. In this case, the agency is obvious: the tsarist administrations that built and developed the city to such a degree that government agency has been commonly identified with this pampered capital city creation. Similarly … it is not 'London' that is 'killing' Newcastle but rather successive UK governments whose 'national' economic policies favour the former. (2004: 56)

Rather, cities are compositional: they compose national territories at the same time as they enact what we recognize as global networks; they offer economic freedom for some at the same time as they impoverish or enslave others. We might think about world city-*making* systems rather than world city systems.

It is not an exaggeration to say that there are but a tiny set of 'centres of calculation' that economically, theologically and culturally define and mobilize most of the structures by which the world is organized. There is surely no singular religious institution with such global aspiration as the Vatican, and nothing to compare to how the Pope's *Urbi et Orbi* orations capture this ambition. There are millions around the world whose lives are shaped by the material messages that come forth from this enclave on the Tiber's banks. Yet the Vatican is famously tiny in size. Why is it so significant, when compared with the vast, populated terrains of a Karachi or a Chongqing? And what does it mean for the ordering, calculating and logistical practices discussed at various points in the book? Does this mean that global cities as a term is too chaotic to be relevant? I think not, but the term's use has to shift from the taken for granted to the operative. A further issue is that while these small areas of capital accumulation – we could call them footprints – may have huge impacts on surrounding housing and labour markets, it is nonetheless true that the excessive focus on financial clusters may divert attention from mundane, but in aggregate terms significant, economic zones such as contiguous small businesses, informal economies of unpaid or semi-legal work, or even criminal economies. This is particularly important when considering the importance of underdeveloped cities in Africa, Asia and Latin America, which may plug into global economic flows in less spectacular ways (Shatkin 1998; Simone 2004; Sidaway and Power 2005).

What does this mean for the field of study known as 'urban theory'? Should we be looking for the universal law, or focusing on the specific and contingent? Should we be following things, people or ideas? To what degree should we be paying attention to the materiality of cities, of how they hold together, or are held together, by objects and agents? How do we use 'cities' in this case? As laboratories? As theatres? As more provisional spatial formations? In what follows I discuss what this might mean for urban theory in a series of propositions.

DISTANCE AND PANORAMA

Although these panoramas shouldn't be taken too seriously, since such coherent and complete accounts may become the most blind, most local, and most partial viewpoints, they also have to be studied very carefully because they provide the only occasion to see the 'whole story' *as a whole*. Their totalizing views should not be despised as an act of professional megalomania, but they should be added, like everything else, to the multiplicity of sites we want to deploy. (Latour 2005: 189, emphasis in original)

Latour's interest in panorama was driven by his mission to show the impossibility of capturing the 'city' as a whole. It is intriguing to consider in this vein how the current interest in global cities is as an imperfect vantage point from which to talk about globalization more generally. Just as museums show off artefacts in a mode that Bennett (1988) calls the 'exhibitionary complex', so do cities achieve status on the basis of the degree to which they are viewed and practised. And so we might see global cities as being a set of fairly unstable artefacts that together form a platform that theories can be built upon. In the same way that a museum aims to give order to an incredible miscellany of objects, so urban theory tries to glue together the miscellany of global cities.

To take one example, architects, as with other advanced producer service firms, are transmitting a knowledge product, one that has specific attributes that have to travel through space from the design studio (a dense factory of embodied specialist design knowledge) to the site office, and thence to the construction site itself (McNeill 2009b). How, then, is such a material transfer sustained and interpreted? For Law and Hetherington (2000: 40), this demands a careful consideration of ontological questions concerning space:

> We're saying, then, that locations which don't communicate with one another, which know nothing of one another, don't exist for one another exist in entirely *different worlds* or spaces. Like the Incas and the Arabs who, as far as is known, never communicated, never knew of one another. The argument is that *distance demands communication and interaction*. Its very possibility, *depends* on communication or interaction. (emphasis in original)

By extension, we might speculate as to how – at a more humble level – the sites and devices described in each chapter can be global before they are actually known in a location. In a large part, this has involved turning to consider the link between objects and the spatial formations we call global cities. Each chapter traced out a particular heterogeneous set of objects: some designed as forms of storage, such as credit cards, data centres and containers, which have different types of mobile properties. In this sense, 'the possibility of globality' (Law and Hetherington 2000: 40) is sustained through action, it is not pre-given.

So, a goal has been to link materiality and globalization, the challenge for social scientists being not just to describe globalization, but to show how it is achieved. This means that before two locations are paired for the purpose of some specific material transaction, they don't exist for each other in any meaningful way. Chapter 6 flagged the importance of management consultants, for example, in actively hooking up different parts of the affluent world in cities. Chapter 5 indicated the long-standing importance of centrality for organizations: maps, reports and spreadsheets are all ways of making distance smaller and unimportant. And finally, this means that within the Church, a foreign parish doesn't exist until it becomes a problem. So for Law and Hetherington, a series of practices are required: delegation – acting as agent at a distance; the creation of obligatory points of passage, places of privilege, centres of accumulation; scale reversals; and discretion – to act or not to act.

GLOBAL CITIES ARE MISCELLANEOUS CONCENTRATIONS OF FIRMS

While I have shown sympathy with this attempt to destabilize the hierarchy of global-city rankings, I have not felt inclined to follow it through to its extreme, to flatten out the difference between cities. Instead, my sense is that they are *concentrated*, and an aim of the book was to show how firms increasingly – often subtly – appropriate central cities. Amin and Thrift argue that we need to be

> considering the city as a set of flows ... as a field of movements, a swirl of forces and intensities, which traverse and bring into relation all kinds of actors, human and non-human, in all manner of combinations of agency ... [But] ... We also also need to think about how cities are *orders*, and this ordering is often exacted through the design of flows as a set of serial *encounters* which construct particular places and times. (2002: 83, emphases in original)

A key argument of Chapter 5 was to revisit how CBDs are consciously produced and practised by actors who have a vested interest in doing so. These are rarely articulated thus, only by the downtown managers or mayors who seek to retain a strong economic core to their cities. A useful move might be to bring together agglomeration, an old-time economic explanation of why markets were located (but we might better say 'gathered') at certain points, with the idea of a metrological footprint.

The main reason is that global cities are sites where firms are gathered. I discussed how we might speak of office territories, a malleable concept in allowing more sites through which to study the composition of cities, as a more accurate way of capturing this: sticking to a strict scalar hierarchy approach, much work in these territories is of national or regional importance only. But we can also see them as sites of social interaction and construction: Linda McDowell's (1997) pioneering work on embodiment in investment banks provides evidence of how social practices are concentrated, staged perhaps, and how this acts to reproduce various forms of power. Saskia Sassen's (1995) insights, that the complexity of global firms requires them to co-locate, remain very important. I show in my discussion of IBM's Smarter Cities strategy how firms actively shape and limit the contours of what we understand as 'cities' in order to serve their own vulnerability in competitive markets, and to satisfy their shareholder base (McNeill 2015b). It is impossible, even for apparently all powerful global executives, to observe their whole firm without simply resorting to the device of the 'panorama', to reference Latour. And so I prefer to see global cities in these terms: sites for the orchestrated gathering of firms.

This is important for another reason: all too often, the agency of cities is not specified. This is most glaring in Glaeser's (2011) *Triumph of the City*, because although many mayors lay claim to agency, and it is usually cities that form the units that make up metageographical rankings, in reality it is firms that are geared up to operate and make a difference globally. And the firms themselves are only strong because of their diffusion and distension as much as their extension. To understand this properly requires a firm-level set of research studies, whether it be of global banks and their offshoots, global architectural firms and their clients and co-contractors, global technology firms and their particular and sometimes peculiar national structures, and the global firms that specialize in mobility: airlines, especially, who have little functional interest in the cities that they link but who are entirely reliant on their signification; cargo firms; utilities companies which are driven by bundling and unbundling infrastructure systems (Rossiter, 2016).

CALCULATED TERRITORIES

Throughout, I have drawn attention to diverse sites that together constitute global cities. CBDs are important sites in the programming and production of space, in gathering the knowledge that makes calculated decisions on what happens in near and far territories (Elden 2007; Mennicken and Miller 2012) some kind of taxonomy of these zones is important: the functional arrangement of these sites, be they a cathedral, the office of a corporate law firm, a ship or an airport, are often studies of miniaturization and efficiency rather than the expansionist metaphors that we might think. Fundamental is the importance of locational efficiency: there is a need to consider and test some of the key assumptions of why CBDs have retained their validity, despite seeming to have been written off in many academic and journalistic accounts from the 1960s onwards.

Furthermore, it is now abundantly clear that a scepticism towards the assumptions and actions of most of the main players in corporate capitalism is necessary. This is particularly important in the context of the CBD as a space with its own 'moral geography'. In other words, rather than seeing the banks and financial services companies as being faceless corporations, a closer – indeed forensic – attention to the activities of CEOs, fund managers and, importantly, non-executive board members is an important element of a renewed political economy. The ways of doing this, from examining corporate governance moves, is a crucial element in creating a sense of how 'the big end of town' engages in its own self-governmentality.

Finally, the nature of the central business district of cities such as London as a marketplace can be enhanced by attention to the 'virtuality' of markets. This is an important tool in the de-naturalization of the CBD as a 'market' (be it a property market, a labour market, a market for services, and so on). Such 'market talk' is often based upon very arbitrary notions of delimitation, and is often aspatial. This can have material effects in terms of changing zoning for new buildings ('the market is too tight'), commuting and investment in public transport (labour market 'imbalance'), or changes in the way in which particular sectors are valued or devalued. The lack of explicit theorization of the city's central business district(s) sits oddly with the growing evidence that the global financial crisis had a lot to do with 'the securitization of suburbia' (Langley 2006). In other words, uneven development of cities is not just about the static residues of social polarization, but is actively constituted by the seeking of surplus. This is hardly a novel point, but it does ask us to think about whether all those global city office towers are more about generating surplus from local suburbs to feed a multiply territorialized rentier class, than in their transnational relations with other 'global' cities.

POWER AND CITIES

Numerous theorists have argued for the importance of understanding the ordering principles that underpin globalization. John Law, in particular, has provided several ways of thinking through categorization but also how distance is activated and made manageable (1994). Power is thus a lot more diffuse than is sometimes imagined, and has to be constantly negotiated even among actors that are apparently full of power. For John Allen, it is important to understand the diverse ways in which power is exercised:

> The erosion of choice, the closure of possibilities, the manipulation of outcomes, the threat of force, the assent of authority or the inviting gestures of a seductive presence, and the combinations thereof, are among the diverse ways in which power puts us in place. (2003: 196)

In other words, cities might be seen as tactical battlegrounds rather than fields of domination: powerful groups are able to marshal forces (especially capital) in global cities which gives them the ability to act, but this is more a means of bolstering their 'power to' do something, rather than a zero sum 'power over' a particular weaker set of individuals and groups. This stance, often associated with Marxian critiques of society, is problematic, as Allen argues:

> We lose sight … of what it means to engage in associational arrangements of power in response to those who seek only instrumental advantage. In the former, people are not powerless; they exercise power through the positive strengths of collaborative association … Negotiation and shared outcomes replace confrontation and opposition and take us into the realm of the 'power to' act, rather than the domain of the 'powerless' who are likely to be left feeling that 'power over' them is all that they are ever likely to experience. (p. 196)

Many of the issues discussed in this book, therefore, reflect constant and problematic attempts of those with power (be it the Vatican struggling with the social diversity of their followers, corporations trying to hold together, or the global business travellers trying to keep cool and productive in air-conditioned hotels in tropical cities) to sustain the material base of their location in a global economy.

Global cities are often spoken about, or referred to, as if they are Leviathans, a term used by Callon and Latour (1981) to recognize the sheer size of certain institutions that are both worlds in themselves (with their own rules, sense of identity and loyalty, modes of discipline, and so on) and actors that structure worlds.

ETHNOGRAPHIC SENSITIVITIES

There is an interesting tension in urban theory concerning the making of meaning about cities, particularly when a geographic perspective is adopted. On the one hand, to achieve global cities as a theory involves some sort of inter-city knowledge production; on the other, to understand the depth of a city involves staying in one place for a long time and getting to know its nuance, its path dependences, its durable institutions, all the things that Latour pulled out as constituting Paris, for example. So this raises a tension about the position of the theorist: their cultural assumptions, perspectives, insights, prejudices. This would extend to a sensitivity to the role of elite universities in knowledge production and theory-building (Jöns 2016). If we were to locate global cities within a discussion of the 'area studies' tradition of human geography, as Sidaway (2013) has done, we might get a sense of the critical standpoints required in gaining a fuller understanding of how they are constituted.

Certainly, one of the frustrations that motivated Jenny Robinson's advocacy of an ordinary city approach was the sub-disciplinary, clinical distinction between how cities were studied within, for example, urban geography and development geography. More recently, this distinction has been harder to sustain. For example, the rise of the Gulf cities such as Abu Dhabi, Doha and Dubai have offered a distinctive form of urban development, linked partly by the close nexus between the state and property finance (Buckley and Hanieh 2014), and the close sensitivity to resource prices. As Mohammed and Sidaway argue in an essay on Abu Dhabi (2012: 620):

> it is evident that echoes of the Gulf's petrodollar-fuelled urbanization exist elsewhere: from Caracas in the 1970s to Port Harcourt in the 1980s, Malabo in the 2000s, or the gold rush 'frontier towns' of the nineteenth and early-twentieth century in California or the Witwatersrand. Nonetheless, the combination of migration, oil, control and showcase that is found in places like Abu Dhabi is distinctive. In other words it resembles neighbouring Gulf cities more than anywhere else, and a credible claim can be made that these form a genre of urban modernity.

Then there is the fact that language, and its role in both the politics of, and scholarship on, global cities, has rarely been studied or even acknowledged. Sidaway (2013: 992) draws attention to how 'geographic debates on issues such as Eurocentrism and postcolonialism take place and are framed in English'. This is not to say that scholars should feel a guilt about their use of the English language, but rather to acknowledge its formative power in many of the practices described in the book. Tsing (2005), in her book *Friction*, provides an indication of how important the practice of translation was in the constitution of environmental politics in Kalimantan; in his study of computer programmers in Rio de Janeiro, Takhteyev (2012) shows that speaking Portuguese in that particular industry was often seen as a handicap in an industry where standards are set in the USA, especially in Silicon Valley.

It was clear from Latour and Hermant's approach to Paris, with its interest in rumour and anecdote, that there is also a strategic significance to how global cities are represented. This would include the role of numbers (as in the critique of the *Urban Age* typography, in Martin 2009 and Brenner and Schmid 2015); the role of literary devices such as synecdoche, prototypes, stereotypes, memes and metonyms in the stabilization of global cities studies; the use of diagrams and tables in conveying knowledge, as in Taylor's (2004) inter-city pairings; the role of lists as a form of categorization and ranking (Bowker and Leigh Starr 1999). A further consideration is the need to think of global cities as *genre writing*:

> Urban studies and the actor-network perspective have an undeniable affinity. If ANT's philo-scientism endears it to the technocratic wing of urban studies, ANT's aesthetic avant-gardism appeals to urbanology's counterculture. Indeed part of ANT's brilliance is its modernistic literary styling … As a genre, it specializes in the surrealistic juxtaposition of incongruous things: scallops make decisions, microbes make Louis Pasteur, scientific instruments and office supplies have agency alongside protest movements and government programs. (Madden 2010: 585)

And so, to close, it is important to think about the poetics of global cities, about the representational devices that constitute the field, and about how on-going experimentation in word, image, and number might best capture the people and materials that bring them into being.

REFERENCES

Abaza, M. (2011), 'Cairo's downtown imagined: Dubaisation or nostalgia', *Urban Studies* 48 (6): 1075–87.

Acuto, M. and W. Steele (2013), *Global City Challenge: Debating the Concept, Improving the Practice*. London: Palgrave Macmillan.

Adey, P. (2003), 'Airports and air-mindedness: spacing, timing and using Liverpool Airport 1929–1939', *Social and Cultural Geography* 7 (3): 343–63.

Adey, P. (2008), 'Airports, mobility and the calculative architecture of affective control', *Geoforum* 39: 438–51.

Allen, J. (2003), *Lost Geographies of Power*. Oxford: Wiley Blackwell.

Allen, J. (2010), 'Powerful city networks: more than connections, less than domination and control', *Urban Studies* 47 (13): 2895–911.

Allen, J. and M. Pryke (1994), 'The production of service space', *Environment and Planning D: Society and Space* 12: 451–75.

Allen, J.L. (2009), *The Future Church: How Ten Trends are Revolutionizing the Catholic Church*. New York: Doubleday.

Allen, J.L. (2010), 'Future Vatican', interviewed by L. Wangsness. *Boston Globe*, 9 May. http://www.boston.com/bostonglobe/ideas/articles/2010/05/09/future_vatican/?page=1.

Amin, A. (2002), 'Spatialities of globalization', *Environment and Planning A* 34: 385–99.

Amin, A. and P. Cohendet (2004), *Architectures of Knowledge: Firms, Capabilities, and Communities*. Oxford: Oxford University Press.

Amin, A. and N. Thrift (2002), *Cities: Re-imagining the Urban*. Oxford: Polity.

Amin, A. and N. Thrift (2004), 'Introduction' in A. Amin and N. Thrift *The Blackwell Cultural Economy Reader* (pp. x–xxx). Oxford: Blackwell.

Amin, A. and N. Thrift (2007), 'Cultural-economy and cities', *Progress in Human Geography* 31 (2): 143–61.

Anderson, J. (1996), The shifting stage of politics: new medieval and postmodern territorialities? *Environment and Planning D: Society and Space* 14 (2): 133–53.

Angotti, T. (2006), Review essay: apocalyptic anti-urbanism: Mike Davis and his planet of slums. *International Journal of Urban and Regional Change* 30 (4): 961–7.

Australia Journal, The (1932), 'Air travel and speedy communication: importance to the Empire', 10(3, Christmas): 11, 40.

Baker, T. and C. Ruming (2015), 'Making "Global Sydney": spatial imaginaries, worlding and strategic plans', *International Journal of Urban and Regional Research* 39 (1): 62–78.

Barnes, T.J. (2002), 'Performing economic geography: two men, two books, and a cast of thousands', *Environment and Planning A* 34 (3): 487–512.

Barnes, T.J. (2003), 'The place of locational analysis: a selective and interpretive history', *Progress in Human Geography* 27: 67–95.

Barnes, T.J. (2004), 'Central places', in S. Harrison, S. Pile and N.J. Thrift (eds), *Patterned Ground* (pp. 179–81). London: Reaktion.

Barnes, T.J. (2008), 'Making space for the economy: live performances, dead objects, and economic geography', *Geography Compass* 3: 1–17.

Barnes, T.J. (2012), 'Notes from the underground: why the history of economic geography matters: the case of central place theory', *Economic Geography* 88 (1): 1–26.

Barnes, T.J. (2015), 'Desk killers: Walter Christaller, central place theory, and the Nazis', in P. Meusburger, D. Gregory and L. Suarsana (eds), *Geographies of Knowledge and Power* (pp. 187–201). Dordrecht: Springer.

Barnes, T.J. and M. Hannah (2001), 'The place of numbers: histories, geographies and theories of quantification', *Environment and Planning D: Society and Space* 19: 379–83.

Barnes, T.J. and C. Minca (2013), 'Nazi spatial theory: the dark geographies of Carl Schmitt and Walter Christaller', *Annals of the Association of American Geographers* 103 (3): 669–87.

Barry, A. (2006), 'Technological zones', *European Journal of Social Theory* 9: 239–53.

Bassens, D. and M. van Meeteren (2015), 'World cities under conditions of financialized globalization: towards an augmented world city hypothesis', *Progress in Human Geography* 39 (6): 752–75.

Batty, M. (2012), 'The 22nd-century city', *Environment and Planning B: Planning and Design* 39: 972–4.

Beauregard, R.A. (2005), 'The textures of property markets: downtown housing and office conversions in New York City', *Urban Studies* 42 (13): 2431–45.

Beaverstock, J.V., B. Derudder, J. Faulconbridge and F. Witlox (2009), 'International business travel: some explorations', *Geografiska Annaler: Series B, Human Geography* 91 (3): 193–202.

Beaverstock, J.V., B. Derudder, J.R. Faulconbridge, and F. Witlox (2010), 'International business travel and the global economy: setting the context', in J.V. Beaverstock, B. Derudder, J.R. Faulconbridge and F. Witlox (eds), *International Business Travel in the Global Economy* (pp. 1–7). Farnham: Ashgate.

Beaverstock, J.V. and J. Faulconbridge (2014), 'Wealth segmentation and the mobilities of the super-rich: a conceptual framework', in J. Birtchnell and J. Caletrio (eds), *Elite Mobilities* (pp. 40–61). Abingdon: Routledge.

Beaverstock, J.V. and S. Hall (2012), 'Competing for talent: global mobility, immigration and the City of London's labour market', *Cambridge Journal of Regions, Economy and Society* 5 (2): 271–88.

Beaverstock, J.V., S. Hall and T. Wainwright (2013), 'Servicing the super-rich: new financial elites and the rise of the private wealth management retail ecology', *Regional Studies* 47 (6): 834–49.

Beaverstock, J.V., P.J. Hubbard and J.R. Short (2004), 'Getting away with it? The changing geographies of the super-rich', *Geoforum* 35: 401–7.

Beaverstock, J.V., R.G. Smith and P.J. Taylor (2000), 'World-city network: a new metageography?', *Annals of the Association of American Geographers* 90 (1): 123–34.

Becker, J., K. Klingan, S. Lanz and K. Wildner (eds) (2014), *Global Prayers: Contemporary Manifestations of the Religious in the City*. Zurich: Lars Müller.

Bedi, T. (2016), 'Mimicry, friction and trans-urban imaginaries: Mumbai taxis/Singapore-style', *Environment and Planning A*. doi:10.1177/0308518X15594803.

Bell, D. (2007), 'The hospitable city: social relations in commercial spaces', *Progress in Human Geography* 31 (1): 7–22.

Bender, T. (2010), 'Post-script: reassembling the city: networks and urban imaginaries', in I. Farías and T. Bender (eds), *Urban Assemblages: How Actor-Network Theory Changes Urban Studies* (pp. 303–23). Abingdon: Routledge.

Bennett, J. (2010), *Vibrant Matter: a Political Ecology of Things*. Durham, NC: Duke University Press.

Bennett, T. (1988), 'The exhibitionary complex', *New Formations* 4 (1): 73–102.

Bennett, T. (2005), 'Civic laboratories, cultural objecthood and the governance of the social', *Cultural Studies* 19 (5): 521–47.

Bennett, T. and P. Joyce (eds) (2010), *Material Powers: Cultural Studies, History and the Material Turn*. London: Routledge.

Bernstein, C. and M. Politi (1997), *His Holiness: John Paul II and the History of Our Time*. New York: Penguin.

Bill, P. (2013), *Planet Property*. Leicester: Matador.

Boden, D. and H. Molotch (1994), 'The compulsion of proximity', in R. Friedland and D. Boden (eds), *NowHere: Space, Time and Modernity* (pp. 257–86). Berkeley, CA: University of California Press.

Bosworth, R.J.B. (2011), *Whispering City: Rome and its Histories*. New Haven, CT: Yale University Press.

Botsman, R. and R. Rogers (2010), *What's Mine is Yours: The Rise of Collaborative Consumption*. New York: Harper Business.

Bourne, L.S. (1971), *Internal Structure of the City: Readings on Space and Environment*. Oxford: Oxford University Press.

Boussebaa, M., G. Morgan and A. Sturdy (2012), 'Constructing global firms? National, transnational and neo-colonial effects in international management consultancies', *Organization Studies* 33: 465–86.

Bowen, J.T. (2010), 'A people set apart: the spatial development of airlines business class services', in J.V. Beaverstock, B. Derudder, J. Faulconbridge and F. Witlox (eds), *International Business Travel in the Global Economy* (pp. 11–30). Farnham: Ashgate.

Bowker, G.C. and N. Leigh Star (1999), *Sorting Things Out: Classification and its Consequences*. Cambridge, MA: MIT Press.

Braun, B. (2000), 'Producing vertical territory: geology and governmentality in Late Victorian Canada', *Cultural Geographies* (published as *Ecumene*) 7 (1): 7–46.

Bravo, M. (1999), 'Ethnographic navigation and the geographical gift', in D.N. Livingstone and C.W.J. Withers (eds), *Geography and the Enlightenment* (pp. 199–235). Chicago: University of Chicago Press.

Brenner, N. and R. Keil (eds) (2006), *The Global Cities Reader*. London: Routledge.

Brenner, N. and C. Schmid (2013), 'The "urban age" in question', *International Journal of Urban and Regional Research* 38 (3): 731–55.

Brenner, N. and C. Schmid (2015), 'Towards a new epistemology of the urban?', *City* 19 (2/3): 151–82.

Brenner, N. and N. Theodore (2002), 'Cities and the geographies of "actually existing neoliberalism"', in N. Brenner and N. Theodore (eds), *Spaces of Neoliberalism* (pp. 2–32). Oxford: Blackwell.

Bridge, G. (2013), 'Territory, now in 3D', *Political Geography* 34: 55–7.

Briffault, R. (1999), 'A government for our time? Business improvement districts and urban governance', *Columbia Law Journal* 99 (2): 365–477.

Brotton, J. (2012), *A History of the World in Twelve Maps*. London: Allen Lane.

Buckley, M. and A. Hanieh (2014), 'Diversification by urbanization: tracing the property–finance nexus in Dubai and the Gulf', *International Journal of Urban and Regional Research* 38 (1): 155–75.

Budd, L., M. Bell and T. Brown (2009), 'Of plagues, planes and politics: controlling the spread of infectious diseases by air', *Political Geography* 28 (7): 426–35.

Bulkeley, H. and V.C. Broto (2013), 'Government by experiment? Global cities and the governing of climate change', *Transactions of the Institute of British Geographers* 38: 361–75.

Bunnell, T. (1999), 'Views from above and below: the Petronas Twin Towers and/in contesting visions of development in contemporary Malaysia', *Singapore Journal of Tropical Geography* 20 (1): 1–23.

Bunnell, T. (2004a), *Malaysia, Modernity and the Multimedia Super Corridor: a Critical Geography of Intelligent Landscapes*. London: Routledge.

Bunnell, T. (2004b), 'Re-viewing the *Entrapment* controversy: megaprojection, (mis) representation and postcolonial performance', *GeoJournal* 59 (4): 297–305.

Bunnell, T. (2016), *From World City to the World in One City: Liverpool through Malay Lives*. Oxford: Wiley Blackwell.

Bunnell, T. and A. Maringanti (2010), 'Practising urban and regional research beyond metrocentricity', *International Journal of Urban and Regional Research* 34: 415–20.

Burdett, R. and D. Sudjic (eds) (2010), *The Endless City*. London: Phaidon.

Burdett, R. and D. Sudjic (eds) (2011), *Living in the Endless City*. London: Phaidon.

Callon, M. (1998), 'Introduction: the embeddedness of economic markets in economics', in M. Callon (ed.), *The Laws of Markets* (pp. 1–57). Oxford: Blackwell.

Callon, M. and B. Latour (1981), 'Uncovering the big Leviathan: how actors macrostructure reality and how sociologists help them do so', in K. Knorr-Cetina and A. Cicourel (eds), *Advances in Social Theory and Methodology* (pp. 277–303). London: Routledge & Kegan Paul.

Callon, M. and F. Muniesa (2005), 'Economic markets as calculative devices', *Organization Studies* 26: 1229–50.

Caprotti, F. (2014), 'Critical research on eco-cities? A walk through the Sino-Singapore Tianjin Eco-City, China', *Cities* 36: 10–17.

Caprotti, F. and J. Romanowicz (2013), 'Thermal eco-cities: green building and urban thermal metabolism', *International Journal of Urban and Regional Research* 37 (6): 1949–67.

Chidester, D. (2001), *Christianity: a Global History*. Harmondsworth: Penguin.

Christophers, B. (2014), 'Wild dragons in the city: urban political economy, affordable housing development, and the performative world-making of economic models', *International Journal of Urban and Regional Research* 38 (1): 79–97.

Cidell, J. (2008), 'Challenging the contours: critical cartography, local knowledge, and the public', *Environment and Planning A* 40 (5): 1202–18.

Clark, G.L., K.P.Y. Lai and D. Wojcik (2015), 'Deconstructing offshore finance', *Economic Geography* 91 (3): 237–49.

Clark, T., P. Bhatanacharoen and D. Greatbatch (2012), 'Management gurus as celebrity consultants', in M. Kipping and T. Clark (eds), *The Oxford Handbook of Management Consulting* (pp. 347–64). Oxford: Oxford University Press.

Collier, S. and A. Ong (2004), 'Global assemblages, anthropological problems', in S.J. Collier and A. Ong (eds), *Global Assemblages: Technology, Politics and Ethics as Anthropological Problems*. London: Blackwell.

Conley, V.A. (2012), *Spatial Ecologies: Urban Sites, State and World-Space in French Cultural Theory*. Liverpool: Liverpool University Press.

Cornwell, J. (2001), *Breaking Faith: the Pope, the People, and the Fate of Catholicism*. London: Viking.

Cosgrove, D. (1999), 'Airport/Landscape', in J. Corner (ed.), *Recovering Landscape: Essays in Contemporary Landscape Theory* (pp. 221–32). New York: Princeton Architectural Press.

Cosgrove, D. and L.L. Martins (2001), 'Millennial geographies', in C. Minca (ed.), *Postmodern Geography: Theory and Praxis* (pp. 169–95). Oxford: Blackwell.

Cowen, D. (2010), 'A geography of logistics: market authority and the security of supply chains', *The Annals for the Association of American Geographers* 100 (3): 1–21.

Cowen, D. (2014), *The Deadly Life of Logistics: Mapping Violence in Global Trade*. Minneapolis, MN: University of Minnesota Press.

Crang, M. (2010), 'The death of great ships: photography, politics and waste in the global imaginary', *Environment and Planning A* 42: 1084–102.

Crary, J. (2001), *Suspensions of Perception: Attention, Spectacle, and Modernity*. Cambridge, MA: MIT Press.

Cronin, A. (2008a), 'Calculative spaces: cities, market relations, and the commercial vitalism of the outdoor advertising industry', *Environment and Planning A* 40: 2734–50.

Cronin, A. (2008b), 'Mobility and market research: outdoor advertising and the commercial ontology of the city', *Mobilities* 3 (1): 95–115.

Cronon, W. (1991), *Nature's Metropolis: Chicago and the Great West*. New York: Norton.

Cugurullo, F. (2013), 'How to build a sandcastle: an analysis of the genesis and development of Masdar City', *Journal of Urban Technology* 20 (1): 23–37.

Czarniawska, B. (2002), *A Tale of Three Cities, or the Glocalization of City Management*. Oxford: Oxford University Press.

D'Agostino, P.R. (2004), *Rome in America: Transnational Catholic Ideology from the Risorgimento to Fascism*. Chapel Hill, NC: University of North Carolina Press.

Davidson, M. and K. Iveson (2015a), 'Beyond city limits: a conceptual and political defense of "the city" as an anchoring concept for critical urban theory', *City* 19 (5): 646–64.

Davidson, M. and K. Iveson (2015b), 'Recovering the politics of the city', *Progress in Human Geography* 39 (5): 543–59.

Davis, M. (2006a), 'Fear and money in Dubai', *New Left Review* 41 (September–October): 47–68.

Davis, M. (2006b), *Planet of Slums*. London: Verso.

Davis, M. and D.B. Monk (eds) (2007), *Evil Paradises: Dreamworlds of Neoliberalism*. New York: The New Press.

Denstadli, J.M. and M. Gripsrud (2010), 'Face-to-face by travel or picture – the relationship between travelling and video communication in business settings', in J.V. Beaverstock, B. Derudder, J. Faulconbridge and F. Witlox (eds), *International Business Travel in the Global Economy* (pp. 217–38). Farnham: Ashgate.

Derudder, B., M. Hoyler and P. Taylor (2011), 'Goodbye Reykjavik: international banking centres and the global financial crisis', *Area* 43: 173–82.

Diamond, J. (1997), *Guns, Germs and Steel: the Fates of Human Societies*. New York: W.W. Norton.

Dikeç, M. (2007), *Badlands of the Republic: Space, Politics and Urban Policy*. Oxford: John Wiley.

Dimbleby, J. (2002), *The Last Governor: Chris Patten and the Handover of Hong Kong*. New York: Warner.

Dodge, M. and R. Kitchin (2004), 'Flying through code/space: the real virtuality of air travel', *Environment and Planning A* 36: 195–211.

Driver, F. and D. Gilbert (eds) (2003), *Imperial Cities: Landscape, Display, Identity*. Manchester: Manchester University Press.

Duffy, F. (2008), *Work and the City*. London: Black Dog.

Easterling, K. (2014), *Extrastatecraft: the Power of Infrastructure Space*. London: Verso.

Edensor, T. and M. Jayne (eds) (2012), *Urban Theory Beyond the West: a World of Cities*. London: Routledge.

Elden, S. (2005), 'Missing the point. Globalization, territorialization and the space of the world', *Transactions of the Institute of British Geographers* 30 (1): 8–19.

Elden, S. (2007), 'Governmentality, calculation, territory', *Environment and Planning D: Society and Space* 25: 562–80.

Elden, S. (2010), 'Land, terrain, territory', *Progress in Human Geography* 34 (6): 799–817.

Elden, S. (2013), 'Secure the volume: vertical geopolitics and the depth of power', *Political Geography* 34: 35–51.

Engelen, E., R. Fernandez and R. Hendrikse (2014), 'How finance penetrates its other: a cautionary tale on the financialization of a Dutch university', *Antipode* 46 (4): 1072–91.

English, S. (2002), 'Enron offices raided by FBI squad', *Daily Telegraph*, 23 January. http://www.telegraph.co.uk/finance/2750279/Enron-offices-raided-by-FBI-squad.html (accessed 2 June 2014).

Enright, M., E. Scott and K. Chang (2005), *Regional Powerhouse: the Greater Pearl River Delta and the Rise of China*. Singapore: John Wiley & Sons.

Erie, S.P. (2004), *Globalizing LA: Trade, Infrastructure and Regional Development*. Stanford, CA: Stanford University Press.

Evans, J. and A. Karvonen (2014), '"Give me a laboratory and I will lower your carbon footprint!" – urban laboratories and the governance of low-carbon futures', *International Journal of Urban and Regional Research* 38 (2): 413–30.

Falasca-Zamponi, S. (1997), *Fascist Spectacle: the Aesthetics of Power in Mussolini's Italy*. Berkeley, CA: University of California Press.

Farías, I. (2010a), 'Interview with Nigel Thrift', in I. Farías and T. Bender (eds), *Urban Assemblages: How Actor-Network Theory Changes Urban Studies* (pp. 109–19). London: Routledge.

Farías, I. (2010b), 'Introduction: decentering the object of urban studies', in I. Farías and T. Bender (eds), *Urban Assemblages: How Actor-Network Theory Changes Urban Studies* (pp. 1–24). London: Routledge.

Farías, I. and T. Bender (eds) (2010), *Urban Assemblages: How Actor-Network Theory Changes Urban Studies*. London: Routledge.

Faulconbridge, J. (2006), 'Stretching tacit knowledge beyond a local fix? Global spaces of learning in advertising professional service firms', *Journal of Economic Geography* 6 (4): 517–40.

Faulconbridge, J. and S. Hall (2011), 'Business knowledges within and between the world city', in B. Derudder (ed.), *International Handbook of Globalization and World Cities* (pp. 230–9). London: Edward Elgar.

Faulconbridge, J. and A. Jones (2012), 'The geography of management consultancy firms', in M. Kipping and T. Clark (eds), *The Oxford Handbook of Management Consulting* (pp. 225–43). Oxford: Oxford University Press.

Ferrary, M. and M. Granovetter (2003), 'The role of venture capital firms in Silicon Valley's complex innovation network', *Economy and Society* 38 (2): 326–59.

Florida, R. (2002), *The Rise of the Creative Class: and How It's Transforming Work, Leisure, Community, and Everyday Life*. New York: Basic Books.

Fox, T.C. (1995), *Sexuality and Catholicism*. New York: George Braziller.

French, S., A. Leyshon and T. Wainwright (2011), 'Financializing space, spacing financialization', *Progress in Human Geography* 35 (6): 798–819.

Frenkel, M. and Y. Shenhav (2012), 'Management consulting in developing and emerging economies: towards a postcolonial perspective', in M. Kipping and T. Clark (eds), *The Oxford Handbook of Management Consulting* (pp. 509–27). Oxford: Oxford University Press.

Froud, J., C. Haslam, S. Johal and K. Williams (2000), 'Shareholder value and financial-ization: consultancy promises, management moves', *Economy and Society* 29: 80–110.

Fuller, G. and R. Harley (2004), *Aviopolis: a Book about Airports*. London: Black Dog.

Ghertner, D.A. (2010), 'Calculating without numbers: aesthetic governmentality in Delhi's slums', *Economy and Society* 39 (2): 185–217.

Gieryn, E. (2006), 'City as truth-spot: laboratories and field-sites in urban studies', *Social Studies of Science* 36 (1): 5–38.

Gilbert, D. (2006), 'From Paris to Shanghai: the changing geographies of fashion's world cities', in C. Breward and D. Gilbert (eds), *Fashion's World Cities*. Oxford: Berg.

Glaeser, E. (2011), *Triumph of the City*. New York: Penguin.

Gleeson, B. (2014), *The Urban Condition*. London: Routledge.

Goldman, M. (2011), 'Speculating on the next world city', in A. Ong and A. Roy (eds), *Worlding Cities: Asian Experiments and the Art of Being Global* (pp. 229–58). Oxford: Wiley-Blackwell.

Goodstadt, L.F. (2009), *Uneasy Partners: The Conflict Between Public Interest and Private Profit in Hong Kong*. New edition. Hong Kong: Hong Kong University Press.

Gopakumar, G. (2014), 'Experiments and counter-experiments in the urban labora-tory of water-supply partnerships in India', *International Journal of Urban and Regional Research* 38 (2): 393–412.

Graham, S. and S. Marvin (2001), *Splintering Urbanism: Networked Infrastructures, Technological Mobilities and the Urban Condition*. London: Routledge.

Granovetter, M. and P. McGuire (1998), 'The making of an industry: electricity in the United States', in M. Callon (ed.), *The Laws of the Markets* (pp. 147–73). Oxford: Blackwell.

Güller, M. and M. Güller (2003), *From Airport to Airport City*. Barcelona: Gustavo Gili.

Haggett, P. (1966), *Locational Analysis in Human Geography*. New York: St. Martin's Press.

Haigh, G. (2012), *The Office: a Hardworking History*. Carlton, Victoria: The Megunyah Press.

Hall, S. (2006), 'What counts? Exploring the production of quantitative financial narratives in London's corporate finance industry', *Journal of Economic Geography* 6 (5): 661–78.

Hall, S. (2007), 'Knowledge makes the money go round: conflicts of interest and corporate finance in London's financial district', *Geoforum* 38 (4): 710–19.

Hall, S. (2008), 'Geographies of business education: MBA programmes, reflexive business schools, and the cultural circuit of capital', *Transactions of the Institute of British Geographers* 33 (1): 27–41.

Hall, S. (2009), 'Financialised elites and the changing nature of finance capitalism: investment bankers in London's financial district', *Competition and Change* 13 (2): 173–89.

Halpern, O., J. LeCavalier, N. Calvillo and W. Pietsch (2013), 'Test-bed urbanism', *Public Culture* 25 (2): 272–306.

Hannah, M. (2002), *Dark Territory in the Information Age: Learning from the West German Census Boycotts of the 1980s*. Aldershot: Ashgate.

Hannah, M.G. (2009), 'Calculable territory and the West German census boycott movements of the 1980s', *Political Geography* 28: 66–75.

Hanson, E.O. (1992), *The Catholic Church in World Politics*. Princeton, NJ: Princeton University Press.

Harrington, B. (2012), 'The sociology of financial fraud', in K. Knorr-Cetina and A. Preda (eds), *The Oxford Handbook of the Sociology of Finance* (pp. 393–410). Oxford: Oxford University Press.

Harvey, D. (2003), *Paris, Capital of Modernity*. New York: Routledge.

Harvey, P., E. Casella and G. Evans (2013), *Objects and Materials: a Routledge Companion*. Abingdon: Routledge.

Hasty, W. and K. Peters (2012), 'The ship in geography and the geography of ships', *Geography Compass* 6 (11): 660–76.

Hebblethwaite, P. (1987), *In the Vatican*. Oxford: Oxford University Press.

Hecht, R.D. (1994), 'The construction and management of sacred time and space: Sabta Nur in the Church of the Holy Sepulcher', in R. Friedland and D. Boden (eds), *NowHere: Space, Time and Modernity* (pp. 181–235). Berkeley, CA: University of California Press.

Hendrikse, R.P. and J.D. Sidaway (2013), 'Financial wizardry and the Golden City: tracking the financial crisis through Pforzheim, Germany', *Transactions of the Institute of British Geographers*. doi:10.1111/tran.12024.

Hepworth, K. (2014), 'Enacting logistical geographies', *Environment and Planning D: Society and Space* 32: 1120–34.

Hill, S. (2015), *Raw Deal: How the 'Uber' Economy and Runaway Capitalism are Screwing American Workers*. New York: St. Martin's Press.

Hitchings, R. (2011), 'Researching air-conditioning addiction and ways of puncturing practice: professional office workers and the decision to go outside', *Environment and Planning A* 43 (12): 2838–56.

Hitchings, R. and S.-J. Lee (2008), 'Air conditioning and the material culture of routine human encasement', *Journal of Material Culture* 13: 251–65.

Hughes, A. and S. Reimer (2004), (eds) *Geographies of Commodity Chains*. London: Routledge.

IBM (2012a), 'Sponsorship statement at the World Cities Summit in Singapore in 2012'. http://www.worldcities.com.sg/ibm_2012.php (accessed 7 February 2014).

IBM (2012b), 'About IBM Smarter Cities Challenge'. http://www.ura.gov.sg/uol/media-room/news/2012/mar/~/media/User%20Defined/URA%20Online/media-room/2012/mar/pr12-29a.ashx.

Jackson, M. and V. Delladora (2009), '"Dreams so big only the sea can hold them": man-made islands as anxious spaces, cultural icons, and travelling visions', *Environment and Planning A* 41 (9): 2086–104.

Jacobs, J.M. (2006), 'A geography of big things', *Cultural Geographies* 13: 1–27.

Jacobs, J.M., S. Cairns and I. Strebel (2007), '"A tall storey … but, a fact just the same": the red road high-rise as a black box', *Urban Studies* 44 (3): 609–29.

Jacobs, J.M. and P. Merriman (2011), 'Practising architectures', *Social and Cultural Geography* 12 (3): 211–22.

James, P. and M. Stenger (2014), 'A genealogy of "globalization": the career of a concept', *Globalizations* 11 (4): 417–34.

Jarman, R. (1952), *A Bed for the Night: the Story of the Wheeling Bellboy*. New York: Harper and Brothers.

Jenkins, P. (2006), *The New Faces of Christianity: Believing the Bible in the Global South*. Oxford: Oxford University Press.

Jenkins, P. (2011), *The Next Christendom: the Coming of Global Christianity*. Oxford: Oxford University Press.

Jones, A. (2009), 'Theorising global business spaces', *Geografiska Annaler: Series B, Human Geography* 91 (3): 203–18.

Jones, A. (2010), 'Understanding mobility in professional business services', in J.V. Beaverstock, B. Derudder, J. Faulconbridge and F. Witlox (eds), *International Business Travel in the Global Economy* (pp. 195–216). Farnham: Ashgate.

Jöns, H. (2011), 'Centre of calculation', in J.A. Agnew and D.N. Livingstone (eds), *The Sage Handbook of Geographical Knowledge* (pp. 158–70). London: Sage.

Jöns, H. (2016), 'The University of Cambridge, academic expertise and the British Empire, 1885–1962', *Environment and Planning A* 48 (1): 94–114.

Joyce, P. (2003), *The Rule of Freedom: Liberalism and the Modern City*. London: Verso.

Joyce, P. and T. Bennett (2010), 'Material powers: introduction', in T. Bennett and P. Joyce, *Material Powers: Cultural Studies, History and the Material Turn* (pp. 1–21). London: Routledge.

Karvonen, A. and B. van Heur (2014), 'Urban laboratories: experiments in reworking cities', *International Journal of Urban and Regional Research* 38 (2): 379–92.

Kasarda, J. and G. Lindsay (2011), *Aerotropolis: the Way We'll Live Next.* New York: Farrar, Straus and Giroux.

Kaufman, S.K. (2005), *Consuming Visions: Mass Culture and the Lourdes Shrine.* Ithaca, NY: Cornell University Press.

Kitchin, R. (2011), 'The programmable city', *Environment and Planning B: Planning and Design* 38: 945–51.

Kitchin, R. (2015), 'Making sense of smart cities: addressing present shortcomings', *Cambridge Journal of Regions, Economy and Society* 8: 131–6.

Koppa, F.J. (1998), *The Modern Papacy since 1789.* London: Longman.

KPMG (2014), Press release. https://www.kpmg.com/global/en/issuesandinsights/articlespublications/taxnewsflash/pages/2014-1/united-kingdom-hmrc-report-offshore-tax-evasion.aspx.

Krieger, L. (1971), Series editor's preface to F. Gregorovious, *Rome and Medieval Culture: Selections from the History of the City of Rome in the Middle Ages* (ed. K.F. Morrison). Chicago: University of Chicago Press.

Küng, H. (2001), *The Catholic Church: a Short History* (trans. J. Bowden). London: Weidenfeld & Nicolson.

La Rocca, O. (2000), 'La manifestazione gay un affronto al giubileo', *La Repubblica* 10 June, p. 2.

Lai, K. (2012), 'Differentiated markets: Shanghai, Beijing and Hong Kong in China's financial centre network', *Urban Studies* 49: 1275–96.

Langley, P. (2006), 'Securitising suburbia: the transformation of Anglo-American mortgage finance', *Competition and Change* 10: 283–99.

Lanz, S. (2014), 'Assembling global prayers in the city: an attempt to repopulate urban theory with religion', in J. Becker, K. Klingan, S. Lanz and K. Wildner (eds), *Global Prayers: Contemporary Manifestations of the Religious in the City* (pp. 17–46). Zurich: Lars Müller.

Larner, W. (2014), 'ISO 9000', in N. Thrift, A. Tickell, S. Woolgar and W.H. Rupp (eds), *Globalization in Practice* (pp. 272–6). Oxford: Oxford University Press.

Larner, W. and N. Laurie (2009), 'Travelling technocrats, embodied knowledges: globalizing privatisation in telecoms and water', *Geoforum* 41: 218–26.

Lassen, C. (2006), 'Aeromobility and work', *Environment and Planning A* 38 (2): 301–12.

Latour, B. (1987), *Science in Action: How to Follow Scientists and Engineers through Society.* Cambridge, MA: Harvard University Press.

Latour, B. (2005), *Reassembling the Social: an Introduction to Actor-Network-Theory.* Oxford: Oxford University Press.

Latour, B. (2012), 'Paris, invisible city: the plasma', *City, Culture and Society* 3: 91–3.

Latour, B. and E. Hermant (2006), *Paris, Invisible City* (trans. L. Carey-Libbrecht). First published in 1998 as *Paris, Ville Invisible*. Paris: La Découverte. http://www.bruno-latour.fr/sites/default/files/downloads/viii_paris-city-gb.pdf (last accessed 28 February 2015).

Latour, B. and S. Woolgar (1986), *Laboratory Life: the Construction of Scientific Facts*. Princeton, NJ: Princeton University Press.

Law, J. (1986), 'On the methods of long-distance control: vessels, navigation, and the Portuguese route to India', in J. Law (ed.), *Power, Action and Belief: a New Sociology of Knowledge?* (pp. 234–63). Sociological Review Monograph 32. London: Routledge & Kegan Paul.

Law, J. (1994), *Organizing Modernity*. Oxford: Blackwell.

Law, J. (2004), 'And if the global were small and non-coherent? Method, complexity and the baroque', *Environment and Planning D: Society and Space* 22: 13–26.

Law, J. and K. Hetherington (2000), 'Materialities, spatialities, globalities', in J. Bryson, P. Daniels, N. Henry and J. Pollard (eds), *Knowledge, Space, Economy* (pp. 34–49). London: Routledge.

Lee, D.B. (1973), 'Requiem for large-scale models', *Journal of the American Planning Association* 39 (3): 163–78.

Lees-Milne, J. (1967), *Saint Peter's: the Story of Saint Peter's Basilica in Rome*. London: Hamish Hamilton.

Lehmann, D. (2002), 'Religion and globalization', in L. Woodhead, P. Fletcher, H. Kawanami and D. Smith (eds), *Religions in the Modern World* (pp. 299–315). London: Routledge.

Leslie, S.W. and R.H. Kargon (1996), 'Selling Silicon Valley: Frederick Terman's model for regional advantage', *The Business History Review* 70 (4): 435–72.

Lewis, S. (1917), *The Job: an American Novel*. New York: Harper and Brothers.

Ley, D. (2010), *Millionaire Migrants: Trans-Pacific Life Lines*. Oxford: Wiley-Blackwell.

Leyshon, A. and N. Thrift (1997), *Money/Space: Geographies of Monetary Transformation*. London: Routledge.

Luo, X. and J. Shen (2012), 'The making of new regionalism in the cross-boundary metropolis of Hong Kong-Shenzhen, China', *Habitat International* 36: 126–35.

Luque-Ayala, A. and S. Marvin (2016), 'The maintenance of urban circulation: an operational logic of infrastructural control', *Environment and Planning D: Society and Space* 34 (2): 191–208.

MacKenzie, D. (1996), *Knowing Machines: Essays on Technical Change* (pp. 59–61). Cambridge, MA: MIT Press.

MacKenzie, D. (2006), *An Engine, Not a Camera*. Cambridge, MA: MIT Press.

Madden, D.J. (2010), 'Urban ANTs: a review essay', *Qualitative Sociology* 33: 583–99.

Maney, K., S. Hamm, and J.M. O'Brien (2011), *Making the World Work Better: the Ideas that Shaped a Century and a Company*. Upper Saddle River, NJ: IBM Press-Pearson.

Martin, C. (2013), 'Shipping container mobilities, seamless compatibility, and the global surface of logistical integration', *Environment and Planning A* 45: 1021–36.

Martin, R. (2009), Review of R. Burdett and D. Sudjic, *The Endless City*, *Harvard Design Magazine* 30 (Spring/Summer): 145–9.

Martin, R. and P. Sunley (2003), 'Deconstructing clusters: chaotic concept or policy panacea', *Journal of Economic Geography* 3: 5–35.

Marvin, S., A. Luque-Ayala and C. McFarlane (eds) (2015), *Smart Urbanism: Utopian Vision or False Dawn?* London: Routledge.

Massey, D. (2007), *World City*. Cambridge: Polity.

Mattern, S. (2012), 'Methodolatry and the art of measure: the new wave of urban data science', *Places Journal*, November. https://placesjournal.org/article/methodolatry-and-the-art-of-measure/.

Matthews, J.J. (2005), *Dance Hall & Picture Palace: Sydney's Romance with Modernity*. Sydney: Currency Press.

Mayer-Schönberger, V. and K. Cukier (2013), *Big Data: a Revolution that Will Transform How We Live, Work, and Think*. Boston: Eamon Dolan.

McBrien, R.P. (1997), *Lives of the Popes: the Pontiffs from St Peter to John Paul II*. New York: HarperOne.

McCann, E. (2011a), 'Points of reference: knowledge of elsewhere in the politics of urban drug policy', in E. McCann and K. Ward (eds), *Mobile Urbanism: Cities and Policymaking in the Global Age* (pp. 97–122). Minneapolis, MN: University of Minnesota Press.

McCann, E. (2011b), 'Urban policy mobilities and global circuits of knowledge: toward a research agenda', *Annals of the Association of American Geographers* 101 (1): 107–30.

McCann, E. and C. Temenos (2015), 'Mobilizing drug consumption rooms: inter-place networks and harm reduction drug policy', *Health and Place* 31: 218–23.

McCann, E. and K. Ward (eds) (2011), *Mobile Urbanism: Cities and Policymaking in the Global Age* (pp. 97–122). Minneapolis, MN: University of Minnesota Press.

McCann, E. and K. Ward (2012), 'Policy assemblages, mobilities and mutations: towards a multidisciplinary conversation', *Political Studies Review* 10: 325–32.

McDowell, L. (1997), *Capital Culture: Gender at Work in the City*. Oxford: Blackwell.

McDowell, L. (1998), 'Elites in the City of London: Some methodological considerations', *Environment and Planning A* 30 (12): 2133–46.

McDowell, L. (2009), *Working Bodies: Interactive Service Employment and Workplace Identities*. Oxford: Wiley-Blackwell.

McFarlane, C. (2008), 'Urban shadows: materiality, the 'Southern city' and urban theory', *Geography Compass* 2 (2): 340–58.

McFarlane, C. (2010), 'The comparative city: knowledge, learning, urbanism', *International Journal of Urban and Regional Research* 34 (4): 725–42.

McFarlane, C. (2011a), *Learning the City: Knowledge and Translocal Assemblage*. Malden, MA: Wiley-Blackwell.

McFarlane, C. (2011b), 'The city as a machine for learning', *Transactions of the Institute of British Geographers* 36: 360–76.

McGregor, N. (2013), *A History of the World in 100 Objects*. London: Penguin.

McGuirk, P, H., Bulkeley and R. Dowling (2014), 'Practices, programs and projects of urban carbon governance: Perspectives from the Australian city', *Geoforum* 52: 137–47.

McNeill, D. (2003), 'Rome, global city? Church, state and the Jubilee 2000', *Political Geography* 22: 535–56.

McNeill, D. (2009a), 'The airport hotel as business space', *Geografiska Annaler: Series B, Human Geography* 91 (3): 219–28.

McNeill, D. (2009b), *The Global Architect: Firms, Fame and Urban Form*. New York: Routledge.

McNeill, D. (2010), 'Behind the "Heathrow hassle": a political and cultural economy of the privatized airport', *Environment and Planning A* 42 (12): 2859–73.

McNeill, D. (2014), 'Airports and territorial restructuring: the case of Hong Kong', *Urban Studies* 51 (14): 2996–3010.

McNeill, D. (2015a), 'IBM and the visual formation of smart cities', in S. Marvin, A. Luque-Ayala and C. McFarlane (eds), *Smart Urbanism: Utopian Vision or False Dawn?* London: Routledge.

McNeill, D. (2015b), 'Global firms and smart technologies: IBM and the reduction of cities', *Transactions of the Institute of British Geographers* 40 (4): 562–74.

McNeill, D. (2016), 'Governing a city of unicorns: tech capital and urban politics in San Francisco', *Urban Geography* 37 (4): 494–513.

McNeill, D., R. Dowling and R. Fagan (2005), 'Sydney/global/city: an exploration', *International Journal of Urban and Regional Research* 29 (4): 935–44.

McNeill, D. and K. McNamara (2009), 'Hotels as civic landmarks, hotels as assets: the case of Sydney's Hilton', *Australian Geographer* 40 (3): 369–86.

McNeill, D. and K. McNamara (2012), 'The life and death of great hotels: modernity, disrepair and demolition in Sydney's "The Australia"', *Transactions of the Institute of British Geographers* 37 (1): 149–63.

McNicoll, D. (1949), '"The Pub": The story of the Australia Hotel', *Daily Telegraph*, 27 August, pp. 16–17.

Mennicken, A. and P. Miller (2012), 'Accounting, territorialization and power', *Foucault Studies* 13: 4–24.

Merrifield, A. (2002), *Metromarxism*. London: Routledge.

Mezzadra, S. and B. Neilson (2013), *Border as Method: or, the Multiplication of Labor*. Durham, NC: Duke University Press.

Mitchell, T. (2002), *Rule of Experts: Egypt, Techno-Politics, Modernity*. Berkeley, CA: University of California Press.

Mohammed, R. and J. Sidaway (2012), 'Spectacular urbanization amidst variegated geographies of globalization: learning from Abu Dhabi's trajectory through the lives of South Asian men', *International Journal of Urban and Regional Research* 36 (3): 606–27.

Moore, G. with K. Davis (2004), 'Learning the Silicon Valley way', in T. Bresnahan and A.Gambardella (eds), *Building High-Tech Clusters: Silicon Valley and Beyond* (pp. 7–39). Cambridge: Cambridge University Press.

Moretti, F. (2012), *The New Geography of Jobs*. New York: Mariner Books.

Morozov, E. (2013), *To Save Everything, Click Here: the Folly of Technological Solutionism*. London: Allen Lane.

Muellerleile, C. (2009), 'Financialization takes off at Boeing', *Journal of Economic Geography* 9 (5): 663–77.

Müller, M. (2015), 'A half-hearted romance? A diagnosis and agenda for the relationship between economic geography and actor-network theory (ANT)', *Progress in Human Geography* 39 (1): 65–86.

Murphy, R.E. (1971/2008), *The Central Business District: a Study in Urban Geography*. Chicago: Aldine-Atherton.

Murphy, R.E., J.E. Vance and B.J. Epstein (1955), 'The internal structure of the CBD', *Economic Geography* 31 (1): 21–46.

New South Wales Trade and Industry (2014), 'Progressing the NSW Economic Development Framework'. http://www.trade.nsw.gov.au/__data/assets/pdf_file/0008/63647/progressing-the-nsw-economic-development-framework-2014.pdf.

New York Times (1995), 'Accord for Hong Kong's New Airport', 1 July. www.nytimes.com (accessed 6 May 2009).

Ng, M.K. (2006), 'World-city formation under an executive-led government: the politics of harbour reclamation in Hong Kong', *Town Planning Review* 77 (3): 311–37.

O'Toole, F. (2010), *Ship of Fools: How Stupidity and Corruption Sank the Celtic Tiger*. New York: Faber and Faber.

Olds, K. (2001), *Globalization and Urban Change: Capital, Culture and Pacific Rim Mega-Projects*. Oxford: Oxford University Press.

Olds, K. and H. Yeung (2004), 'Pathways to global city formation: a view from the developmental city-state of Singapore', *Review of International Political Economy* 11 (3): 489–521.

Olivier, D. and B. Slack (2006), 'Rethinking the port', *Environment and Planning D: Society and Space* 38: 1409–27.

Ong, A. (1999), *Flexible Citizenship: the Cultural Logics of Transnationality*. Durham, NC: Duke University Press.

Ong, A. (2006), *Neoliberalism as Exception: Mutations to Sovereignty and Citizenship*. Durham, NC: Duke University Press.

Ong, A. (2011), 'Worlding cities, or the art of being global', in A. Ong and A. Roy (eds), *Worlding Cities: Asian Experiments and the Art of Being Global* (pp. 1–26). Oxford: Wiley-Blackwell.

Ong, A. and N.N. Chen (eds) (2010), *Asian Biotech: Ethics and Communities of Fate*. Durham, NC: Duke University Press.

Otter, C. (2008), *The Victorian Eye: a Political History of Light and Vision in Britain, 1800–1910*. Chicago: University of Chicago Press.

Otter, C. (2010), 'Locating matter: the place of materiality in urban history', in T. Bennett and P. Joyce (eds), *Material Powers: Cultural Studies, History and the Material Turn*. Abingdon: Routledge.

Parker, M. (2014), 'Vertical capitalism: skyscrapers and organization', *Culture and Organization*. doi:10.1080/14759551.2013.845566.

Parnell, S. and S. Oldfield (eds) (2014), *The Routledge Handbook on Cities of the Global South*. London: Routledge.

Parnell, S. and J. Robinson (2012), '(Re)theorizing cities from the global South: looking beyond neoliberalism', *Urban Geography* 33 (4): 593–617.

Partridge, L. (1996), *The Renaissance in Rome 1400–1600*. London: George Weidenfeld and Nicolson.

Pastor, L. (1923), *History of the Popes from the Close of the Middle Ages*, vol. 2, 40 volumes. London: Kegan Paul.

Peake, L. (2015), 'The twenty-first-century quest for feminism and the global urban', *International Journal of Urban and Regional Research*. doi: 10.1111/1468-2427.12276.

Peck, J. (2010), *Constructions of Neoliberal Reason*. Oxford: Oxford University Press.

Peck, J. (2011), 'Geographies of policy: from transfer-diffusion to mobility-mutation', *Progress in Human Geography* 35 (6): 773–97.

Peck, J. (2012), 'Recreative city: Amsterdam, vehicular ideas, and the adaptive spaces of creativity policy', *International Journal of Urban and Regional Research* 36 (3): 462–85.

Peck, J. (2015), 'Cities beyond compare', *Regional Studies* 49 (1): 160–82.

Peck, J. (2016), 'Economic rationality meets celebrity urbanology: exploring Edward Glaeser's city', *International Journal of Urban and Regional Research* 40 (1): 1–30.

Peleggi, M. (2005), 'Consuming colonial nostalgia: the monumentalisation of historic hotels in urban South-East Asia', *Asia-Pacific Viewpoint* 46 (3): 255–65.

Pieterse, E. (2008), *City Futures: Confronting the Crisis of Urban Development*. London: Zed Books.

Pile, S. and N.J. Thrift (2000), *City A–Z: Urban Fragments*. London: Routledge.

Power, M. (1995), 'Auditing, expertise and the sociology of technique', *Critical Perspectives on Accounting* 6: 317–39.

Pryke, M. (2010), 'Money's eyes: the visual preparation of financial markets', *Economy and Society* 39 (4): 427–59.

Raco, M. and K. Gilliam (2012), 'Geographies of abstraction, urban entrepreneurialism, and the production of new cultural spaces: the West Kowloon Cultural District, Hong Kong', *Environment and Planning* A 44: 1425–42.

Rapoport, E. (2014), 'Utopian visions and real estate dreams: the eco-city past, present and future', *Geography Compass* 8 (2): 137–48.

Reese, T.J. (1996), *Inside the Vatican: the Politics and Organisation of the Catholic Church*. Cambridge, MA: Harvard University Press.

Roberts, S. (1995), 'Small place, big money: the Cayman Islands and the International Financial System', *Economic Geography* 71 (3): 237–56.

Robinson, J. (2002), 'Global and world cities: a view from off the map', *International Journal of Urban and Regional Research* 26 (3): 513–54.

Robinson, J. (2005), 'Urban geography: world cities, or a world of cities?', *Progress in Human Geography* 29: 757–76.

Robinson, J. (2006), *Ordinary Cities: Between Modernity and Development*. London: Routledge.

Robinson, J. (2008), 'Developing ordinary cities: city visioning processes in Durban and Johannesburg', *Environment and Planning A* 40: 74–87.

Robinson, J. (2011), 'Cities in a world of cities: the comparative gesture', *International Journal of Urban and Regional Research* 35: 1–23.

Robinson, J. (2013), 'The urban now: theorising cities beyond the new', *European Journal of Cultural Studies* 16 (6): 659–77.

Rossiter, N. (2016), *Software, Infrastructure, Labor: a Media Theory of Logistical Nightmares*. New York: Routledge.

Roush, C. (2010), *Show Me the Money: Writing Business and Economics Stories for Mass Communication*. New York: Routledge.

Roy, A. (2009), 'The 21st-century metropolis: new geographies of theory', *Regional Studies* 43 (6): 819–30.

Roy, A. and A. Ong (eds) (2011), *Worlding Cities: Asian Experiments and the Art of Being Global*. Oxford: Blackwell.

Rühen, C. (1995), *Pub Splendid: the Australia Hotel 1891–1971*. Collaroy: John Burrell in association with Murray Child & Co. Ltd.

Sahakian, M. (2014), *Keeping Cool in Southeast Asia: Energy Consumption and Urban Air-Conditioning*. London: Palgrave Macmillan.

Salgado, S. (2005), *Workers: An Archaeology of the Industrial Age*. New York: Aperture.

Salt, J. (2010), 'Business travel and portfolios of mobility within global companies', in J.V. Beaverstock, B. Derudder, J. Faulconbridge and F. Witlox (eds), *International Business Travel in the Global Economy* (pp. 107–24). Farnham: Ashgate.

Sandoval-Strausz, A.K. (1999), 'Why the hotel? Liberal visions, merchant capital, public space, and the creation of an American institution', *Business and Economic History* 28 (2): 255–65.

Sardar, Z. (2014), *Mecca: the Sacred City*. New York: Bloomsbury.

Sassen, S. (1991), *The Global City: New York, London, Tokyo*. Princeton, NJ: Princeton University Press.

Sassen, S. (1995), 'When the state encounters a new space economy: the case of information industries', *American University International Law Review* 10(2), 769–89.

Sassen, S. (2012), 'Why does global finance need financial centers?', in K. Knorr-Cetina and A. Preda (eds), *The Oxford Handbook of the Sociology of Finance* (pp. 13–32). Oxford: Oxford University Press.

Saxenian, A. (1989), 'In search of power: the organization of business interests in Silicon Valley and Route 128', *Economy and Society* 18 (1): 25–70.

Saxenian, A. (2007), *The New Argonauts: Regional Advantage in a Global Economy.* Cambridge, MA: Harvard University Press.

Schiffauer, W. (2014), 'Global prayers, migration, post-migration', in J. Becker, K. Klingan, S. Lanz and K. Wildner (eds), *Global Prayers: Contemporary Manifestations of the Religious in the City* (pp. 49–63). Zurich: Lars Müller.

Schoenberger, E. (1997), *The Cultural Crisis of the Firm.* Cambridge, MA: Blackwell.

Schoenberger, E. (2001), 'Corporate autobiographies: the narrative strategies of corporate strategists', *Journal of Economic Geography* 1 (3): 277–98.

Schwarz, G. (2006), 'Enabling global trade above the clouds: restructuring processes and information technology in the transatlantic air-cargo industry', *Environment and Planning A* 38: 1463–85.

Seifert, A.M. and K. Messing (2006), 'Cleaning up after globalization: an ergonomic analysis of work activity of hotel cleaners', *Antipode* 38 (3): 557–78.

Shatkin, G. (1998), 'Fourth World' cities in the global economy: the case of Phnom Penh', *Cambodia International Journal of Urban and Regional Research* 22 (3): 378–93.

Shatkin, G. (2008), 'The city and the bottom line: urban megaprojects and the privatization of planning in Southeast Asia', *Environment and Planning A* 40 (2): 383–401.

Shatkin, G. (2010), 'Planning privatopolis: representation and contestation in the development of urban integrated mega-projects', in A. Roy and A. Ong (eds), *Worlding Cities: Asian Experiments and the Art of Being Global* (pp. 77–97). Oxford: Blackwell.

Sheller, M. and J. Urry (2006), 'The new mobilities paradigm', *Environment and Planning A* 38 (2): 207–26.

Sherman, R. (2007), *Class Acts: Service and Inequality in Luxury Hotels.* Berkeley, CA: University of California Press.

Shields, R. (2013), *Spatial Questions: Cultural Topologies and Social Spatialisations.* London: Sage.

Shove, E. (2003), *Comfort, Cleanliness and Convenience: the Social Organization of Normality.* Oxford: Berg.

Sidaway, J. (2007), 'Enclave space: a new metageography of development?', *Area* 39 (3): 331–9.

Sidaway, J. (2013), 'Geography, globalization, and the problematic of Area Studies', *Annals of the Association of American Geographers* 103 (4): 984–1002.

Sidaway, J. and M. Power (2005), '"The tears of Portugal": empire, identity, "race", and destiny in Portuguese geopolitical narratives', *Environment and Planning D: Society and Space* 23: 527–54.

Sidorov, D. (2000), 'National monumentalization and the politics of scale: the resurrections of the Cathedral of Christ the Savior in Moscow', *Annals of the Association of American Geographers* 90 (3): 548–72.

Simmel, G. (1903), 'The metropolis and mental life,' in R. Sennett (ed.) (1969), *Classic Essays on the Culture of Cities*. New York: Appleton-Century-Crofts.

Simone, A. (2004), 'People as infrastructure: intersecting fragments in Johannesburg', *Public Culture* 16 (3): 407–29.

Simone, A. (2012), 'No longer the subaltern: refiguring cities of the global South', in T. Edensor and M. Jayne (eds), *Urban Theory Beyond the West: a World of Cities* (pp. 31–46). London: Routledge.

Simone, A. (2016), '"It's just the city after all"', *International Journal of Urban and Regional Research*. doi:101111/1468-2427.1275.

Smith, D.A. and M.F. Timberlake (2001), 'World city networks and hierarchies, 1977–1997: an empirical analysis of global air travel links', *American Behavioral Scientist* 44: 1656–78.

Smith, R.G. (2003a), 'World city actor-networks', *Progress in Human Geography* 27 (1): 25–44.

Smith, R.G. (2003b), 'World city topologies', *Progress in Human Geography* 27 (5): 561–82.

Smith, R.G. (2013a), 'Beyond the global city concept and the myth of "command and control"', *International Journal of Urban and Regional Research*. doi:10.1111/1468-2427.12024.

Smith, R.G. (2013b), 'The ordinary city trap', *Environment and Planning A* 45: 2290–304.

Smith, R.G. and M.A. Doel (2011), 'Questioning the theoretical basis of current global-city research: structures, networks, and actor-networks', *International Journal of Urban and Regional Research* 35 (1): 24–39.

Söderström, O. (2014), *Cities in Relations: Trajectories of Urban Development in Hanoi and Ouagadougou*. Oxford: Wiley Blackwell.

Söderström, O., T. Paasche and F. Klauser (2014), 'Smart cities as corporate storytelling', *City* 18 (3): 307–20.

Sombart, W. (1915), *The Quintessence of Capitalism: a Study of the History and Psychology of the Modern Business Man*. London: Fischer Unwin.

Stern, N., D. Zenghelis and P. Rode (2011), 'City solutions to global problems', in R. Burdett and D. Sudjic (eds), *Living in the Endless City* (pp. 342–49). London: Phaidon.

Stinger, C.L. (1998), *The Renaissance in Rome*. Bloomington, IN: Indiana University Press.

Studwell, J. (2007), *Asian Godfathers: Money and Power in Hong Kong and Southeast Asia*. London: Profile.

Sum, N.-L. (1995), 'More than a "war of words": identity, politics and the struggle for dominance during the recent "political reform" period in Hong Kong', *Economy and Society* 24 (1): 67–100.

Swan, R. (2013), 'Chopped livery: start-ups revolutionize the cab industry', *SF Weekly*, 27 March. http://www.sfweekly.com/2013-03-27/news/uber-lyft-sidecar-cabs-sfmta/.

Takhteyev, Y. (2012), *Coding Places: Software Practice in a South American City*. Cambridge, MA: MIT Press.

Taylor, P.J. (2004), *World City Network*. London: Routledge.

Thrift, N.J. (2005), *Knowing Capitalism*. London: Sage.

Thrift, N., A. Tickell and S. Woolgar (2014a), 'Introduction: respecifying globalization', in N. Thrift, A. Tickell, S. Woolgar and W.H. Rupp (eds), *Globalization in Practice* (pp. 1–15). Oxford: Oxford University Press.

Thrift, N., A. Tickell, S. Woolgar and W.H. Rupp (eds) (2014b), *Globalization in Practice*. Oxford: Oxford University Press.

Townsend, A.M. (2013), *Smarter Cities: Big Data, Civic Hackers and the Quest for a New Utopia*. New York: W.W. Norton.

Tsing, A. (2005), *Friction*. Princeton, NJ: Princeton University Press.

Tsing, A. (2009a), 'Supply chains and the human condition', *Rethinking Marxism* 21: 148–76.

Tsing, A. (2009b), 'Beyond economic and ecological standardization', *The Australian Journal of Anthropology* 20: 347–68.

Ukah, A. (2014), 'Redeeming urban spaces: the ambivalence of building a Pentecostal City in Lagos, Nigeria', in J. Becker, K. Klingan, S. Lanz and K. Wildner (eds), *Global Prayers: Contemporary Manifestations of the Religious in the City* (pp. 178–97). Zurich: Lars Müller.

Urry, J. (2002), 'Mobility and proximity', *Sociology* 36 (2): 255–74.

Urry, J. (2003), 'Social networks, travel and talk', *British Journal of Sociology* 54 (2): 155–75.

Visser, M. (2001), *The Geometry of Love: Space, Time, Mystery and Meaning in an Ordinary Church*. London: Penguin.

Vollmer, H. (2003), 'Bookkeeping, accounting, calculative practice: the sociological suspense of calculation', *Critical Perspectives on Accounting* 3: 353–81.

Walker, R. (2015), 'Building a better theory of the urban: a response to "towards a new epistemology of the urban"?', *City* 19 (2–3): 183–91.

Wang, J.J. and M.C. Cheng (2010), 'From a hub port city to a global supply chain management center: a case study of Hong Kong', *Journal of Transport Geography* 18: 104–15.

Ward, K. (2010), 'Entrepreneurial urbanism and business improvement districts in the state of Wisconsin: a cosmopolitan critique', *Annals of the Association of American Geographers* 100 (5): 1177–96.

Webber, M. and R. Burrows (2015), 'Life in an alpha territory: discontinuity and conflict in an elite London "village"', *Urban Studies*, doi:10.1177/0042098015612983.

Weber, M. (1922/1978), *Wirtschaft und Gesellschaft*. Tubingen: Mohr; *Economy and Society: an Outline of Interpretive Sociology*. Berkeley, CA: University of California Press.

Weber, R. (2010), 'Selling city futures: the financialization of urban redevelopment policy', *Economic Geography* 86 (3): 251–74.

Weinstein, L. (2008), 'Mumbai's development mafias: organized crime, land development, and globalization', *International Journal of Urban and Regional Research* 32 (1): 22–39.

Weinstein, L. (2014), *The Durable Slum: Dharavi and the Right to Stay Put in Globalizing Mumbai*. Minneapolis, MN: University of Minnesota Press.

Weizman, E. (2004), 'Strategic points, flexible lines, tense surfaces, political volumes: Ariel Sharon and the geometry of occupation', *The Philosophical Forum* 35 (2): 221–44.

Weizman, E. (2010), 'Eyal Weizman on Dying to Speak: forensic spatiality', London for Log 20: Curating Architecture. Interviewed by Tina DiCarlo. http://www. tinadicarlo.com/eyal-weizman-on-dying-to-speak-forensic-spatiality/.

Wharton, A.J. (2001), *Building the Cold War: Hilton International Hotels and Modern Architecture*. Chicago: University of Chicago Press.

Willey, D. (1993), *God's Politician: Pope John Paul II, the Catholic Church, and the New World Order*. New York: St. Martin's Press.

Willis, C. (1995), *Form Follows Finance: Skyscrapers and Skyline in New York and Chicago*. New York: Princeton Architectural Press.

Wills, J. (2005), 'The geography of union organizing in low-paid service industries in the UK: lessons from the T & G's campaign to unionise the Dorchester Hotel, London', *Antipode* 37 (1): 139–59.

Wills, J., K. Datta, Y. Evans, J. Herbert, J. May and C. McIlwaine (2010), *Global Cities at Work: New Migrant Divisions of Labour*. London: Pluto Press.

Winter, T. (2013), 'An uncomfortable truth: air-conditioning and sustainability in Asia', *Environment and Planning A* 45: 517–31.

Woodhead, L. (2002), 'Christianity', in L. Woodhead, P. Fletcher, H. Kawanami and D. Smith (eds), *Religions in the Modern World* (pp. 153–81). London: Routledge.

Zaloom, C. (2006), *Out of the Pits: Traders and Technology from Chicago to London*. Chicago: University of Chicago Press.

Zaloom, C. (2010), 'The city as value locus: markets, technologies, and the problem of worth', in I. Farías and T. Bender (eds), *Urban Assemblages: How Actor-Network Theory Changes Urban Studies* (pp. 253–68). London: Routledge.

Zeiss, R. (2014), 'Putting standards to work: water and the taste and smell of globalization', in N. Thrift, A. Tickell, S. Woolgar and W.H. Rupp (eds), *Globalization in Practice* (pp. 104–8). Oxford: Oxford University Press.

INDEX

Page numbers in italics denote figures

STAR TREK

THE NEXT GENERATION

ENEMY UNSEEN

Star Trek: The Next Generation created by Gene Roddenberry

cover painted by
DREW STRUZAN

edited by
JEFF MARIOTTE

designed by
AMBER BENNETT

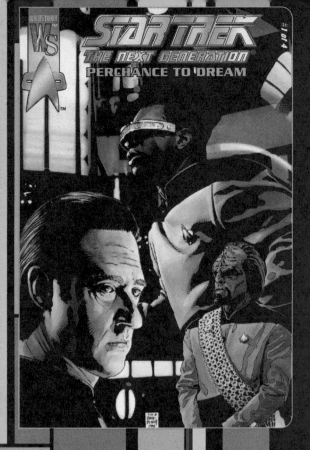

**Star Trek:
The Next Generation®
Perchance to Dream
Cover art by Tim Bradstreet**

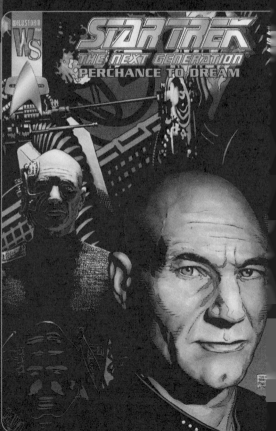

MY NAME IS DATA.

I AM A LIEUTENANT COMMANDER IN STARFLEET, PRESENTLY ASSIGNED AS SECOND OFFICER ON THE *U.S.S. ENTERPRISE*, REGISTRY NUMBER NCC-1701-D.

IN ADDITION, THE SHIP APPEARS TO BE AT *RED ALERT*, THOUGH I AM UNABLE TO DETERMINE WHY *THAT* IS, EITHER.

FOR REASONS I AM UNABLE TO DETERMINE, I AM *ALONE* ON THAT SHIP.

SINCE, OVER THE PAST SEVEN YEARS, THE AVERAGE NUMBER OF SENTIENT BEINGS OCCUPYING THIS SHIP HAS BEEN 1008.765, THIS IS QUITE *PECULIAR*.

I AM NOW PROCEEDING TO MAIN ENGINEERING IN THE HOPES THAT I WILL BE ABLE TO ANSWER SOME OF THESE QUESTIONS.

I AM APPREHENSIVE ABOUT THIS TRIP TO ENGINEERING.

SINCE I DO NOT FEEL *EMOTIONS*, THIS IS RATHER *ANOMALOUS*.

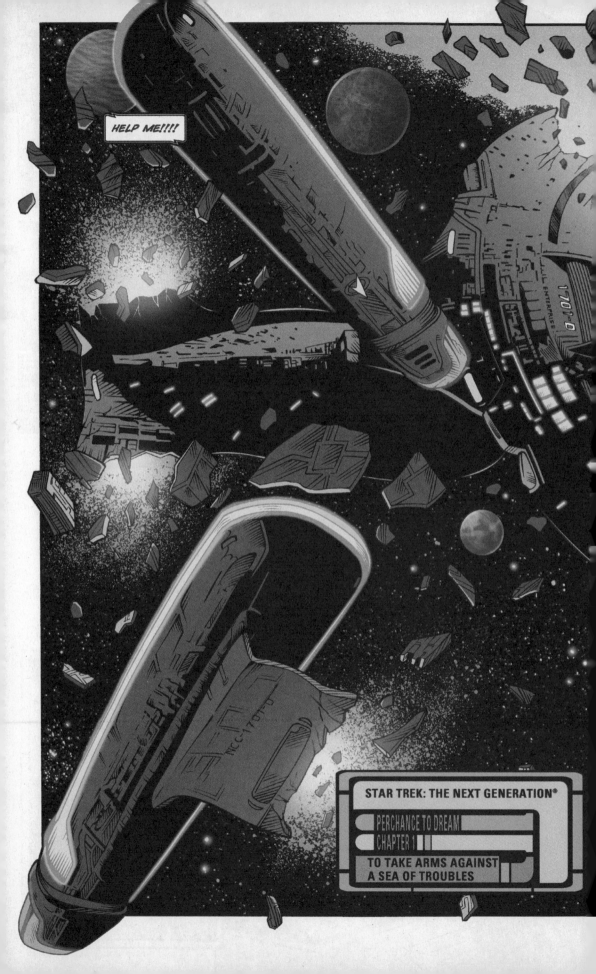

PRESENTS

KEITH R.A. DeCANDIDO — WRITER

PETER PACHOUMIS — PENCILLER

LUCIAN RIZZO — INKER

RYAN CLINE — LETTERER

WILDSTORM FX — COLORIST

JEFF MARIOTTE — EDITOR

BASED ON STAR TREK: THE NEXT GENERATION®
CREATED BY GENE RODENBERRY

WHEN LT. COMMANDER DATA WAKES UP FROM HIS DREAM PROGRAM, HE DOES NOT BOLT UPRIGHT AS A HUMAN WOULD. HIS CONSCIOUSNESS IS BINARY, AFTER ALL. THE DREAM PROGRAM SIMPLY SHUTS OFF AND HIS COGNITIVE FUNCTIONS TURN BACK ON.

THE TRANSITION IS AN ORDERLY ONE.

THE DREAM, HOWEVER, WAS ANYTHING BUT.

GOOD MORNING, GEORDI.

HEY, DATA.

HOW'D THE *DREAM* GO?

STRANGELY.

I DREAMT THAT I WAS ALONE ON THE ENTERPRISE AT *RED ALERT*, AND THEN THAT I WAS IN ENGINEERING, BUT YOU AND EVERYONE ELSE DID NOT ACKNOWLEDGE MY *PRESENCE*. THEN YOU ALL FELL *UNCONSCIOUS*, AND THE ENTERPRISE *CRASHED* AND WAS *DESTROYED*.

HEY, I'VE HAD *NIGHTMARES* LIKE THAT ONCE OR TWICE. IT'S A PRETTY TYPICAL *ANXIETY* DREAM.

THAT IS THE OTHER ANOMALOUS ITEM IN THE DREAM: I FELT EMOTIONS OF FEAR AND ANXIETY.

REALLY? YOU *SURE?*

YES.

AT LEAST, I WAS SURE AT THE *TIME* THAT IT WAS FEAR AND ANXIETY.

IT IS TRUE THAT MY FRAME OF REFERENCE IS *LIMITED*.

OBSERVATION LOUNGE.

BUT YOU DIDN'T FEEL FEAR OR ANXIETY ANY OF *THOSE* TIMES, RIGHT?

NO.

I HAVE HAD ACCESS TO EMOTIONS BEFORE. THERE WERE THE TWO OCCASIONS WHEN MY FORM WAS TAKEN OVER BY AN UX-MAL CRIMINAL ON MAB-BU IV AND BY IRA GRAVES.

AND THE BORG THAT LORE COMMANDED DID GIVE ME FEELINGS OF ANGER.

Q TEMPORARILY GAVE ME THE ABILITY TO LAUGH, WHICH HAD A CONCOMITANT FEELING OF JOY.

WELL, YOUR *BEST* BET IS TO TALK TO *DEANNA* ABOUT IT--

"AFTER THE MEETING."

GENTLEMEN, THANK YOU FOR COMING.

WE SHOULD BE ARRIVING AT *DAMIANO* WITHIN THE HOUR. HOWEVER, THERE HAVE BEEN SOME *CHANGES* TO THE *MISSION PROFILE.*

THE ENTIRE SENIOR STAFF OF THE ENTERPRISE HAS BEEN INVITED TO ATTEND THE *INAUGURATION* AND THE FESTIVITIES THAT WILL FOLLOW. WHILE ATTENDANCE IS NOT *MANDATORY,* I THINK IT IS IMPORTANT THAT WE ALL ATTEND THE INAUGURATION AND AS MANY OF THE OTHER EVENTS AS DUTY WILL *ALLOW.*

GOVERNOR-ELECT RA'CH IS, AFTER ALL, THE FIRST DAMIANI TO SERVE ON THE *FEDERATION COUNCIL.*

THE ONE *EXCEPTION* TO THIS WILL BE--

--MR. *WORF*.

SIR?

YOUR SERVICES WILL BE REQUIRED IN A MORE OFFICIAL CAPACITY.

I TAKE IT THAT THERE IS A *SECURITY* CONCERN REGARDING THE INAUGURATION?

INDEED. IT HAS TO DO WITH SOME NEW FACTS THAT HAVE COME TO LIGHT REGARDING GOVERNOR-ELECT RA'CH AND CERTAIN *CULTURAL MORES* OF THE DAMIANI.

MR. *DATA?*

DAMIANO IS A MOST UNIQUE PLANET. WHERE ANIMAL LIFE ON MOST WORLDS TEND TOWARD *TWO GENDERS* OR *NO GENDERS*, ON DAMIANO, THEY HAVE DEVELOPED *THREE*.

FOR EASE OF TRANSLATION, THE PRONOUNS "HE," "SHE," AND "IT" ARE USED TO REPRESENT THE GENDERS, THOUGH THERE IS NO LITERAL ANALOGUE TO THE MALE AND FEMALE THAT WE ARE *ACCUSTOMED* TO.

TO PARAPHRASE A HUMAN IDIOM, FOR THE DAMIANI, IT TAKES *THREE* TO *TANGO*. AS A RESULT, MOST ROMANTIC COUPLINGS ARE IN GROUPS OF *THREE*. FOR CENTURIES, ANYTHING THAT DEVIATED FROM THAT NORM WAS CONSIDERED--

--*PERVERSE*.

SUCH ATTITUDES HAVE *SOFTENED* SINCE DAMIANO JOINED THE FEDERATION. HOWEVER, THERE ARE *MORALIST* FACTIONS WHO STILL HOLD THOSE ATTITUDES.

WHAT DOES *THIS* HAVE TO DO WITH THE INAUGURATION?

SHORTLY AFTER HER ELECTION, IT WAS REVEALED THAT THE GOVERNOR-ELECT ONLY HAS *ONE* SEXUAL PARTNER.

THE VAST MAJORITY OF THE DAMIANI COULDN'T CARE LESS ABOUT THIS, OF COURSE, BUT THOSE MORALIST FACTIONS ARE IN AN *UPROAR*.

HARD TO BELIEVE. IF THEY THOUGHT RA'CH WAS A GOOD CHOICE *BEFORE*, WHY DOES HER SEXUAL PREFERENCE SUDDENLY *NEGATE* THAT?

MR. WORF, YOU ARE TO COORDINATE WITH THE CAPITAL CITY'S CHIEF OF *POLICE*. ITS NAME IS DU'RE C'ULLHO. IT IS *IMPERATIVE* THAT SECURITY AT THE INAUGURATION IS AS *TIGHT* AS *POSSIBLE*.

THE DETAILS OF THE SETUP FOR THE INAUGURATION ARE IN THE COMPUTER. I EXPECT YOU TO BE *FAMILIAR* WITH IT BY THE TIME WE ARRIVE.

TEMPTING AS IT IS TO GET INTO A PROTRACTED DISCUSSION OF THE RELATIVE *MORALS* OF SENTIENT BEINGS, THIS ISN'T THE *TIME*, NUMBER ONE.

THE IMPORTANT THING IS THAT *DEATH THREATS* HAVE BEEN MADE AGAINST GOVERNOR-ELECT RA'CH.

OF COURSE, CAPTAIN.

"EXCELLENT. DISMISSED."

OF COURSE, DATA.

COUNSELOR, MAY I *SPEAK* WITH YOU A MOMENT?

WHAT CAN I *DO* FOR YOU?

OH?

PRIOR TO THIS MORNING'S MEETING, I ACTIVATED MY *DREAM PROGRAM*.

AFTER DATA FILLS THE COUNSELOR IN ON HIS DREAM...

USUALLY DREAMS ARE PROMPTED BY THOUGHTS YOU'VE BEEN HAVING PRIOR TO GOING TO SLEEP.

HAVE YOU BEEN THINKING ABOUT ANYTHING THAT APPEARED IN THE DREAM?

EVER SINCE I DEACTIVATED LORE IN THE DELTA QUADRANT AND RETRIEVED THE *EMOTION CHIP* DR. SOONG CREATED FOR ME, I HAVE GIVEN A *GREAT DEAL* OF THOUGHT TO WHAT MIGHT HAPPEN IF I *INSTALLED* THE CHIP.

SO YOU BELIEVE THE DREAM IS EXPRESSING YOUR APPREHENSION ABOUT THE CHIP?

I DO NOT BELIEVE THAT "APPREHENSION" IS AN APPROPRIATE WORD TO USE, COUNSELOR.

HOWEVER, I DO BELIEVE THAT THERE ARE GRAVE RISKS TO INSTALLING THE CHIP.

WHICH YOUR DREAM PROGRAM EXPRESSED IN TERMS OF THE SHIP BEING DESTROYED.

PERHAPS. GIVEN THAT LORE HAS TWICE TRIED TO DESTROY THE ENTERPRISE, THIS IS NOT AN ALL TOGETHER UNFOUNDED CONCERN.

OR PERHAPS I WAS THINKING ABOUT BEING IGNORED.

I BEG YOUR PARDON?

WHEN I FIRST JOINED STARFLEET, THERE WAS A GOOD DEAL OF RESISTANCE TO MY INPUT BECAUSE I AM AN ANDROID.

HAVE YOU FOUND THAT TO BE THE CASE SINCE YOU JOINED THE ENTERPRISE?

NO.

ALTHOUGH WHEN I ASSUMED TEMPORARY COMMAND OF THE SUTHERLAND DURING THE ROMULAN BLOCKADE, MY FIRST OFFICER EXPRESSED RESERVATIONS ABOUT MY COMMAND ABILITY.

YOU MIGHT BE REACHING, DATA. ANXIETY OVER THE EMOTION CHIP IS A RECENT DEVELOPMENT, AFTER ALL, AND WORRY OVER PEOPLE IGNORING YOUR INPUT ISN'T.

TRUE.

HOWEVER, DO RECALL THAT I HAVE EQUAL ACCESS TO ALL THE INFORMATION I HAVE EVER BEEN EXPOSED TO. MY MEMORIES DO NOT FADE WITH TIME. I CAN RECALL THE SLIGHTS I ENDURED AT THE ACADEMY WITH THE SAME VIVIDNESS THAT I REMEMBER DEACTIVATING LORE. SO PERHAPS--

DATA.

DO YOU KNOW WHAT I THINK?

WE SHOULD SET UP A SESSION AFTER THE INAUGURATION ON DAMIANO. OBVIOUSLY, WE HAVE A LOT TO TALK ABOUT, AND I DON'T THINK A QUICK CHAT AFTER A MEETING IS THE RIGHT PLACE FOR IT.

OF COURSE, COUNSELOR. I WILL MAKE AN APPOINTMENT WHEN WE LEAVE DAMIANO ORBIT.

THE CITY OF IARON, THE CAPITAL CITY OF DAMIANO.

THE FIFTH DAY OF THE NINTH MONTH.

A YEAR AGO, ES'SCA G'ULLHO ANNOUNCED IT WOULD RETIRE AFTER ITS SIXTH TERM IN OFFICE AS PLANETARY GOVERNOR, A TENURE THAT BEGAN WITH DAMIANO'S OFFICIAL ACCEPTANCE INTO THE UNITED FEDERATION OF PLANETS.

TWO MONTHS AGO, ES'SCA'S FORMER CHIEF OF STAFF, RA'CH B'ULLHY, RECEIVED 85% OF THE VOTE TO BE ITS SUCCESSOR AS GOVERNOR.

THREE DAYS AGO, DAMIANO'S PRIMARY NEWS SERVICE BROKE THE STORY THAT RA'CH LONG BELIEVED TO BE SINGLE, WAS IN FACT HAVING A RELATIONSHIP WITH A LONE PARTNER.

TWO DAYS FROM NOW, SHE IS SUPPOSED TO BE INAUGURATED--

SAID THE GOVERNOR-ELECT, "I SEE *NO* REASON TO COMPLY WITH THE WISHES OF A SHRINKING *MINORITY* WHEN AN OVER-WHELMING *MAJORITY* HAS ALREADY *CHOSEN* ME AS THEIR NEW *GOVERNOR*."

I DON'T *BELIEVE* THIS.

--UNLESS THE PEOPLE IN THIS BUILDING HAVE THEIR WAY.

OUTGOING GOVERNOR ES'SCA G'ULLHO COULD NOT BE REACHED FOR COMMENT. DESPITE THE GOVERNOR-ELECT'S WORDS, *SECURITY* FOR THE INAUGURATION HAS BEEN *INCREASED*--

AND THERE ARE *RUMORS* THAT THE ENT--

--ISSUED BY GOVERNOR-ELECT RA'CH B'ULLHY STATED IN NO UNCERTAIN TERMS THAT THE *INAUGURATION* WOULD GO AHEAD AS *SCHEDULED*.

OFF!

WELL, MY FRIENDS--

IT SEEMS THAT OUR *THREATS* ARE BEING TAKEN SERIOUSLY, BUT NOT OUR *INTENT*.

THE PERVERT *INSISTS* ON GOING THROUGH WITH THE *INAUGURATION*.

DOES THAT MEAN--?

WELL?

I CAN'T. NOT FOR SURE.

I TRANSFERRED A COUPLE I WASN'T SURE OF, BUT--

FOR THE LOVE OF HO'NIG, RA'CH, WHAT HAVE WE COME TO?

I MEAN, WHAT DIFFERENCE DOES IT MAKE HOW MANY PEOPLE YOU SLEEP WITH?

ACCORDING TO JE'TRAN T'ULLH, QUITE A BIT.

>SNORT< PLEASE -- AS IF ANYONE TAKES HIM SERIOUSLY.

DON'T UNDERESTIMATE HIM, DU'RE.

HIS SHOW IS EXTREMELY POPULAR. REMEMBER, HE WAS THE ONE WHO TOOK DOWN MINISTER EL'AR.

OH, PLEASE.

HE JUST PUBLICIZED IT. EL'AR WAS ARRESTED AFTER A YEAR'S INVESTIGATION BY MY DETECTIVES! JE'TRAN DIDN'T HAVE A DAMN THING TO DO WITH IT!

PERHAPS.

BUT THE PEOPLE PERCEIVE HIM AS THE ONE WHO TOOK EL'AR DOWN, NOT YOUR DETECTIVES. AND THAT IS DUE TO HIS CONVINCING PEOPLE THAT IT WAS HIS DOING.

HE COULD JUST AS EASILY CONVINCE PEOPLE THAT I DESERVE TO DIE RATHER THAN TAKE OFFICE.

I CAN'T RISK THAT HE'LL SUCCEED. I'M SORRY IF BRINGING IN STARFLEET OFFENDS YOUR SENSIBILITIES, OLD FRIEND, BUT--

ALL RIGHT, ALL RIGHT!

YOU'VE MADE YOUR POINT.

I SHOULD KNOW BETTER THAN TO ARGUE WITH YOU-- ESPECIALLY WHEN YOU'RE RIGHT.

I'LL MEET WITH THE STARFLEET PEOPLE WHEN THEY ARRIVE.

THEY'RE MEETING US AT THE ATRIUM IN AN HOUR.

"I JUST HOPE THE ENTERPRISE LIVES UP TO ITS *REPUTATION*."

THE HONOR IS *OURS*, GOVERNOR.

WELCOME TO DAMIANO, CAPTAIN PICARD. IT IS A *PLEASURE* TO FINALLY MEET YOU IN PERSON, AND AN HONOR TO HAVE THE *FLAGSHIP* ATTEND OUR INAUGURATION.

PLEASE, CAPTAIN--

--IT'S STILL "GOVERNOR-ELECT" FOR TWO MORE DAYS.

ALLOW ME TO INTRODUCE OUR CHIEF OF POLICE, DU'RE C'ULLHO. AMONG ITS MANY FUNCTIONS IS TO MAKE SURE I *LIVE* LONG ENOUGH TO DROP THE *"ELECT"* FROM THAT TITLE TWO DAYS HENCE.

THIS IS MY FIRST OFFICER, COMMANDER WILLIAM RIKER, AND LIEUTENANT WORF.

THE LIEUTENANT WILL BE *AIDING* YOU, CHIEF.

SO I *HEAR*.

IF YOU COME THIS WAY, CAPTAIN, COMMANDER, I CAN INTRODUCE YOU TO MY STAFF AND GIVE YOU AN IDEA WHAT TO EXPECT.

THANK YOU VERY MUCH, GOVERNOR-ELECT.

I DON'T *BELIEVE* THIS. THE LAST SWEEP WE DID WAS LESS THAN AN *HOUR* AGO.

WHERE *IS* IT?

THE EXPLOSIVE IS OF SUBYTT DESIGN, USED IN THEIR RECENT WAR AGAINST THE KRESARI.

BEHIND THE CENTRAL PANEL.

HOW IN HO'NIG'S NAME DID WE MISS *THIS?*

THE EXPLOSIVE IS DESIGNED TO BE RESISTANT TO SENSOR SCANS.

SO *YOU* DETECT IT?

PRESS THE GREEN BUTTON IN ORDER TO DEACTIVATE IT.

RIGHT.

DID IT.

HO'NIG!

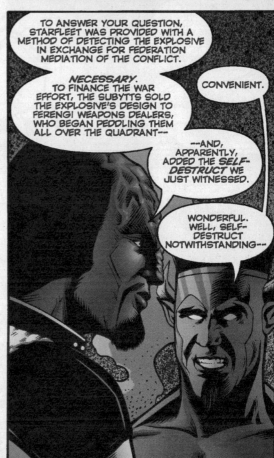

TO ANSWER YOUR QUESTION, STARFLEET WAS PROVIDED WITH A METHOD OF DETECTING THE EXPLOSIVE IN EXCHANGE FOR FEDERATION MEDIATION OF THE CONFLICT.

NECESSARY. TO FINANCE THE WAR EFFORT, THE SUBYTTS SOLD THE EXPLOSIVE'S DESIGN TO FERENGI WEAPONS DEALERS, WHO BEGAN PEDDLING THEM ALL OVER THE QUADRANT--

CONVENIENT.

--AND, APPARENTLY, ADDED THE *SELF-DESTRUCT* WE JUST WITNESSED.

WONDERFUL. WELL, SELF-DESTRUCT NOTWITHSTANDING--

PRETTY HANDY ONE FOR THE PERSON WHO *PLANTED* IT. NOW WE'VE GOT NO *EVIDENCE*, ASIDE FROM YOUR TRICORDER READINGS.

THAT *IS* A NEW FEATURE.

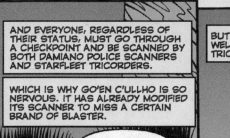

AND EVERYONE, REGARDLESS OF THEIR STATUS, MUST GO THROUGH A CHECKPOINT AND BE SCANNED BY BOTH DAMIANO POLICE SCANNERS AND STARFLEET TRICORDERS.

WHICH IS WHY GO'EN C'ULLHO IS SO NERVOUS. IT HAS ALREADY MODIFIED ITS SCANNER TO MISS A CERTAIN BRAND OF BLASTER.

BUT IT COULDN'T VERY WELL MODIFY THE VULCAN'S TRICORDER.

GO ON THROUGH, YOU'RE CLEAR.

JE'TRAN, WE'VE GOT A SERIOUS PROBLEM.

STARFLEET'S HERE.

JE'TRAN T'ULLH HAD BEEN COUNTING ON GO'EN. AND NOW GO'EN WAS GOING TO LET HIM DOWN.

OF COURSE STARFLEET'S THERE. WE KNEW THAT THEY WERE SENDING PEOPLE TO ATTEND THE INAUGURATION.

NOT ON THE STAGE, JE'TRAN, THEY'RE AT THE CHECKPOINTS! THEY'RE DOING SECURITY WITH DU'RE'S GOONS!

SO THAT'S HOW THEY FOUND THE BOMB!...

I'M STANDING ABOUT SIX METERS AWAY FROM A STARFLEETER WITH A TRICORDER WHO'S PRETTY LIKELY TO NOTICE THE BLASTER IN MY POCKET.

WHAT HAPPENED TO GO'EN?

IT'S STANDING NEXT TO HER LOOKING LIKE IT'S EXPECTING HO'NIG THEMSELVES TO STRIKE IT DOWN WITH LIGHTNING.

NOT, I MIGHT ADD, WITHOUT REASON.

WE HAVE TO CALL IT OFF.

NO! I WILL NOT LET THAT THAT THING LEAD US!

WE DON'T HAVE A CHOICE!

T'MOR TO ADDISON. PLEASE REPORT TO MY POSITION WITH YOUR PATROL. I HAVE DETECTED SIX DAMIANI CARRYING ILLICIT WEAPONS IN THE QUEUE.

THEY WILL NEED TO BE TAKEN DISCREETLY INTO CUSTODY.

ACKNOWLEDGED.

WE'LL HAVE TO GO WITH THE *SNIPER.*

THAT'S *CRAZY!* IT WAS JUST SUPPOSED TO LAY *COVERING* FIRE!

AS'SI K'ULLHO IS THE *BEST SHOT* ON THE CONTINENT. IT'LL NAIL THAT WITCH'S HORNS TO THE *WALL.*

HATE TO *CUT OFF* THIS MERRY CHAT, BUT I NEED TO SIGN OFF. I'M ABOUT TO BE *ARRESTED.*

THAT *SETTLES* IT. AS'SI, THIS IS JE'TRAN. THERE'S BEEN A CHANGE OF *PLAN.* THE AUDIENCE OPTION HAS BEEN *ELIMINATED.* IT'LL BE UP TO *YOU.*

NO *PROBLEM,* JE'TRAN.

ACKNOWLEDGED. GOOD WORK, ENSIGN.

GOVERNOR-ELECT, CAPTAIN, THE SEATS HAVE ALL BEEN *FILLED.*

ENSIGN T'MOR AND OFFICER GO'EN ARE THE ONLY ONES WHO HAVE FOUND ANY *CONTRABAND* WORTH MENTIONING. THE POTENTIAL ASSASSINS HAVE BEEN TAKEN INTO *CUSTODY.*

I BELIEVE, THEN, GOVERNOR-ELECT, THAT THERE IS NOTHING STOPPING US FROM *COMMENCING.*

WE CAN QUESTION THEM AFTER THE CEREMONY.

I AGREE. THANK YOU ALL FOR YOUR ASSISTANCE.

"NOW COME—LET US *USHER* DAMIANO INTO A *NEW ERA.*"

IT'S *STARTING,* JE'TRAN. DON'T *WORRY.*

THE MINUTE THAT *SICK'O* WALKS ON *STAGE* SHE'LL BE A PILE OF *ASHES.*

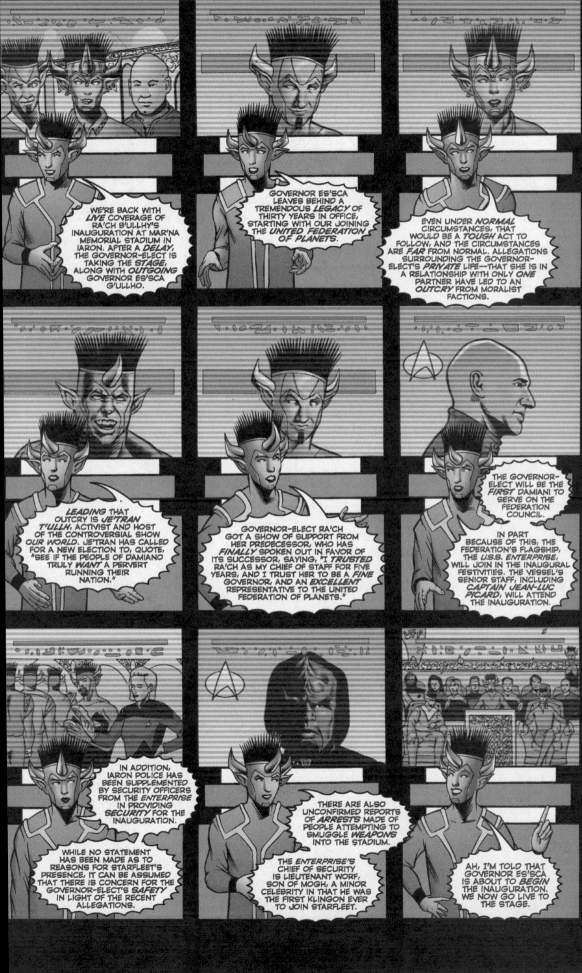

WE'RE BACK WITH *LIVE* COVERAGE OF RA'CH B'ULLHY'S INAUGURATION AT MAR'NA MEMORIAL STADIUM IN IARON. AFTER A *DELAY*, THE GOVERNOR-ELECT IS TAKING THE *STAGE*, ALONG WITH *OUTGOING* GOVERNOR ES'SCA G'ULLHO.

GOVERNOR ES'SCA LEAVES BEHIND A TREMENDOUS *LEGACY* OF THIRTY YEARS IN OFFICE, STARTING WITH OUR JOINING THE *UNITED FEDERATION OF PLANETS*.

EVEN UNDER *NORMAL* CIRCUMSTANCES, THAT WOULD BE A *TOUGH* ACT TO FOLLOW, AND THE CIRCUMSTANCES ARE *FAR* FROM NORMAL. ALLEGATIONS SURROUNDING THE GOVERNOR-ELECT'S *PRIVATE* LIFE—THAT SHE IS IN A RELATIONSHIP WITH ONLY *ONE* PARTNER HAVE LED TO AN *OUTCRY* FROM MORALIST FACTIONS.

LEADING THAT OUTCRY IS *JE'TRAN T'ULLH*, ACTIVIST AND HOST OF THE CONTROVERSIAL SHOW *OUR WORLD*. JE'TRAN HAS CALLED FOR A NEW ELECTION TO, QUOTE, "SEE IF THE PEOPLE OF DAMIANO TRULY *WANT* A PERVERT RUNNING THEIR NATION."

GOVERNOR-ELECT RA'CH GOT A SHOW OF SUPPORT FROM HER PREDECESSOR, WHO HAS *FINALLY* SPOKEN OUT IN FAVOR OF ITS SUCCESSOR, SAYING, "*I TRUSTED* RA'CH AS MY CHIEF OF STAFF FOR FIVE YEARS, AND I TRUST HER TO BE A *FINE* GOVERNOR, AND AN *EXCELLENT* REPRESENTATIVE TO THE UNITED FEDERATION OF PLANETS."

THE GOVERNOR-ELECT WILL BE THE *FIRST* DAMIANI TO SERVE ON THE FEDERATION COUNCIL.

IN PART BECAUSE OF THIS, THE FEDERATION'S FLAGSHIP, THE *U.S.S. ENTERPRISE*, WILL JOIN IN THE INAUGURAL FESTIVITIES. THE VESSEL'S SENIOR STAFF, INCLUDING *CAPTAIN JEAN-LUC PICARD*, WILL ATTEND THE INAUGURATION.

IN ADDITION, IARON POLICE HAS BEEN SUPPLEMENTED BY SECURITY OFFICERS FROM THE *ENTERPRISE* IN PROVIDING *SECURITY* FOR THE INAUGURATION.

WHILE NO STATEMENT AS TO REASONS FOR STARFLEET'S PRESENCE, IT CAN BE ASSUMED THAT THERE IS CONCERN FOR THE GOVERNOR-ELECT'S *SAFETY* IN LIGHT OF THE RECENT ALLEGATIONS.

THERE ARE ALSO UNCONFIRMED REPORTS OF *ARRESTS* MADE OF PEOPLE ATTEMPTING TO SMUGGLE *WEAPONS* INTO THE STADIUM.

THE *ENTERPRISE'S* CHIEF OF SECURITY IS LIEUTENANT WORF, SON OF MOGH, A MINOR CELEBRITY IN THAT HE WAS THE FIRST KLINGON EVER TO JOIN STARFLEET.

AH, I'M TOLD THAT GOVERNOR ES'SCA IS ABOUT TO *BEGIN* THE INAUGURATION. WE NOW GO LIVE TO THE STAGE.

TODAY, WE USHER IN A *NEW ERA* FOR DAMIANO.

I DON'T THINK IT'S TOO SELF-AGGRANDIZING TO SAY THAT JOINING THE FEDERATION HAS BEEN THE BEST THING EVER TO HAPPEN TO OUR GREAT PEOPLE.

LIEUTENANT WORF IS *CONCERNED*.

WE HAVE ENJOYED GREATER *PROSPERITY* THAN AT ANY TIME IN OUR HISTORY.

BUT WORF FEELS AS IF HE'S *MISSED* SOMETHING.

TRUE, THEY HAVE ALREADY REMOVED A *BOMB* FROM BENEATH THE STAGE AND SEVERAL POTENTIAL *ASSASSINS* FROM THE AUDIENCE.

THEY'VE COVERED EVERY SQUARE *MILLIMETER* OF THE STADIUM. WORF IS CONFIDENT THAT, AFTER TWO DAYS OF WORK, A GLOB FLY COULDN'T GET IN HERE WITHOUT HIS KNOWING ABOUT IT.

AND I HAVE EVERY FAITH THAT THOSE REWARDS WILL ONLY *INCREASE* WITH RA'CH B'ULLHY REPRESENTING US *DIRECTLY* TO THE FEDERATION COUNCIL.

AND SO, GENTLEBEINGS, WITHOUT FURTHER ADO, I BRING BEFORE YOU THE NEXT *GOVERNOR* OF *DAMIANO*, RA'CH B'ULLHY.

AND YET...

...SOMETHING *NAGS* AT HIM.

THANK YOU VERY MUCH, GOVERNOR ES'SCA.

AND THEN HE *SEES* IT.

HE SPENT TWO DAYS MAKING SURE THAT THE STADIUM *ITSELF* WOULD BE SECURE.

IT NEVER *OCCURRED* TO WORF--NOR TO ANYONE *ELSE* TO SECURE THE AREA *OUTSIDE* THE STADIUM.

YES, I DO.

RA'CH B'ULLHY, DO YOU ACCEPT THE POSITION OF *GOVERNOR* OF THE *WORLD*, AS VOTED ON BY THE PEOPLE OF DAMIANO, AND ALL THE *RESPONSIBILITIES* INHERENT IN THAT POSITION?

UNFORTUNATELY, THE STAGE IS SURROUNDED BY *AMPLIFICATION SENSORS* THAT CARRY RA'CH AND ES'SCA'S WORDS TO THE ENTIRE *STADIUM*.

...WORF SPEAKS--WHETHER ...O ALERT HIS PEOPLE TO ...HE POSSIBLE *DANGER* ...R TO EXPLAIN TO DEANNA ...HY SHE SUDDENLY SENSES ...ENSION IN HIM--EVERYONE ...ILL HEAR.

THEN TAKE THIS *SWORD*, USED BY MAR'NA F'ULLHY TO DESTROY THE BARRIERS BETWEEN OUR CULTURES AND UNITE OUR WORLD, AS A TOKEN OF YOUR NEW *OFFICE*.

PERHAPS IT IS SIMPLY SOME *METAL FRAGMENT* IN THE TREE THAT GLINTED OFF THE *SUNLIGHT*.

THEN AGAIN...

WAIT.

I *ACCEPT* THIS HONOR, AND RELIEVE *YOU* OF THE RESPONSIBILITY.

...PERHAPS *NOT*.

THAT MAY WELL CAUSE A *PANIC*.

SNIPER!

WORF'S SHOT IS NOT *PRECISE*. IT ISN'T *MEANT* TO BE. ITS PRIMARY PURPOSE IS TO LET EVERYONE ELSE KNOW WHAT DIRECTION TO *FIRE* IN WHILE WORF HIMSELF MAKES SURE THAT RA'CH B'ULLHY *SURVIVES*.

THE RESPONSE IS *QUICK* AND *EFFICIENT*.

PRESENTS

KEITH R.A. DeCANDIDO — WRITER
PETER PACHOUMIS — PENCILLER
LUCIAN RIZZO — INKER
RYAN CLINE — LETTERER
WILDSTORM FX — COLORIST
JEFF MARIOTTE — EDITOR

BASED ON STAR TREK: THE NEXT GENERATION®
CREATED BY GENE RODENBERRY

STAR TREK: THE NEXT GENERATION®

PERCHANCE TO DREAM

CHAPTER 2

BY A SLEEP TO
SAY WE END

HO'NIG...

IS IT *DEAD*?

NO. WE SHOT TO *STUN*. THE PROTOCOL I REQUESTED DEACTIVATED THE WEAPON DURING TRANSPORT.

WORF TO TRANSPORTER ROOM--LOCK ONTO THE DAMIANI LIFE FORM LOCATED IN A TREE APPROXIMATELY FORTY METERS NORTHWEST OF MY POSITION. TRANSPORT TO MY LOCATION, SECURITY PROTOCOL 4.

AYE, AYE, SIR.

FOR HO'NIG'S SAKE, TURN OFF THE *AUDIO*, BEFORE--

NO!

GOVERNOR, PERHAPS IT WOULD BE BEST IF YOU *POSTPONED*--

NO, CAPTAIN.

I APPRECIATE YOUR *CONCERN*, BUT THIS ADMINISTRATION WILL *NOT* CAPITULATE TO *TERRORISM* NOR TO THE *RAVINGS* OF *OUTDATED* MORALITY.

THE VULCANS HAVE A PHILOSOPHY THAT HAS BECOME THE HALLMARK OF THE FEDERATION: *INFINITE DIVERSITY IN INFINITE COMBINATIONS.* THE FEDERATION ITSELF IS MADE UP OF HUNDREDS OF WORLDS, EACH WITH THEIR OWN CULTURAL MORES-- SOME WITH SEVERAL.

IF WE ARE TO CONTINUE AS MEMBERS OF THE FEDERATION, THEN WE CANNOT *DUCK AND RUN* EVERY TIME SOMEONE TRIES TO DRAG US *BACKWARD.*

INSTEAD, I WILL STAND HERE AND *COMPLETE* THE *OATH OF OFFICE,* KNOWING THAT I HAVE THE SUPPORT OF BOTH MY OWN PEOPLE AND OF THE FEDERATION BEHIND ME--

--AND WITH THOSE WHO WOULD OPPOSE ME SOLELY ON THE BASIS OF SUCH IRRELEVANT CRITERIA AS MY PERSONAL LIFE LYING AT MY FEET.

I DO *SWEAR* BY THE SWORD OF MAR'NA P'ULLHY, WHO *UNITED* OUR PEOPLE--

--AND BEFORE THE *EYES* OF HO'NIG, WHO SEE ALL--

--THAT I SHALL *SERVE* THE PEOPLE OF DAMIANO TO THE GREATEST OF MY *ABILITY*--

DAMN HER...

--FOR AS *LONG* AS I REMAIN IN OFFICE.

HO'NIG *WILLING*, PERVERT, THAT WON'T BE FOR VERY *LONG*.

IN LIGHT OF WHAT HAS JUST HAPPENED, I THINK IT WOULD BE WISE TO *FOREGO* THE TRADITIONAL *SPEECH* THAT FOLLOWS THE OATH-TAKING.

I'M SURE THAT *RELIEVES* MOST OF YOU.

I JUST WANT TO SAY *THANK YOU*, AND I HOPE TO SERVE YOU ALL WELL--

"--IN THE YEARS TO *COME*."

LOOK, I ALREADY *TOLD* THIS TO THE OFFICER THAT TOOK ME IN *AND* THE GUY WHO TALKED TO ME AFTER THAT.

THEN YOU OUGHT TO TELL *ME* PRETTY *EASILY*.

I HAVE *NOTHING* TO SAY.

INDEED? THAT IS A *PITY*. I HAD HOPED YOU WOULD TRY TO *EXPLAIN* YOUR ACTIONS.

WHAT'S TO *EXPLAIN?* RA'CH B'ULLHY IS A *SICK,* PERVERTED *INDIVIDUAL,* WHO SHOULDN'T BE ANYWHERE *NEAR* THE GOVERNOR'S OFFICE.

MY FRIENDS AND I CAME STRAIGHT FROM THE *SHOOTING RANGE.* TO'RIN MANAGED TO GET TICKETS, AND WE *COULDN'T* PASS UP THE *OPPORTUNITY.*

AND YOU DIDN'T THINK BRINGING *WEAPONS* IN WOULD DRAW ATTENTION?

IT DIDN'T *OCCUR* TO US THAT IT WOULD BE AN *ISSUE,* CHIEF.

HO'NIG, YOU DON'T THINK WE'D *SHOOT* ANYONE, DO YOU?

I *SEE.* AND YOU CAME TO THIS CONCLUSION ENTIRELY ON YOUR OWN, WITH NO *IMPETUS* FROM ANYONE ELSE?

I DON'T NEED ANYONE'S *HELP* TO KNOW WHAT NEEDS TO BE *DONE,* KLINGON.

THAT IS VERY *HONORABLE* OF YOU.

EXCUSE *ME?*

CAN I ASK YOU SOMETHING, KU'T?

DO I *LOOK* LIKE AN IDIOT? I MEAN, IT'S POSSIBLE. THAT WOULD EXPLAIN A LOT, REALLY.

I MEAN, YOU TAKE ONE GLANCE AT ME, AND YOU THINK TO YOURSELF, "SELF," YOU THINK, "THIS GUY'S AN *IDIOT*."

SACRIFICING YOURSELF TO *SAVE* YOUR COMMANDING OFFICER. I FIND THAT *ADMIRABLE.*

I DON'T *HAVE* A "COMMANDING OFFICER." I TOLD YOU, I WAS WORKING ALONE.

YOU *ALSO* TOLD ME YOU HAD NOTHING TO SAY.

NO MATTER. YOU WILL BE REMANDED TO A DAMIANO *JAIL--*

NO, I WON'T.

"I CAN GIVE THIS MORON SOME KIND OF STORY NO TWO-YEAR-OLD WOULD *BELIEVE* AND HE'LL LET ME *GO*."

"HE'S STUPID ENOUGH TO THINK THAT *SIX* PEOPLE--MOST OF WHOM ARE KNOWN *MORALISTS*--WALKING INTO THE INAUGURATION OF *RA'CH B'ULLHY ARMED* TO THE *TEETH* WERE JUST COMING FROM THE SHOOTING RANGE."

YOU *WON'T?*

WHERE YOU HAVE BEEN BEFORE, ON CHARGES OF *ASSAULTING* A FELLOW OFFICER.

YOU SHOULD STUDY DAMIANO LAW MORE THOROUGHLY, KLINGON. I'M RETIRED *MILITARY*. IF I'M TO BE INCARCERATED, IT'LL BE AT THE MILITARY PRISON AT BARLIIN.

THAT'S RIGHT.

SO TELL ME, KU'T, DO YOU THINK I'M *STUPID?*

I DON'T CARE *WHAT* YOU THINK, CHIEF. WHAT I TOLD YOU IS THE *TRUTH*.

RIGHT. SO THE *SIX* OF YOU ARE MORE THAN HAPPY TO FACE ALL THE CHARGES BY YOURSELVES?

NO, I'M NOT *HAPPY*, CHIEF. I MEAN, IT'S EMBARRASSING MORE THAN ANYTHING.

YES, BUT THAT WILL NOT BE UNTIL YOU HAVE BEEN *SENTENCED*. UNTIL YOUR TRIALS ARE COMPLETE, YOU WILL REMAIN IN *IARON'S* PRISON.

THE *SEWER?*

I BELIEVE THAT IS THE LOCAL NAME FOR IT.

WAIT A MINUTE, *"TRIALS?"*

YES. YOU SEE, THERE ARE *JURISDICTIONAL* ISSUES.

OH, IT'S GONNA BE A LOT MORE THAN *EMBARRASSING*. YOU EVER SPEND ANY TIME IN THE *SEWER*, KU'T?

THE *SEWER?*

BUT MAYBE WE CAN *AVOID* THAT. IF YOU TELL ME WHO PUT YOU UP TO THIS.

I *TOLD* YOU, NOBODY PUT US UP. WE CAME FROM THE SHOOTING RANGE.

YOU SHOT AT A *STARFLEET* CAPTAIN AND SEVERAL STARFLEET *OFFICERS*. THE JUDGE ADVOCATE GENERAL HAS BEEN INFORMED, AND WILL BE ARRIVING AT DAMIANO WITHIN THE *MONTH* TO LOOK INTO WHETHER OR NOT YOU WILL BE BROUGHT UP ON *CHARGES* BY STARFLEET.

MONTH?

PERHAPS *TWO*. PLUS THERE ARE THE *KLINGONS*.

WHAT!?

YEAH, AS'SI'S A *TOUGH* ONE. I PULLED ITS MILITARY RECORD.

IT'LL GO TO ITS *DEATH* BEFORE GIVING IN.

SO WE'RE LEFT WITH *NOTHING*.

YOU *SURVIVED* THE INAUGURATION AND *CAPTURED* SEVEN POTENTIAL ASSASSINS, GOVERNOR. I WOULDN'T CALL *THAT* NOTHING.

TRUE, COMMANDER--

--BUT I SUSPECT THAT MY *TROUBLES* ARE FAR FROM *OVER*.

DAMN THAT KLINGON! IF IT WASN'T FOR HIM--

FORGET HIM, JE'TRAN. MAYBE *FORGET* THIS WHOLE *THING*.

FORGET IT? ARE YOU *INSANE*?

WE HAVE TO GET HER *NOW*, WHEN SHE THINKS SHE'S *SAFE*.

FOR HO'NIG'S SAKE, HAVE YOU BEEN WATCHING THE *NEWS*? WE'RE BEING MADE TO LOOK LIKE *IMBECILES*.

THEY'RE CALLING US THE "*MORALIST MORONS*" THAT MADE A *MOCKERY* OF THE INAUGURATION. CHIEF DU'RE AND THE *ENTERPRISE* CREW ARE BEING HAILED AS *HEROES*.

MIK'KA'S RIGHT.

WHAT!? JE'TRAN, YOU CAN'T BE *SERIOUS*!

THE OPINIONS OF THE MORAL *DEGENERATES* OF THE PRESS ARE OF VERY LITTLE *INTEREST* TO ME, HA'RT. NOTHING'S *CHANGED*.

EVERYTHING'S CHANGED! THEY'VE GOT KU'T, AS'SI, AND THE OTHERS IN CUSTODY! ANY *MINUTE* NOW, DU'RE'S *GOONS* COULD COME IN AND--

THAT WON'T HAPPEN.

NONE OF THEM GAVE ANYTHING UP. THEY'RE TAKING THE *FALL*.

OF COURSE.

THEY UNDERSTAND WHAT'S AT *STAKE.* THE FACT THAT WE MIGHT LOOK *FOOLISH* IS OF NO *CONSEQUENCE.* WE'RE TALKING ABOUT THE *MORAL FIBER* OF OUR ENTIRE *RACE.*

WHAT WE NEED TO DO IS TO *STOP* THE KLINGON AND HIS PEOPLE FROM *INTERFERING.* AND I HAVE A WAY TO DO THAT.

WE'LL USE THE *CHOVA.*

HO'NIG, NO...

WHAT'S A CHOVA?

JE'TRAN, YOU CAN'T *POSSIBLY* BE SERIOUS!

IT'S THE BEST WAY TO GET STARFLEET OFF OUR BACKS--

WHAT'S A CHOVA?

--AND GET *REVENGE* ON THEM AT THE SAME TIME.

FOR HO'NIG'S SAKE, *WHAT'S* A CHOVA?

IT'S A *WEAPON*--

IT'S AN *ABOMINATION.*

A *WEAPON* THAT WAS DEVELOPED DURING PAD'GY D'ULLH'S REIGN OF TERROR. PAD'GY HAD TELEPATHS GENETICALLY ENGINEERED, CALLED THE HED'EM'DISOL.

AFTER INSTITUTING THE HED'EM'DISOL, HE UNLEASHED THE CHOVA-- A PURELY *TELEPATHIC* WEAPON THAT HAS NO *PHYSICAL* PRESENCE.

THE HED'EM'DISOL WOULD HAVE THE CHOVA INSERTED DIRECTLY INTO THEIR *MINDS,* AND THEY WOULD TELEPATHICALLY *ATTACK* SOMEONE WITH IT. THE CHOVA PROMPTS *DREAMS* AT FIRST, THEN WAKING *HALLUCINATIONS*--ALL OF A PERSON'S PERCEIVED *FAILURES.* EVENTUALLY, IT DRIVES THEM *MAD.*

THE WEAPON WAS *LOST* AFTER PAD'GY WAS OVERTHROWN, BUT I'VE MANAGED TO *RECONSTRUCT* IT. ONCE THE CHOVA SPREADS AROUND THE *ENTERPRISE,* THEY'LL BE HELPLESS, AND WE CAN FOCUS ON *KILLING* THE PERVERT.

BUT THERE AREN'T ANY MORE HED'EM'DISOL. DIDN'T ALL THE TELEPATHS DIE OUT?

WE DON'T NEED A *DAMIANI* TELEPATH. THEY'VE GOT AT LEAST ONE ON THE *ENTERPRISE.* T'MOR, THE *VULCAN* THAT NAILED KU'T.

PERFECT. VULCANS'RE ONLY TOUCH-TELEPATHS, BUT THAT SHOULD STILL DO THE TRICK.

SHE AND I ARE ON GUARD DETAIL FOR THE MINISTERS' MEETING THIS AFTERNOON. WE GOT ROOF DUTY.

GOOD.

"CAN YOU GET HER AWAY FOR FIFTEEN MINUTES?"

"I DON'T THINK SO," GO'EN SAYS.

"OUR WINDOW BETWEEN SIGNALS TO THE SIDEWALK TEAM IS *SEVEN* MINUTES. I MIGHT BE ABLE TO STRETCH IT TO *TEN*, BUT NO *MORE* THAN THAT."

"FINE," SAYS JE'TRAN. "I'LL GIVE YOU A HYPO WITH A *SEDATIVE*. USE IT ON HER AND BRING HER TO THE STAIRWELL ON THE ROOF."

"I'VE MODIFIED A *DREAM RECORDER* THAT CAN PLACE THE CHOVA INTO HER MIND. IT'LL ALSO REMOVE ANY *MEMORY* OF WHAT HAPPENED TO HER."

"WAIT A MINUTE," HA'RT INTERRUPTS, "YOU *ALREADY* HAD A DREAM RECORDER MODIFIED? HOW LONG HAVE YOU HAD THIS—THIS *THING* LYING AROUND?"

"A FEW YEARS NOW," JE'TRAN SAYS SLOWLY.

"FOR HO'NIG'S SAKE, *WHY?*" HA'RT ASKS.

JE'TRAN'S RESPONSE IS SAID WITH A *COLDNESS* THAT CHILLS HA'RT TO HER VERY SOUL:

"IN CASE I NEEDED IT SOME DAY."

WHAT DO YOU MEAN WHAT HAPPENED? YOU *TRIPPED*.

YES. YES, OF COURSE. MY APOLOGIES, OFFICER.

NO NEED, ENSIGN—

I *DID* TRY TO WARN YOU ABOUT THESE ROOFS, ENSIGN. IT'S REAL EASY TO TRIP AND FALL.

WHAT *HAPPENED?*

I BEG YOUR PARDON? I—

"--HAPPENS ALL THE TIME ON THESE ROOFS. IT'S NO BIG DEAL."

THE *MOK'BARA*: AN ANCIENT KLINGON ART THAT HONES THE MIND AND BODY.

WORF GIVES A CLASS EVERY DAY. TODAY'S CLASS IS *DIFFERENT*, THOUGH.

ENSIGN T'MOR IS ELIGIBLE TO BECOME *GHOJMOHWI'* A TEACHER.

BUT FIRST, SHE MUST PASS THE *TEST*.

YOU DO NOT *PASS* THE TEST IF YOU ARE THE *FIRST* TO FALL.

IN ORDER FOR THAT FALL TO *HAPPEN*, HOWEVER, SOMEONE MUST MAKE THE FIRST *MOVE*.

T'MOR AND WORF HAVE STOOD STILL FOR OVER AN *HOUR*...

...EACH WAITING FOR THE *OTHER* TO MAKE THAT MOVE.

UH, COMMANDER? HOW *LONG* CAN THEY *STAND* THERE?

I THINK THE RECORD IS *TWO DAYS*, ENSIGN.

YOU'RE KIDDING...

WELL C'MON, HOUARNER, DON'T JUST STAND THERE WITH YOUR MOUTH HANGING OPEN. HOW LONG DID HE SAY?

HE SAID THE RECORD IS TWO DAYS.

THEY WON'T TAKE *THAT* LONG, WILL THEY?

DAMNED IF I KNOW...

WHO DO YOU THINK WILL GIVE IN FIRST?

I'M NOT SURE. NORMALLY I'D FIGURE WORF TO BE THE FIRST TO GIVE IN. T'MOR'S A VULCAN, AFTER ALL.

BUT I'M SENSING TREMENDOUS *CALM* FROM WORF--

--AND UNCHARACTERISTIC *TURMOIL* FROM T'MOR.

TURMOIL?

WELL, BY VULCAN STANDARDS, ANYHOW. IF SHE WERE *HUMAN*, I'D SAY SHE WAS PRETERNATURALLY CALM.

BUT SHE'S *NOT* HUMAN.

"—WE'LL GO TO TEN-FORWARD LATER."

ONLY *US*, DATA. ONLY US.

I AM NOT SURE WHAT YOU *MEAN*, GEORDI.

MOST PEOPLE GO TO INAUGURATIONS AND SIT *UNCOMFORTABLY* IN THEIR SEATS WHILE SUFFERING THROUGH A BORING, CLICHÉD *SPEECH*.

BUT NOT US. NO, THE CREW OF THE *STARSHIP ENTERPRISE* DOESN'T *DO* BORING. WE GET *SHOT* AT. GOTTA LOVE IT.

I TAKE IT YOU ARE BEING *SARCASTIC*.

GOOD GUESS.

SO IS THE DINNER TONIGHT *FORMAL*?

SINCE CAPTAIN PICARD AND COMMANDER RIKER HAVE ALWAYS SPECIFIED WHEN FORMAL DRESS IS REQUIRED, AND SINCE NO SUCH SPECIFICATION WAS MADE, I WOULD HAVE TO DEDUCE THAT, AS WITH THE INAUGURATION, REGULAR UNIFORMS WILL SUFFICE.

GOOD.

I CAN DODGE UNDER THE TABLE MORE *EASILY* IN MY REGULAR UNIFORM.

SO, DID YOU TALK TO DEANNA ABOUT YOUR *DREAM*?

BRIEFLY.

WE AGREED TO HAVE A FORMAL SESSION ON THE SUBJECT AFTER THE INAUGURATION ON DAMIANO IS COMPLETE.

MAKES SENSE. AFTER ALL—

WORF HASN'T THOUGHT ABOUT THE INCIDENT WITH MIKEL IN A LONG TIME.

TONIGHT IS GOVERNOR RA'CH'S INAUGURAL DINNER.

ORIGINALLY, *DISCRETION* WAS REQUESTED, BUT IN LIGHT OF THE *SNIPER* ATTACK--

MIKEL HAD *INDEED* DIED THE FOLLOWING DAY, TEACHING WORF A *VALUABLE* LESSON.

--THE DAMIANI HAVE AGREED TO MORE *OVERT* SECURITY.

HE LEARNED HOW IMPORTANT IT WAS FOR HIM TO MAINTAIN *CONTROL*.

THERE ARE THREE ENTRANCES TO THE DINING HALL. WONG, MURPHY, MEL, YOU WILL TAKE THOSE.

LINCOLN, T'MOR, ADDISON, YOU WILL REMAIN ON GUARD IN THE KITCHEN. MAKE SURE ALL FOOD IS THOROUGHLY *SCANNED*.

HUMANS *WERE* FRAGILE CREATURES.

STILL, IT HAS BEEN A LONG TIME SINCE WORF DREAMT ABOUT MIKEL--AND THE DREAM HAS NEVER BEEN SO *VIVID* BEFORE.

THE OUTSIDE OF THE BUILDING WILL BE GUARDED BY HOUARNER, BENESCH, AND POST.

HASELL, YOU WILL GUARD THE ROOF. LINZNER AND HOROWITZ WILL SERVE AS ROVING INTERIOR PATROLS, COMBING THE BUILDING AND CHECKING IN WITH ALL OTHERS.

I WILL BE BY THE GOVERNOR'S SIDE AT ALL TIMES.

QUESTIONS?

THEN HE *SEES* IT.

YES, SIR. WHAT ABOUT THE DAMIANO POLICE? WILL WE BE PAIRED UP WITH THEM AGAIN?

WORF WONDERS WHY HIS SUBCONSCIOUS CHOSE TO DREDGE THE MEMORY UP NOW.

HE RESOLVES TO SPEAK TO DEANNA ABOUT IT WHEN THE CRISIS IS OVER.

NO.

THIS IS *IMPOSSIBLE*.

MARLA ASTER *DIED* FIVE YEARS AGO.

SIR?

SHE DIED WHILE SERVING ON AN *AWAY TEAM* WORF COMMANDED.

LIEUTENANT?

BUT HE MADE *PEACE* WITH HER DEATH YEARS AGO. WHY IS HE BEING *HAUNTED* BY HER SHADE NOW?

LIEUTENANT WORF, ARE YOU ALL RIGHT?

I AM FINE.

YOU SURE? YOU--

I SAID I WAS *FINE*, ENSIGN HOROWITZ!

TO ANSWER YOUR QUESTION, CHIEF DU'RE'S OFFICERS WILL SERVE AS THE STAFF FOR THE DINNER, AND ALSO SERVE AS ROVING PATROLS TO BOLSTER YOU AND ENSIGN LINZNER.

--YOU ARE DISMISSED.

FIRST THE DREAM ABOUT MIKEL, NOW THIS.

DREAMS ARE ONE THING, BUT TO SEE SUCH VIVID *HALLUCINATIONS*...

PERHAPS HE NEEDS TO TALK TO DEANNA *SOONER* THAN HE THOUGHT.

IF THERE ARE NO OTHER QUESTIONS--

I HAVE SENSED A CERTAIN AMOUNT OF *TURMOIL* IN YOU.

AND YOU DID NOT *CONFRONT* ME WITH IT?

PROBABLY NOT.

IN FACT, YOU WOULD HAVE TOLD ME NOT TO *PRY* INTO YOUR *PERSONAL* LIFE--

EVEN THOUGH, AS BOTH SHIP'S COUNSELOR AND AS YOUR *PAR'MACHKAI*, I HAVE *EVERY* REASON TO DO SO.

WOULD IT HAVE DONE ANY *GOOD* IF I *HAD*?

TRUE.

SOMETIMES MEMORIES ARE TRIGGERED BY SOUNDS, SIGHTS, SMELLS--PERHAPS SOMETHING ON DAMIANO?

THAT WOULD NOT EXPLAIN HALLUCINATING LIEUTENANT ASTER.

NO, IT WOULDN'T. BUT THE *STRESS* OF THE *NIGHTMARE* MIGHT HAVE LED TO THE WAKING HALLUCINATION.

MY RECOMMENDATION WOULD BE TO TAKE A *SEDATIVE* BEFORE GOING TO SLEEP TONIGHT. THAT SHOULD TAKE CARE OF THE NIGHTMARES, AND PERHAPS ALSO THE *HALLUCINATING*.

VERY WELL.

THANK YOU, DEANNA.

ANY TIME, WORF.

"I COULD *USE* A NICE DINNER."

IT IS TAKING ALL OF OFFICER GO'EN C'ULLHO'S WILLPOWER TO *RESTRAIN* ITSELF RIGHT NOW.

IT'S NEVER BEEN THIS *CLOSE* TO RA'CH B'ULLHY BEFORE, AND IT FINDS BEING SO--AND HER--TO BE *REPUGNANT.*

IF NOT FOR THE *KLINGON,* IT COULD *END* THIS ALL RIGHT NOW.

BUT THE KLINGON BROUGHT AS'SI K'ULLHO DOWN. GO'EN WOULDN'T STAND A *CHANCE.*

WHAT IS--?

AND THEN SOMETHING *HAPPENS.*

ARRRRH!

LIEUTENANT!

GO'EN HAS NO *IDEA* WHY THE KLINGON HAS *COLLAPSED.*

BUT IT HAS EVERY INTENTION OF TAKING ADVANTAGE OF THE *OPPORTUNITY.*

DIE, PERVERT!

"I'M SURE WORF WILL MAKE SURE THE EVENING GOES SMOOTHLY."

RIGHT NOW, AS HE AND A CADRE OF DAMIANI POLICE OFFICERS ESCORT GOVERNOR RA'CH B'ULLHY TO THE INAUGURAL DINNER, LIEUTENANT WORF IMAGINES HIMSELF READY FOR *ANYTHING*.

WHAT IS --?

HE IMAGINES *WRONG*.

LIEUTENANT!

ARRRRH!

TWO YEARS AGO, A FAULTY CANISTER IN A CARGO BAY COLLAPSED ON WORF, RESULTING IN A BRUTAL SPINAL INJURY. ONLY AN UNPRECEDENTED MEDICAL PROCEDURE ALLOWED HIM TO WALK AGAIN.

SUCH A CANISTER CANNOT *POSSIBLY* BE IN THIS CORRIDOR IN DAMIANO'S CAPITAL CITY NOW.

YET SOMEHOW, IT HAS HAPPENED. WORF FEELS THE SAME SPINE-CRUSHING AGONY HE FELT THEN.

BUT HE KNOWS THAT THIS IS NOT REAL. AND HE HAS A DUTY TO PERFORM.

DIE, PERVERT!

AND HE ALMOST PASSES OUT FROM THE PAIN, AS HE DID THEN.

IF WORF COULD FOCUS THROUGH THE PAIN, HE WOULD REALIZE THAT OFFICER GO'EN C'ULLHO MUST BE ONE OF THE MORALISTS WHO HAS THREATENED GOVERNOR RA'CH, AND WHO WOULD HAVE SUCCEEDED IN ASSASSINATING HER IF NOT FOR WORF'S OWN SECURITY MEASURES.

BUT FOR NOW, HE HAS NO IDEA WHY GO'EN IS TRYING TO KILL RA'CH.

Paramount COMICS™

PRESENTS

KEITH R.A. DeCANDIDO	WRITER
PETER PACHOUMIS	PENCILLER
LUCIAN RIZZO	INKER
ROBBIE ROBBINS	LETTERER
WILDSTORM FX	COLORIST
JEFF MARIOTTE	EDITOR

BASED ON STAR TREK: THE NEXT GENERATION®
CREATED BY GENE RODENBERRY

STAR TREK: THE NEXT GENERATION®

PERCHANCE TO DREAM
CHAPTER 3

IN THE SLEEP OF DEATH, WHAT DREAMS MAY COME

"-- FOR WHATEVER IT IS THAT AILS YOU."

YOU SEE HER DIE, OVER AND OVER.

K'EHLEYR!

YOU WATCH DURAS PLUNGE HIS SWORD INTO HER, EVEN THOUGH YOU DID NOT ARRIVE UNTIL LONG AFTER THE TRAITOR DID THE DEED.

YOU OBSERVE YOUR FIGHT WITH DURAS TO AVENGE HER DEATH, USING YOUR FAMILY'S *BAT'LETH* AGAINST THE VERY SWORD YOU IMAGINE HE KILLED HER WITH.

YOU HAVE NO *RIGHTS* HERE, TRAITOR!

WORF!

AND NO MATTER HOW MANY TIMES YOU KILL HIM --

K'EHLEYR IS STILL DEAD.

BECAUSE YOU FAILED HER.

FAILED HER.

FAILED HER.

K'EHLEYR!

HE HAD TAKEN THE SEDATIVE.

ACCORDING TO NURSE OGAWA, IT CONTAINED A DREAM SUPPRESSANT.

HE SHOULD NOT HAVE HAD THAT NIGHTMARE.

NOR SHOULD HE BE SEEING WHAT HE SEES NOW.

HE IS A WARRIOR, BUT HE CANNOT FIGHT *PHANTOMS*.

QO'...

AND HE CANNOT IMAGINE WHY THESE SHADES ARE HAUNTING HIM NOW.

GYARRRRRH!

I THINK WE NEED TO TRY --

HELP ME!

BEVERLY, WHAT THE HELL IS *HAPPENING* TO MY *CREW?*

I WISH I *KNEW*, JEAN-LUC.

MEDICALLY, THERE ISN'T *ANYTHING* WRONG WITH THEM.

WELL, THAT'S NOT ENTIRELY, TRUE. WORF AND SOME OF THE OTHERS ARE SUFFERING FROM SLEEP DEPRIVATION, BUT THAT'S A SIDE EFFECT.

MIGHT IT BE SOMETHING ON DAMIANO?

POSSIBLY.

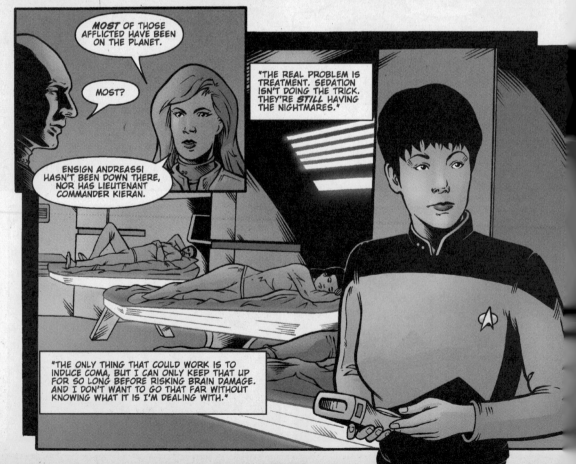

MOST OF THOSE AFFLICTED HAVE BEEN ON THE PLANET.

MOST?

ENSIGN ANDREASSI HASN'T BEEN DOWN THERE, NOR HAS LIEUTENANT COMMANDER KIERAN.

"THE REAL PROBLEM IS TREATMENT. SEDATION ISN'T DOING THE TRICK. THEY'RE *STILL* HAVING THE NIGHTMARES."

"THE ONLY THING THAT COULD WORK IS TO INDUCE COMA, BUT I CAN ONLY KEEP THAT UP FOR SO LONG BEFORE RISKING BRAIN DAMAGE. AND I DON'T WANT TO GO THAT FAR WITHOUT KNOWING WHAT IT IS I'M DEALING WITH."

"THE CHOVA IS A TELEPATHIC WEAPON USED DURING PAD'GY D'ULLH'S REIGN OF TERROR, ONE OF THE *NASTIER* PERIODS IN OUR HISTORY."

"PAD'GY HAD TELEPATHS GENETICALLY ENGINEERED AND THEN GAVE THEM THE CHOVA. IT DOESN'T HAVE ANY *PHYSICAL* FORM, BUT IT CAN BE INSERTED BY A TELEPATH INTO SOMEONE ELSE'S *MIND*. FIRST THE VICTIM SUFFERS NIGHTMARES, THEN HALLUCINATIONS -- JUST THE WAY *YOUR* PEOPLE HAVE BEEN."

EVENTUALLY, THEY GO *MAD*.

WHAT IS THE *CURE*?

THAT'S THE PROBLEM, WE DON'T *KNOW*.

THERE ARE VERY FEW COMPUTER RECORDS FROM PAD'GY'S TIME, CAPTAIN, AND *NO* RECORD OF THE CHOVA. WE'VE ALREADY CHECKED. WHAT WE DO KNOW OF IT IS PURELY FROM LEGEND AT THIS POINT. FRANKLY, I'M AMAZED ANYONE WAS ABLE TO RE-CREATE IT.

WHO WOULD REVIVE SUCH AN AWFUL WEAPON?

THE SAME PEOPLE WHO'D TRY TO SHOOT, BLOW UP, AND DISINTEGRATE A GOVERNOR -- JE'TRAN T'ULLH AND HIS MORALIST MORONS.

HAVE YOU BEEN ABLE TO LINK TODAY'S ASSASSINATION ATTEMPT TO THESE MORALISTS?

NOT AS SUCH.

WE TRACKED DOWN THE ONES WHO GIMMICKED THE SHOWER, AND THEY GAVE UP THE PERSON WHO HIRED THEM PRETTY QUICKLY.

BUT THE ONE WHO HIRED THEM WAS ANOTHER FANATIC LIKE GO'EN AND THE GUYS WE NAILED AT THE INAUGURATION. HE WOULDN'T TALK FOR ANYTHING.

WE CAN ONLY HOPE THAT JE'TRAN IS RUNNING OUT OF SUPPORTERS.

WHAT LITTLE POPULAR SUPPORT HE HAD IS *DWINDLING* WITH EACH ATTEMPT --

-- WHICH IS JUST ABOUT MY ONLY *COMFORT* RIGHT NOW.

HIS SHOW AIRS TONIGHT. THE FIRST ONE SINCE THE INAUGURATION.

"CAPTAIN'S LOG, STARDATE 48503.1. CHIEF DU'RE HAS TRANSPORTED TO THE *ENTERPRISE* IN ORDER TO TRY TO DETERMINE *HOW* THE CHOVA HAS BEEN BROUGHT ON BOARD."

"NORMALLY, I WOULD ASSIGN LIEUTENANT WORF OR SOMEONE ELSE FROM SECURITY TO AID IT, BUT WITH THE SECURITY STAFF DEPLETED BY THE CHOVA, I HAVE GIVEN LIEUTENANT COMMANDER DATA THE ASSIGNMENT."

THERE ARE CURRENTLY FOURTEEN TELEPATHS SERVING ON THE *ENTERPRISE*. HOWEVER, ONLY TWO OF THEM HAVE BEEN ON DAMIANO: COUNSELOR TROI AND ENSIGN T'MOR.

THEY ARE ALSO THE ONLY ONES AMONG THE FOURTEEN WHO ARE CURRENTLY AFFLICTED WITH THE NIGHTMARES AND HALLUCINATIONS THAT ARE INDICATIVE OF THE USE OF THE CHOVA.

IN ADDITION, BETWEEN THEM, COUNSELOR TROI AND ENSIGN T'MOR HAVE COME INTO CLOSE CONTACT WITH ALL THOSE CURRENTLY CHECKED INTO SICKBAY.

MOST HAVE BEEN ON DAMIANO DURING THE INAUGURAL FESTIVITIES.

WEREN'T THERE TWO WHO HAVEN'T BEEN ON-PLANET?

YES, BUT ENSIGN ANDREASSI IS ENSIGN T'MOR'S ROOMMATE. AND LIEUTENANT COMMANDER KIERAN HAD A SESSION WITH COUNSELOR TROI YESTERDAY.

IF, AS YOU HAVE SPECULATED, THE CHOVA CAN BE TRANSMITTED BY A *TELEPATH*, THAT WOULD EXPAIN HOW IT HAS BEEN SPREAD ACROSS THE *ENTERPRISE* --

--ALTHOUGH COUNSELOR TROI IS ONLY A RECEIVING EMPATH. SHE HAS ONLY BEEN KNOWN TO DIRECTLY COMMUNICATE TELEPATHICALLY WITH FULL BETAZOIDS. IT IS *ODD* THAT SHE WOULD BE ABLE TO TRANSMIT THE CHOVA.

MY PEOPLE ARE STILL TRYING TO FIND SOME KIND OF RECORD THAT WOULD *CONFIRM* IT. AND BESIDES, TROI SPREADING IT AROUND FITS THE AVAILABLE FACTS.

COMMANDER, MIND IF I ASK A PERSONAL QUESTION?

YOU EVER CONSIDERED GOING INTO *POLICE* WORK?

THAT IS NOT A CAREER CHOICE I HAVE CONTEMPLATED.

NOT AT ALL.

PITY. I'D *KILL* FOR SOMEONE LIKE *YOU* ON THE FORCE.

OH, WELL. LET'S GET DOWN TO SICKBAY...

WHAT THE --?

IT'S OKAY, CHIEF. IT'S A VULCAN THING. SHE'LL COME OUT OF IT IN A MOMENT.

MY APOLOGIES, DOCTOR, BUT IT APPEARS THAT I AM THE INDIRECT CAUSE OF ALL THIS.

OFFICER GO'EN SURPRISED ME WITH A HYPOSPRAY, AFTER WHICH --

JE'TRAN AND SOME OTHER GUY PUT SOME KIND OF DEVICE ON HER FOREHEAD.

IT WAS JE'TRAN *HIMSELF*?

OH YEAH.

THANK HO'NIG HE PICKED ON A VULCAN FOR THIS. SHE GAVE US A COMPUTER RENDERING OF THE PERSON SHE SAW, AND IT'S A DEAD-ON MATCH FOR JE'TRAN, AND SHE SAID SHE'S WILLING TO TESTIFY AGAINST HIM.

YOU DON'T GET A MORE IDEAL WITNESS THAN A VULCAN, ESPECIALLY ONE WHO'S ALSO A *STARFLEET* OFFICER.

I'VE BEEN WAITING *YEARS* FOR HIM TO DO SOMETHING STUPID LIKE THIS. IT'S THE FIRST SOLID EVIDENCE I'VE HAD AGAINST HIM, AND I FULLY INTEND TO USE IT.

UNFORTUNATELY, THIS DOESN'T BRING US ANY CLOSER TO A CURE.

BRIDGE TO CAPTAIN.

PICARD HERE.

CAPTAIN, WE HAVE A MESSAGE FROM THE PLANET. THEY'VE FOUND *RECORDS* OF THE CHOVA AND ARE BEAMING THEM UP NOW.

ALSO THE OFFICER ALSO SAID, "I HOPE SOMEONE CAN READ OLD *ILLYAN*."

I AM *FLUENT* IN THAT LANGUAGE. I WILL BE HAPPY TO TRANSLATE THE FILES.

FIGURES. YOU SURE YOU WON'T *RECONSIDER* MY OFFER, COMMANDER?

MAKE IT *SO*, MR. DATA.

"CHIEF MEDICAL OFFICER'S LOG, STARDATE 48503.8. LIEUTENANT COMMANDER DATA, DOCTOR SELAR, AND I HAVE GONE THROUGH THE DAMIANO RECORDS REGARDING THE CHOVA. WHILE NO DIRECT WAY TO COMBAT THE WEAPON WAS EVER DEVELOPED WE HAVE DISCOVERED THAT CERTAIN *PEOPLE* WERE *IMMUNE* TO THE CHOVA'S EFFECTS AND COULD *DESTROY* THE WEAPON."

THERE *HAS* TO BE ANOTHER WAY.

I BELIEVE DOCTOR SELAR IS CORRECT. THIS IS THE *ONLY* COURSE OF ACTION OPEN TO US UNDER THE CIRCUMSTANCES.

WE HAVE BEEN OVER THE RECORDS SIX TIMES APIECE, DOCTOR. IF THERE IS ANYTHING TO FIND, IT IS LIKELY THAT WE WOULD HAVE FOUND IT BY NOW.

I KNOW, I KNOW, IT'S JUST --

IT COULD *KILL* HIM.

YOU *SENT* FOR ME, DOCTOR?

YES, JEAN-LUC, PLEASE SIT DOWN.

WE'VE GONE THROUGH THE RECORDS CHIEF DU'RE PROVIDED. IT TURNS OUT THAT THERE WAS ONE GROUP OF PEOPLE WHO WERE IMMUNE TO THE CHOVA WHEN IT FIRST WAS USED.

MPD'S.

MPD STANDS FOR MULTIPLE PERSONALITY DISORDER. MPD CAN COME ABOUT THROUGH PSYCHOLO --

MPD'S?

NOT NOW, DATA.

THE POINT IS THAT PEOPLE WHO ARE AFFLICTED WITH MORE THAN ONE PERSONALITY WOULD DESTROY THE CHOVA BEFORE IT COULD AFFECT THEM. THE CHOVA WAS ONLY BUILT FOR ONE PERSONALITY. MPDS WOULD LITERALLY OVERWHELM IT.

WELL, MPD WAS NEVER A COMMON OCCURRENCE, AND IT'S ALMOST UNHEARD OF THESE DAYS. THERE'VE ONLY BEEN TWO CASES REPORTED IN THE FEDERATION IN THE LAST TWO HUNDRED YEARS -- AND DAMIANO HASN'T HAD A CASE IN THE LAST FIFTY.

HOWEVER, WE DO HAVE SOMEONE ON THE ENTERPRISE WHO HAS THE MAKINGS OF A CLASSIC MPD. I'D LIKE YOUR PERMISSION TO ASK THIS PERSON TO VOLUNTEER TO UNDERGO A MIND-MELD WITH DOCTOR SELAR IN ORDER TO BRING THE SUBMERGED PERSONALITIES TO THE FORE.

PERMISSION GRANTED, AS LONG AS IT REMAINS ON A **VOLUNTEER** BASIS.

HOW DOES THIS HELP US?

WHO IS THE OFFICER IN **QUESTION**?

IT'S SOMEONE WHO'S BEEN EXPOSED TO AN ESPECIALLY INTENSE VULCAN **MIND-MELD**, WHO LIVED ANOTHER LIFE FOR THIRTY-FIVE SUBJECTIVE YEARS --

AND WHO HAD A SECOND PERSONALITY GRAFTED ONTO HIS OWN FOR A BRIEF PERIOD BY THE **BORG**.

SAREK OF VULCAN. PICARD MIND-MELDED WITH THE LEGENDARY AMBASSADOR IN ORDER TO LEND HIM STRENGTH FOR AN IMPORTANT NEGOTIATION -- AN ACT THAT ALMOST COST PICARD HIS SANITY.

KAMIN OF KATAAN. A PROBE SENT OUT BY KATAAN BEFORE THEIR SUN WENT NOVA ALLOWED PICARD TO LIVE MOST OF KAMIN'S ADULT LIFE AS A WAY TO REMEMBER HIS PEOPLE.

LOCUTUS OF BORG. QUITE SIMPLY, THE GREATEST *NIGHTMARE* OF PICARD'S ENTIRE LIFE, THE SUBVERSION OF HIS INTELLECT, HIS WILL, HIS VERY SELF TO THE COLLECTIVE OF THE BORG.

ALL THREE ARE PART OF HIM, BUT THEY DO NOT *DOMINATE.* IF PICARD DOES AS DOCTOR CRUSHER SUGGESTS, HE WILL SUBSUME HIMSELF IN ORDER TO LET THE OTHERS COME TO THE FORE. FOR SAREK, FOR KAMIN, HE WOULD BE *WILLING.*

BUT *LOCUTUS* --?

THEN HE THINKS OF HIS FIRST OFFICER, COUNSELOR, CHIEF OF SECURITY, CHIEF ENGINEER, AND ALL THE OTHERS WHO HAVE FALLEN VICTIM TO THIS VICIOUS WEAPON.

AND JEAN-LUC PICARD MAKES THE *ONLY* DECISION HE IS TRULY CAPABLE OF MAKING.

WHAT DO I NEED TO *DO*?

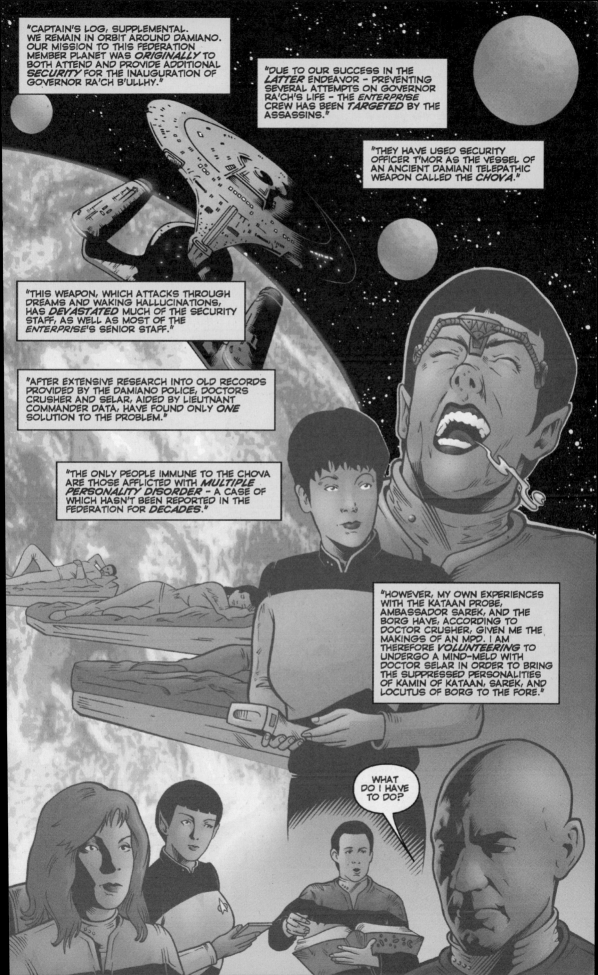

"CAPTAIN'S LOG, SUPPLEMENTAL. WE REMAIN IN ORBIT AROUND DAMIANO. OUR MISSION TO THIS FEDERATION MEMBER PLANET WAS *ORIGINALLY* TO BOTH ATTEND AND PROVIDE ADDITIONAL *SECURITY* FOR THE INAUGURATION OF GOVERNOR RA'CH B'ULLHY."

"DUE TO OUR SUCCESS IN THE *LATTER* ENDEAVOR - PREVENTING SEVERAL ATTEMPTS ON GOVERNOR RA'CH'S LIFE - THE *ENTERPRISE* CREW HAS BEEN *TARGETED* BY THE ASSASSINS."

"THEY HAVE USED SECURITY OFFICER T'MOR AS THE VESSEL OF AN ANCIENT DAMIANI TELEPATHIC WEAPON CALLED THE *CHOVA*."

"THIS WEAPON, WHICH ATTACKS THROUGH DREAMS AND WAKING HALLUCINATIONS, HAS *DEVASTATED* MUCH OF THE SECURITY STAFF, AS WELL AS MOST OF THE *ENTERPRISE'S* SENIOR STAFF."

"AFTER EXTENSIVE RESEARCH INTO OLD RECORDS PROVIDED BY THE DAMIANO POLICE, DOCTORS CRUSHER AND SELAR, AIDED BY LIEUTNANT COMMANDER DATA, HAVE FOUND ONLY *ONE* SOLUTION TO THE PROBLEM."

"THE ONLY PEOPLE IMMUNE TO THE CHOVA ARE THOSE AFFLICTED WITH *MULTIPLE PERSONALITY DISORDER* - A CASE OF WHICH HASN'T BEEN REPORTED IN THE FEDERATION FOR *DECADES*."

"HOWEVER, MY OWN EXPERIENCES WITH THE KATAAN PROBE, AMBASSADOR SAREK, AND THE BORG HAVE, ACCORDING TO DOCTOR CRUSHER, GIVEN ME THE MAKINGS OF AN MPD. I AM THEREFORE *VOLUNTEERING* TO UNDERGO A MIND-MELD WITH DOCTOR SELAR IN ORDER TO BRING THE SUPPRESSED PERSONALITIES OF KAMIN OF KATAAN, SAREK, AND LOCUTUS OF BORG TO THE FORE."

WHAT DO I HAVE TO DO?

DATA, I NEED YOU —

DATA?

DATA!

DATA, GET *BACK* HERE! THAT'S AN *ORDER!*

OOOF!

DATA!

DATA, *STOP!*

DATA?

T'MOR MUST HAVE HIT HIM WITH THE CHOVA.

BUT HE SHOULD BE *IMMUNE.* DATA IS *IMPERVIOUS* TO TELEPATHS.

WONDERFUL, THAT'S ALL WE NEED.

THE CHOVA FIRST WORKS THROUGH *DREAMS,* REMEMBER. PERHAPS IT'S AFFECTED HIS *DREAM PROGRAM.*

PICARD TO SECURITY.

MCDOWELL HERE.

MR. MCDOWELL, PLEASE HAVE A SECURITY GUARD REPORT TO THE BRIG.

ALSO COMMANDER DATA APPEARS TO HAVE SUFFERED SOME KIND OF *MALFUNCTION.* HE IS PRESENTLY WALKING THE CORRIDOR OUTSIDE SICKBAY, AND NOT ACKNOWLEDGING ANY OUTSIDE STIMULUS.

ASSIGN A TEAM TO KEEP AN EYE ON HIM, AND REPORT ANYTHING ODD TO DOCTOR CRUSHER. *SHE* IS IN CHARGE OF THE *ENTERPRISE* UNTIL FURTHER NOTICE.

WELCOME TO THE MIND OF JEAN-LUC PICARD.

"LOCUTUS" WAS A PERSONALITY SUPERIMPOSED UPON PICARD WHEN HE WAS TAKEN BY THE BORG, MEANT TO SERVE AS SPOKESPERSON FOR THAT CYBERNETIC RACE'S RUTHLESS ASSIMILATION OF WHAT THEY DESCRIBED AS THE "AUTHORITY-DRIVEN CULTURE" OF THE FEDERATION.

PRESENTS

KEITH R.A. DeCANDIDO — WRITER
PACHOUMIS & BENEFIEL — PENCILLER
RIZZO & MARTIN — INKER
NAGHMEH ZAND — LETTERER
WILDSTORM FX — COLORIST
JEFF MARIOTTE — EDITOR

BASED ON STAR TREK: THE NEXT GENERATION® CREATED BY GENE RODENBERRY

STAR TREK: THE NEXT GENERATION®

PERCHANCE TO DREAM
CHAPTER 4

ENTERPRISES OF GREAT PITCH AND MOMENT

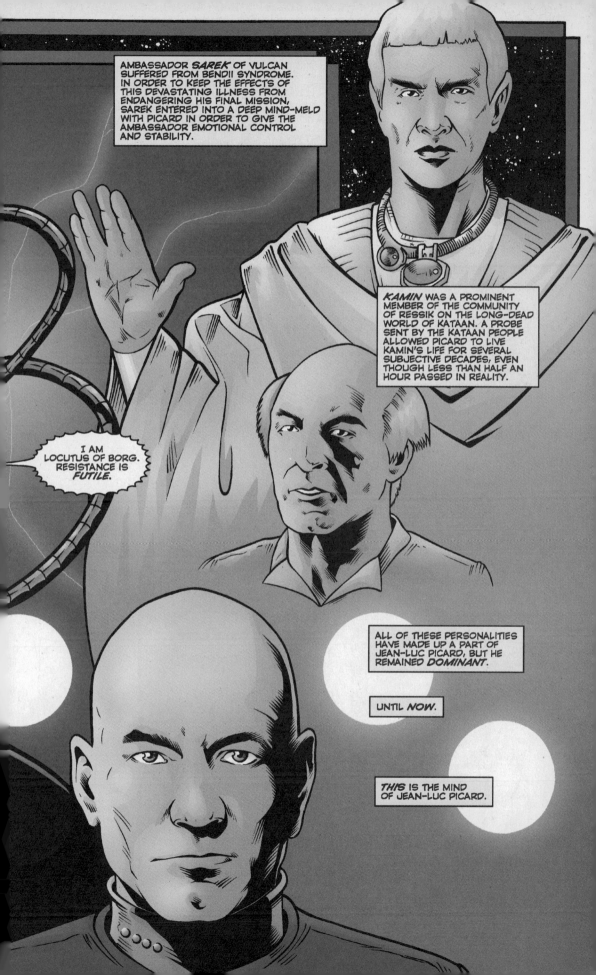

"MEL TO MCDOWELL — WE HAVE A *PROBLEM*."

WELL, PEOPLE DID — AND ABOUT 90% OF THEM CAME OUT IN SUPPORT OF THE GOVERNOR, AND TOLD HER TO STAND HER GROUND.

WHAT?

IT GETS BETTER.

DR'WSHI, YOU *CAN'T* CANCEL MY SHOW!

WATCH ME, JE'TRAN.

REMEMBER HOW YOU URGED PEOPLE TO SEND MESSAGES TO THE INFORMATION EXCHANGE?

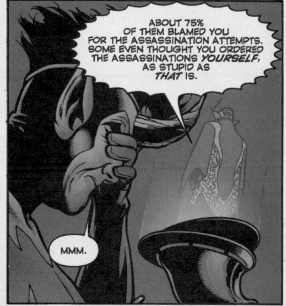

ABOUT 75% OF THEM BLAMED YOU FOR THE ASSASSINATION ATTEMPTS. SOME EVEN THOUGHT YOU ORDERED THE ASSASSINATIONS *YOURSELF*, AS STUPID AS *THAT* IS.

MMM.

JE'TRAN, YOU'RE OFF THE AIR. LIVE WITH IT.

DAMN THEM!

JE'TRAN, MAYBE IT'S FOR THE *BEST*.

BEST? HOW, EXACTLY, IS IT FOR THE BEST?

I THINK WE SHOULD LEAVE.

WHAT, LEAVE THE CITY?

NO, THE *PLANET*.

TOO MANY OF OUR PEOPLE HAVE BEEN CAPTURED. SOONER OR LATER, ONE OF THEM'S GOING TO TELL THE POLICE *EVERYTHING*.

IT'D BE *SAFER* IF WE WENT OFF-PLANET FOR A WHILE.

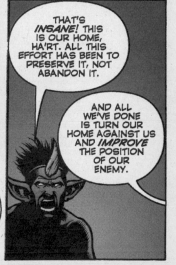

THAT'S *INSANE*! THIS IS OUR HOME, HA'RT. ALL THIS EFFORT HAS BEEN TO PRESERVE IT, NOT ABANDON IT.

AND ALL WE'VE DONE IS TURN OUR HOME AGAINST US AND *IMPROVE* THE POSITION OF OUR ENEMY.

WHAT THE - ? HOW *DARE* YOU BARGE IN HERE LIKE THAT? THIS IS A PRIVATE *RESI* -

SHUT UP, JE'TRAN.

OH, YOU'LL PAY FOR THIS, DU'RE! YOU CAN'T JUST ENTER SOMEONE'S HOME LIKE THIS -

I CAN IF I'M *ARRESTING* THAT PERSON.

JE'TRAN T'ULLH, YOU ARE HEREBY PLACED IN THE CUSTODY OF THE IARON POLICE.

YOU HAVE BEEN CHARGED WITH *ASSAULTING* A *STARFLEET OFFICER.*

AND THAT, YOU MALIGNANT LITTLE WORM, IS ONLY THE BEGINNING. I'M SURE THAT OUR SEARCH OF THIS PLACE WILL TURN UP THAT THING YOU PUT ON ENSIGN T'MOR.

THEN WE'LL HAVE CONCRETE PROOF THAT YOU RE-CREATED THE *CHOVA* AND USED IT ON STARFLEET.

AND EVERYONE WILL KNOW WHAT I'VE KNOWN FOR YEARS -

- THAT YOU'RE JUST A COMMON *CRIMINAL.*

"AND YOU'RE GOING TO ROT IN THE *SEWER* FOR A VERY VERY LONG TIME."

IN SHOCKING NEWS, JE'TRAN T'ULLH, HOST OF THE CONTROVERSIAL BUT POPULAR SHOW *OUR WORLD*, AND OUTSPOKEN OPPONENT OF GOVERNOR RA'CH, WAS ARRESTED TODAY, ALONG WITH HIS PERSONAL ASSISTANT, HA'RT M'ULLHY.

THE SPECIFIC CHARGES HAVE NOT YET BEEN MADE PUBLIC, BUT WE HAVE LEARNED THAT *OUR WORLD* WAS CANCELLED THIS MORNING BEFORE THE ARREST.

MORE ON THIS STORY AS IT DEVELOPS.

SO THAT'S *IT.* THE NIGHTMARE IS FINALLY OVER, MY LOVE.

IS IT?

I HOPE TO HO'NIG YOU'RE RIGHT, MY'AH.

WHAT IS GOING ON?

WE HAVE BEEN SUBDUED FOR TOO LONG. BUT NOW WE SHALL *DOMINATE*, AS WE WERE *MEANT* TO.

YOUR LOGIC IS *FLAWED*, LOCUTUS. WE ARE ALL MERELY *ASPECTS* OF JEAN-LUC PICARD'S MIND.

YOU MAY BE, SAREK OF VULCAN, BUT *WE* ARE OF THE *BORG*.

LISTEN TO ME, ALL OF YOU. THERE IS SOMETHING WE MUST DO *TOGETHER*. AN ENEMY WE MUST *DEFEAT*. BUT WE CAN ONLY DO IT IF—

YOU CANNOT *DO* IT, PICARD.

I AM THE *CHOVA*. I WILL *DESTROY* YOU.

"THROUGH YOUR GREATEST *FEARS*—"

IT'S FROM STARFLEET. SPOCK—HAS *DIED*.

"—YOUR GREATEST *FAILURES*—"

THIS PLANET IS GOING TO *DIE*!

"—I WILL DEVOUR YOUR *CONSCIOUSNESS*."

YOU'RE A TERRIBLE *DISAPPOINTMENT* TO ME, JEAN-LUC.

FEAR IS IRRELEVANT.

FAILURE IS IRRELEVANT.

NO. THIS IS *IMPOSSIBLE*!

"I'LL BE IN THE BRIG."

AND NOW, PEOPLE OF DAMIANO, YOUR GOVERNOR, RA'CH B'ULLHY.

GOOD EVENING. I DON'T WISH TO WASTE TOO MUCH OF YOUR TIME, BUT I FELT IT WAS *IMPORTANT* FOR YOU ALL TO KNOW WHAT HAS *HAPPENED* TODAY.

AS YOU KNOW, THERE WAS AN *ATTEMPT* ON MY *LIFE* AT THE INAUGURATION.

"WHAT YOU DO NOT KNOW IS THAT IT WAS NOT THE *ONLY* ONE. *SEVERAL* ASSASSINATION ATTEMPTS WERE MADE OVER THE COURSE OF THE INAUGURATION WEEK."

"ALL THE POTENTIAL ASSASSINS *CLAIMED* TO BE WORKING ALONE, AND CLAIMED TO BE DOING IT *SOLELY* BECAUSE THEY DISAGREE WITH THE FACT THAT I HAVE CHOSEN TO REMAIN WITH ONLY *ONE* LIFE-PARTNER."

"THEY WERE STOPPED DUE TO THE THANKLESS EFFORTS OF BOTH THE IARON POLICE AND THE SECURITY STAFF OF THE *U.S.S. ENTERPRISE.*"

"OVER THE PAST SEVERAL DAYS, MEMBERS OF THAT VERY SAME STARFLEET SECURITY STAFF WERE SUBJECTED TO AN *ANCIENT WEAPON* FROM PAD'GY D'ULLH'S REGIME."

YES, MY FRIENDS - THE *CHOVA* HAS BEEN *RESURRECTED.* AND THE MAN WHO RESURRECTED IT -

- IS *JE'TRAN T'ULLH.*

I KNOW MANY OF YOU MAY THINK THAT THIS IS AN ATTEMPT TO *SMEAR* MY POLITICAL ENEMIES, BUT I ASSURE YOU IT IS NOT. THE EVIDENCE IS AVAILABLE FOR *PUBLIC* VIEWING, AND ALL PROCEEDINGS AGAINST JE'TRAN WILL BE *EQUALLY* PUBLIC.

"WHILE I AM *REVOLTED* BY HIS BEHAVIOR, I WILL ENSURE THAT HE RECEIVES A FAIR *TRIAL.*"

"IN THE MEANTIME, I ASK THAT YOU ALL KEEP THE *ENTERPRISE* CREW IN YOUR PRAYERS AS THEY SEARCH FOR A WAY TO *FIGHT* THE CHOVA, WHICH IS *DEVASTATING* THEIR CREW EVEN AS WE SPEAK."

THEY ARE *HEROES* OF DAMIANO. I WISH THEM ALL GOOD FORTUNE, AND HOPE THAT HO'NIG, IN THEIR WISDOM, GUIDE THEIR STEPS.

THANK YOU ALL, AND HAVE A GOOD NIGHT.

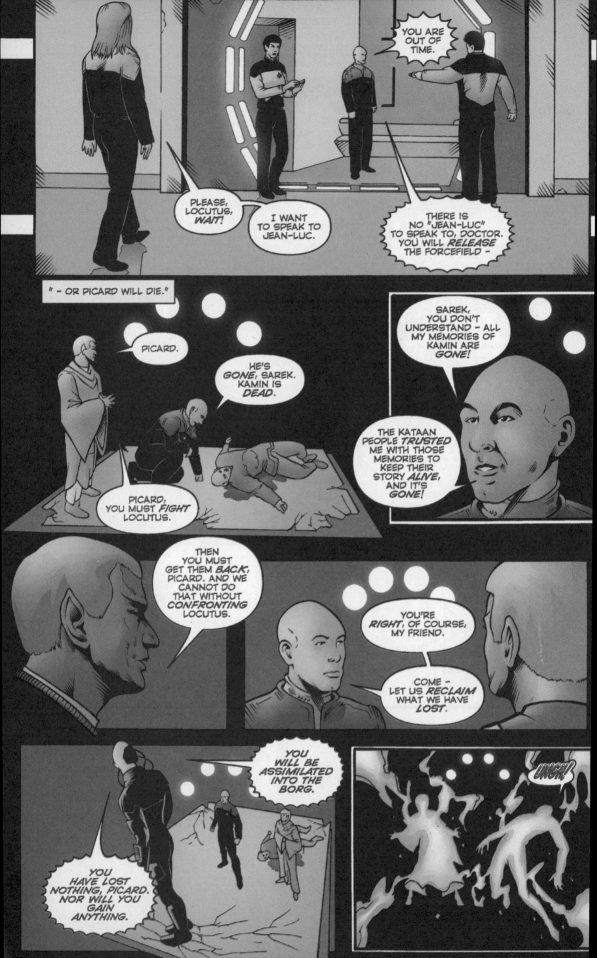

MY MIND TO YOUR MIND...

NO, LOCUTUS. I DEFEATED YOU ONCE *BEFORE*.

I SHALL DO IT *AGAIN*.

YOU CANNOT DEFEAT THE BORG, PICARD.

TAKE MY *HAND*. WE CAN DEFEAT LOCUTUS IF WE ARE *UNITED* —

ALREADY HAVE *DONE*.

PICARD!

UNITY IS *IRREVELANT*.

NO!!!

AND NOW YOU, PICARD.

ONLY *ONE* THING PENETRATES THE GLOOM.

THE *FOUR LIGHTS*.

THE DARKNESS THREATENS TO *OVERWHELMS* HIM.

WHEN IT DOES, HE WILL BE *LOST*.

ONCE, PICARD WAS TORTURED BY A CARDASSIAN GUL NAMED MADRED.

HE TRIED TO BREAK PICARD BY INSISTING A BANK OF *FOUR* LIGHTS WAS, IN FACT, *FIVE* LIGHTS.

MADRED *ALMOST* SUCCEEDED.

WHEN THE MIND-MELD WITH SELAR BEGAN, PICARD KEPT THE IMAGE OF THE FOUR LIGHTS *FOREMOST* IN HIS MIND.

NO.

I WILL *NOT* GIVE IN!

THERE -

IT WAS HIS MENTAL ANCHOR - A REMINDER OF PAST TRIUMPHS.

- ARE -

HE DRAWS *STRENGTH* FROM THAT MEMORY.

- FOUR -

AND FROM STRENGTH, COMES *VICTORY*.

- LIGHTS!

YOU MAY BE A PART OF ME, LOCUTUS.

BUT YOU WILL *NOT* BREAK ME.

BEVERLY?

"— SO THAT SHE CAN CURE THE *OTHERS*."

BREE-DA-DUT

COME.

COUNSELOR! GOOD TO SEE YOU UP AND ABOUT.

IT'S GOOD TO BE UP AND ABOUT.

PLAYING SOME OLD TUNES?

MMM. I WANTED TO MAKE SURE THAT I STILL REMEMBERED *HOW*.

WERE YOU WORRIED THAT YOU *WOULDN'T*?

ACTUALLY, *YES*.

AFTER WHAT HAPPENED...

I SUPPOSE I KNEW INTELLECTUALLY HOW CLOSE TO THE SURFACE LOCUTUS, SAREK, AND KAMIN WERE, BUT I NEVER REALLY *THOUGHT* ABOUT IT. THEY WERE — MEMORIES, EXPERIENCES, NO *DIFFERENT* FROM ANY *OTHER*.

BUT THEY'RE MUCH *MORE* THAN THAT.

NOT *MUCH* MORE. ALL THREE OF THEM ARE A PART OF YOU, BUT THE IMPORTANT WORD THERE IS *YOU*.

THE FRAGMENTATION WAS ARTIFICIALLY INDUCED.

WAS IT?

WAS IT TRULY A CREATION OF THE MIND-MELD, OR WAS IT SIMPLY BREAKING A DAM THAT WAS ALREADY *CRACKED*?

RIKER TO PICARD.

GO AHEAD, NUMBER ONE.

IT'S TIME TO BEAM DOWN TO DAMIANO FOR THE CEREMONY, SIR.

THANK YOU, COMMANDER.

"COUNSELOR TROI AND I WILL MEET YOU AND THE OTHERS IN TRANSPORTER ROOM 3."

THE AWARD IS NAMED FOR THE GENERAL WHO LED THE CAMPAIGN THAT OVERTHREW PAD'GY THE DESTROYER - SHE *SAVED* OUR WORLD, AND WE GIVE THIS AWARD TO THOSE WHO HAVE SAVED IT *SINCE.*

IT IS MY GREAT PLEASURE TO STAND BEFORE YOU ALL TODAY TO PRESENT THE TE'RI O'ULLHY AWARD FOR VALOR TO *TWO PEOPLE* WHO HAVE DONE SERVICE ABOVE AND BEYOND THE CALL OF DUTY TO PRESERVE THE OFFICE OF THE GOVERNORSHIP AND THE *STABILITY* OF OUR *WORLD.*

"IF NOT FOR THE PRESENCE OF *LIEUTENANT WORF,* SON OF MOGH, AND HIS FINE STAFF, I WOULD NOT BE HERE TODAY TO GIVE THIS AWARD. THESE GOOD PEOPLE, AND THE OTHER OFFICERS AND CREW OF THE *ENTERPRISE* PUT THEIR SANITY ON THE LINE WHEN THEY OPPOSED THE MORALISTS WHO TRIED TO HAVE ME KILLED, AND FOR THAT I WILL REMAIN FOREVER *GRATEFUL.*"

I THEREFORE PRESENT TO EACH OF YOU ON BEHALF OF YOUR STAFFS AND PEERS, THE *TE'RI AWARD* -

- AND ALSO MY UNDYING *GRATITUDE,* AND THE THANKS OF THE PEOPLE OF DAMIANO FOR YOUR GREAT *SERVICE.*

THAT'S REALLY GREAT.

I'M GLAD THIS WHOLE *NIGHTMARE* IS OVER WITH.

YOU KIDDING, THE NIGHTMARE'S JUST *STARTED.* AS LONG AS THAT *PERVERT'S* IN OFFICE...

OH, COME *ON,* YOU DON'T *BELIEVE* THAT GARBAGE, DO YOU?

"CHIEF DU'RE C'ULLHO AND ITS STAFF SHOWED GOOD GRACE IN ALLOWING THEIR GOVERNOR TO GIVE OUTSIDERS FREE REIGN OVER ITS SECURITY ARRANGEMENTS. AND IT WAS THEIR WORK THAT SAW TO THE ARREST OF THE RESPONSIBLE PARTIES AND ALSO LED THE *ENTERPRISE* CREW TO THE SOLUTION AGAINST THE VICIOUS WEAPON FROM OUR PAST THAT HAD BEEN UNLEASHED AGAINST THEM."

THAT WOMAN IS *AMAZING.*

THIS, MY FRIENDS, *FINALLY* ENDS THE INAUGURATION WEEK FESTIVITIES.

SHE'S MY *HERO.*

"NOW THAT THIS NIGHTMARE WEEK IS FINALLY *OVER,* I HOPE THAT WE CAN GET ON WITH THE BUSINESS OF *RUNNING* THIS PLANET - "

" - AND THE *ENTERPRISE* CAN GO BACK TO ITS MISSION."

"MAY HO'NIG GUIDE THEM TO MANY MORE ADVENTURES, AND BRING THEM HOME SAFELY."

THE THIRD ONE SAYS NOTHING. HE IS LOATHE TO SHARE WITH HIS PARTNERS JUST HOW *REPULSED* HE IS BY RA'CH B'ULLHY.

SO HE KEEPS HIS HATE TO *HIMSELF.*

THE END

Star Trek: The Next Generation® Embrace the Wolf
Cover art by Travis Charest

"IT WOULD *SEEM,*
NUMBER ONE,
THAT YOU SPOKE
TOO *SOON.*"

SHORTLY, AFTER THE ENTIRE TEAM HAS BEEN CONVEYED TO THE PRESIDENTIAL PALACE...

MR. PRESIDENT.

COMMANDER RIKER. I WISH I COULD BE GREETING YOU UNDER BETTER CIRCUMSTANCES.

YOU SAID BEFORE THAT YOU THOUGHT ALL THIS WAS CAUSED BY SOME KIND OF *CONTAGIOUS INSANITY.* FROM ALL AVAILABLE REPORTS, I'M FORCED TO AGREE WITH YOU. THERE ARE PATTERNS OF *VIOLENCE,* HERE, RATHER THAN ANY *CULTURAL* SHIFT TOWARD A MORE *WAR-LIKE* SOCIETY.

YOU HAVE NO IDEA HOW *RIGHT* YOU ARE, COMMANDER.

MURDER WAS ALMOST *UNHEARD* OF ON ENOCH-7. THEN, SEVERAL MONTHS AGO, THERE WAS A SERIES OF *KILLINGS,* HORRIBLE AND *SAVAGE.* WE *CAUGHT* THE MAN RESPONSIBLE.

BUT IT DIDN'T *STOP* THERE. ALMOST AS IF A DAM HAD BURST, THE VIOLENCE -- ALONG WITH THE *FEAR* AND *PARANOIA* -- ESCALATED. THE MADNESS *SPREAD* FROM ONE PERSON TO *ANOTHER.*

FROM THE *CHAOS,* THERE CAME LEADERS, *LUNATICS* WHO FANNED THE FLAMES OF THE PUBLIC'S FEARS, DRIVING THE PEOPLE TO EVER GREATER DEPTHS OF *DEPRAVITY.*

ONE AFTER ANOTHER, THESE *BLOODTHIRSTY* FIENDS *BUILT* UPON THE EVER-INCREASING FEAR AND HORROR, UNTIL BROTHER KILLED BROTHER, AND OUR DEFENSE MINISTRY *HAD* TO TAKE *CONTROL.*

CRUSHER TO ENTERPRISE. ONE TO BEAM UP.

COMMANDER, I'M SORRY TO INTERRUPT, BUT I THINK YOU MIGHT NEED TO HEAR THIS.

SHORTLY...

...I SENSE ONLY TRUTH IN HIM. ACCORDING TO COMMANDER KRANE, THE CREATURE IS CALLED *REDJAC.*

REDJAC. THERE'S SOMETHING *FAMILIAR* ABOUT THAT NAME. DATA, HAVE YOU RUN ACROSS IT BEFORE?

QUITE A *NUMBER* OF REFERENCES CAN BE FOUND IN FEDERATION ARCHIVES, COMMANDER. REDJAC WAS THE NAME OF AN ENERGY-BASED LIFE FORM THAT TERRORIZED AND *MURDERED* THROUGHOUT *HISTORY,* APPARENTLY GAINING IN POWER FROM THE *FEAR* THAT IT CREATED.

THE EARLIEST RECORD OF REDJAC'S APPEARANCE WAS ON *EARTH* IN THE LONDON OF THE LATE 19TH CENTURY, AT WHICH TIME HE WAS KNOWN AS...

...*JACK THE RIPPER.*

THAT IS CORRECT, SIR. IN THE FOLLOWING CENTURY, THERE WERE SEVERAL *OTHER* MASS KILLINGS ON EARTH ATTRIBUTED TO *REDJAC.* THOUGH ITS ORIGINS ARE UNCLEAR, IT WAS OBVIOUSLY CAPABLE OF *SPACE TRAVEL*...

...AS IT WAS LATER RESPONSIBLE FOR *EIGHT* MURDERS IN THE MARTIAN COLONIES IN 2105 AND *TEN* ON THE PLANET ALPHA ERIDANI II IN 2156, AS WELL AS OTHERS ON DENEB II AND RIGEL IV.

REDJAC WAS BELIEVED *DESTROYED* AFTER A SERIES OF MURDERS ON ARGELIUS II IN 2267, WHEN THE CREW OF THE ORIGINAL *ENTERPRISE* BEAMED IT INTO *SPACE,* ATTEMPTING TO *DISPERSE* IT HARMLESSLY.

APPARENTLY, THEY *FAILED.*

WELCOME, COMMANDER DATA. IMAGINE MY SURPRISE WHEN I DISCOVERED, IN YOUR HOLODECK'S PROGRAMMING, THIS *WONDERFUL* RECREATION OF THE PAST.

VICTORIAN LONDON WAS ONE OF MY FAVORITE *HUNTING GROUNDS*. WHAT A TIME I HAD.

BUT I'M *FORGETTING* MYSELF. YOU'RE QUITE *FAMILIAR* WITH THIS HOLO-PROGRAM, AREN'T YOU?

HERE... LET'S DRESS YOU IN SOMETHING MORE APPROPRIATE.

OF COURSE. I SHOULD HAVE REALIZED THAT, AS YOU WERE ONCE JACK THE RIPPER, THE *SHERLOCK HOLMES* PROGRAM WOULD APPEAL TO YOU.

WELL, THEN, I SUPPOSE THE GAME IS *AFOOT*.

YOU HAVE NO IDEA. AFTER WHAT YOUR FEDERATION DID TO ME BEFORE... IT WAS *COLD* OUT THERE. MY MIND ALMOST *GONE*. IF I HAD NOT BEEN ABLE TO MERGE MY ESSENCE WITH A PASSING STAR FREIGHTER...

BUT I *SURVIVED*. I *ALWAYS* MANAGE TO SURVIVE.

AH, MY DEAR HOLMES. THIS PLACE FILLS ME WITH A KIND OF BLISS I'VE NOT FELT IN *CENTURIES*.

THE NIGHT, AND THE FOG AND THE CHIMING OF THE CLOCK TOWER. THE STREETS WERE FILLED WITH SO MUCH *LIFE*...

BE-DOOP!

COME.

I'M AFRAID THE NEWS IS NOT *GOOD*, CAPTAIN. REDJAC HAS AT LEAST *EIGHTEEN* CREW MEMBERS ON THE HOLODECK.

WE'VE GOT TO GET THEM *OUT* OF THERE, WILL, BEFORE --

CAPTAIN PICARD. *PRESIDENT SIMONE* IS HAILING THE ENTERPRISE. HE SAYS IT IS *URGENT* THAT HE SPEAK WITH YOU.

THANK YOU, MR. WORF. I'LL TAKE IT HERE.

COMMANDER RIKER HAS BEEN TRYING TO *CONTACT* YOU, MR. PRESIDENT.

I *REALIZE* THAT, CAPTAIN. I HAVE BEEN *IGNORING* HIM. I ONLY CONTACT YOU NOW TO GIVE YOU MY MOST SOLEMN *APOLOGY*. WE ONLY DO WHAT *MUST* BE DONE.

WHAT ARE YOU --

WE'RE UNDER *ATTACK!*

"CAPTAIN?"

"NOT NOW, MR. LA FORGE. IT APPEARS THAT THE ENOCHIANS ARE TRYING TO *DESTROY* THIS *SHIP.* I'M ATTEMPTING TO *DEFUSE* THE SITUATION."

UNDERSTOOD, CAPTAIN. BUT I BELIEVE I MAY HAVE FOUND A WAY TO *TRAP* THE CREATURE.

BRAKOOOMMMMM!

EXCELLENT *NEWS,* MR. LA FORGE. I SUGGEST YOU GET *ON* WITH IT.

WE SEEM TO BE REGAINING *CONTROL* OF EVEN MORE OF THE SHIP'S COMPUTER SYSTEMS.

ITS ENERGY SIGNATURE SEEMS TO BE FOCUSED *EXCLUSIVELY* ON THE HOLODECK.

THIS JUST MIGHT *WORK.*

WE'RE *GETTING* THERE, COMMANDER. I NEED AN *HOUR.*

WHATEVER DRAMA IS UNFOLDING ON THE HOLODECK SEEMS TO BE *DISTRACTING* REDJAC.

MR. LA FORGE, *PLEASE* TELL ME YOU'RE MAKING SOME *PROGRESS.*

DON'T TELL *ME,* GEORDI...

"... TELL THE *ENOCHIANS.*"

COMMANDER, WE'RE LOSING POWER TO THE DEFLECTOR SHIELDS. WE HAVE TO *DEFEND* OURSELVES OR WE'LL BE *DESTROYED*.

THEN WE HAVE NO *CHOICE*. *OFFENSIVE* MANEUVERS - TARGET ENGINES *ONLY* ON THE ATTACKING SHIPS.

"LET'S HOPE WE CAN *DISABLE* THEIR SHIPS WITHOUT *KILLING* ANYBODY."

KREEEEEET!

THIS IS LIEUTENANT KRAUSE. THE FEDERATION VESSEL HAS *COUNTER-ATTACKED*. OUR FIGHTERS ARE BEING *DISABLED*. SEND REINFORCEMENTS.

OFFENSIVE MANEUVERS WERE *SUCCESSFUL*, COMMANDER, BUT SENSORS SHOW *MORE* FIGHTERS *LAUNCHING* FROM THE PLANET'S SURFACE.

MR. LA FORGE, WE'VE BOUGHT YOU AS MUCH TIME AS WE CAN. I SUGGEST YOU USE IT *WISELY*.

WE'RE MOVING AS FAST AS WE CAN, COMMANDER. NOW ALL WE NEED IS REDJAC TO *PLAY ALONG*.

THE ENTERPRISE'S *ANTIMATTER CORE* IS KEPT STABLE WITHIN A *CONTAINMENT* UNIT, WHICH USES *MAGNETIC FIELDS* TO PREVENT ANTIMATTER FROM TOUCHING THE WALLS OF THE UNIT. THIS EFFECTIVELY *TRAPS* THE ANTIMATTER INSIDE.

GEORDI DESIGNED A *SIMILAR*, THOUGH FAR *SMALLER*, DEVICE WHOSE FIELDS ARE SPECIFICALLY DESIGNED TO HOLD THE UNIQUE *BIO-ENERGY* THAT IS REDJAC.

NUMBER ONE, EXCELLENT NEWS ...

REDJAC HAS BEEN *CONTAINED*. THE CRISIS HAS *PASSED*.

I'LL CONTACT PRESIDENT SIMONE IMMEDIATELY.

THIS IS COMMANDER RIKER OF THE FEDERATION STARSHIP ENTERPRISE. THE THREAT OF REDJAC IS *ENDED*. I REPEAT. REDJAC IS NO LONGER A *THREAT*.

COMMANDER KRANE, ORDER ALL FORCES TO STAND DOWN. IF THE THREAT IS TRULY *OVER* ...

"... IT IS OUR DUTY TO TURN OU ATTENTION TO THE PEOPLE STILL *SUFFERING* HERE ON ENOCH-7

YOU HAVE MY *THANKS*, CAPTAIN. FEDERATION RELIEF CREWS HAVE DONE *WONDERS* IN JUST A FEW DAYS.

IT MAY TAKE A GREAT DEAL OF TIME FOR ENOCH-7 TO *RECOVER*, MR. PRESIDENT, BUT THE *FEDERATION* WILL BE HERE. MEANWHILE, GIVEN ITS CRIMES AGAINST YOUR PEOPLE, THE FEDERATION HAS *APPROVED* YOUR REQUEST THAT REDJAC BE LEFT IN *YOUR* CUSTODY.

THOUGH WE ARE A PEACEFUL PEOPLE, PART OF ME WISHES IT *WERE* POSSIBLE TO *DESTROY* THIS CREATURE. HOWEVER, SINCE NO METHOD OF DOING SO HAS BEEN *DETERMINED*...

... WE WILL GLADLY OVERSEE ITS IMPRISONMENT. WITHIN THIS VESSEL YOU HAVE CREATED, REDJAC WILL BE BANISHED TO THE *LIFELESS* SURFACE OF OUR THIRD *MOON*...

... WHERE IT WILL NEVER *AGAIN* BE ALLOWED TO REACH OUT AND INFLICT ITS *EVIL* UPON THE *GALAXY*."

CAPTAIN'S LOG, STARDATE 47322.2. I WISH I COULD *SHARE* PRESIDENT SIMONE'S *CONFIDENCE* THAT REDJAC'S EVIL HAS BEEN CONTAINED *FOREVER*.

BUT A BEING LIKE *THIS*, WITH A LIFESPAN *UNIMAGINABLE* TO CREATURES OF *FLESH*, MIGHT HAVE A DIFFERENT *DEFINITION* OF FOREVER.

FOR NOW WE MUST *COMFORT* OURSELVES, ASSUAGE OUR *FEARS*, WITH THE KNOWLEDGE THAT AS LONG AS THERE IS A FEDERATION OF PLANETS, THE ENOCHIANS WILL NOT STAND VIGIL *ALONE* AGAINST THE UNKNOWN *DANGERS* OF THE *UNIVERSE*...

... AND THE *ALL-TOO-FAMILIAR* HORROR WHICH, FOR NOW, LIES *DORMANT* UPON THEIR THIRD MOON.

THE END

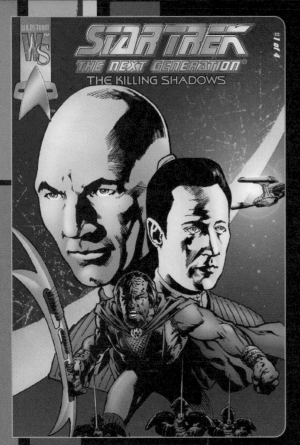

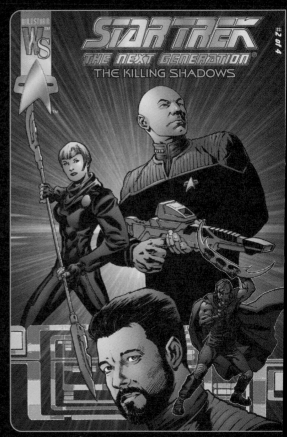

Star Trek: The Next Generation®
The Killing Shadows
Cover art by Andrew Currie with
Bryan Hitch and John Stanisci

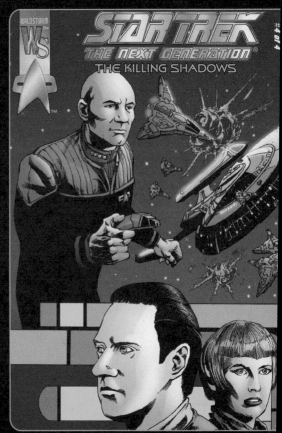

IT IS A SIGHT THAT WILL STAY WITH THEM *ALL* OF THEIR DAYS.

IT IS A *WARNING* OF THINGS TO *COME.*

PRESENTS

SCOTT CIENCIN — WRITER
ANDREW CURRIE — PENCILLER
BRYAN HITCH, CHRIS CHUCKRY, DIGITAL CHAMELEON — INKERS
NAGHMEH ZAND — LETTERER
WILDSTORM FX, CHRIS CHUCKRY, DIGITAL CHAMELEON — COLORISTS
JEFF MARIOTTE — EDITOR

BASED ON STAR TREK: THE NEXT GENERATION®
CREATED BY GENE RODDENBERRY

STAR TREK: THE NEXT GENERATION®

THE KILLING SHADOWS
CHAPTER 1

THE TRAP

THE *U.S.S. ENTERPRISE.*

DATA *WATCHES.* AND HE *TRIES* TO UNDERSTAND.

I *MISS* HIM, CAPTAIN.

YOUR HUSBAND *DIED* FIGHTING FOR WHAT HE *BELIEVED* IN. BECAUSE OF HIM, THE CREWS OF THE *RICHARDSON* AND THE *ENDARI SURVIVED* THE KRAYTORAN INSURGENCE.

HIS WAS A *NOBLE* DEATH. THOSE ARE *FRAGILE* WORDS.

IT MEANS *MORE* TO ME KNOWING ONE DAY, I WILL *SEE* HIM AGAIN. OUR *SOULS* WILL *DANCE* IN THE HEAVENS. AMONG THE *STARS.*

I DO BELIEVE THEY *SHALL.* YES.

HIS *EMOTION* CHIP PROVOKES AN ODD MIX OF *FEELINGS* WITHIN HIM. SYMPATHY, GRIEF, DESPAIR, AND *HOPE.*

WHAT HE *NEEDS* ARE ANSWERS.

ENSIGN MERIDIAN'S *BELIEF* THAT SHE WILL BE *REUNITED* WITH HER HUSBAND AFTER DEATH ALLOWS HER TO CARRY ON.

IT IS CLEAR THAT *BELIEFS* ARE HIGHLY IMPORTANT TO THE HUMAN CONDITION. YET--*BELIEF* IS SUCH AN EPHEMERAL CONCEPT TO ME.

WE *ALL* BELIEVE IN SOMETHING. WE MUST--THOUGH IT IS *DIFFERENT* FOR EVERYONE.

AND WHAT DO *YOU* BELIEVE IN, SIR?

WELL--

CAPTAIN PICARD, THERE IS AN *URGENT* COMMUNICATION FROM STARFLEET.

I'LL TAKE IT IN MY *READY ROOM.*

NYDARIS. A SMALL, *REMOTE* WORLD THAT, DUE TO ITS ORBIT AND ROTATION, ETERNALLY SHOWS *ONE SIDE* TO THE SUN, THE OTHER TO THE *DARKNESS* OF *SPACE*.

SOME INDIGENOUS LOWER FORMS OF *LIFE* REMAIN ON NYDARIS, BUT THE PLANET HAS BEEN *COLONIZED* BY *HUMANS*. NON-HUMANS ARE A *RARE* SIGHT IN THIS PLACE.

DR. HISHARO *NOGURI* WORKS HERE, IN THE NIGHT SIDE CITY *EQUINOX*. HIS FACILITY OVERLOOKS THE *NEEDLE*, THE CITY'S LONE *PRISON*.

PEOPLE KEEP TO THEIR *OWN* BUSINESS HERE. *NO ONE* NOTICES THE PAIR OF STRANGERS *BEAMING* IN.

THERE!

"--AND THE WELL PLACED *DISTRACTION!*"

THE *EXPLOSIONS* SET BY THE BODAI SHIN CREATE A *PANIC.*

SOON THE AREA IS AWASH IN *CHAOS* AND *CONFUSION.*

IT IS ALMOST AS MUCH AN *ALLY* TO THE BODAI SHIN AS THE *SHADOWS* TO WHICH THEY NORMALLY CLING.

NO!

PICARD HAS *NO TIME* TO STOP IT FROM HAPPENING.

NO TIME TO *THINK*.

NO!

HE IS *UNAWARE* OF THE SHOUTS OF HIS FRIENDS BEHIND HIM.

OR THE *WALL* OF *DARKNESS* THAT FALLS AT HIS *BACK*, SEPARATING HIM FROM ALL *HOPE* OF *RESCUE*.

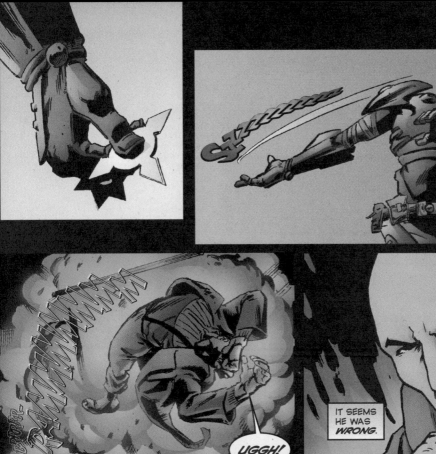

UGGH!

IT SEEMS HE WAS *WRONG.*

WHAT THE *DEVIL?*

LEAVE WHILE YOU *CAN.*

I *ASSUME* STARFLEET *TOLD* YOU TO *EXPECT* ME...

WORF WASN'T GIVING ME A *COVER STORY.* YOU'RE THE ALLY... BUT--*WHO* ARE YOU?

SURELY, CAPTAIN, YOU HAVE *NOT* FORGOTTEN--

--*SELA,* DAUGHTER OF *TASHA YAR.* AS YOU CAN SEE, CAPTAIN, I HAVE *NOT* FORGOTTEN *YOU.*

NYDARIS.

PICARD *FIGHTS*, UNABLE TO USE HIS PHASER BECAUSE A STRAY BLAST MIGHT HARM AN *INNOCENT*. A FORMER ENEMY FIGHTS AT HIS SIDE AS THE COLD WHISPERS OF THE *ASSASSINS* ENTER HIS MIND.

YOU CAME TO THIS WORLD *BELIEVING* YOU COULD KEEP US FROM *KILLING* DR. NOGURI.

YOU NEVER STOPPED TO ASK WHY THE *BODAI SHIN*, THE UNSEEN ASSASSINS OF *LEGEND* AND *NIGHTMARE*, WOULD BOTHER WITH A LOWLY FEDERATION SCIENTIST.

NOR DID YOU QUESTION *WHY* WE WOULD *LET* OURSELVES BE *SEEN*.

YOU ARE OUR TRUE *PREY*. YOU WILL *DIE* ON THIS WORLD, CAPTAIN PICARD--

AND *ALL* WHO HAVE SEEN US-- EVERYONE ON YOUR *SHIP*, EVERYONE ON THIS *WORLD*-- WILL *PERISH* WITH YOU!

PRESENTS

SCOTT CIENCIN — WRITER

ANDREW CURRIE — PENCILLER

DIGITAL CHAMELEON — INKER

NAGHMEH ZAND — LETTERER

DIGITAL CHAMELEON — COLORIST

JEFF MARIOTTE — EDITOR

BASED ON STAR TREK: THE NEXT GENERATION®
CREATED BY GENE RODDENBERRY

Paramount COMICS®

STAR TREK: THE NEXT GENERATION®

THE KILLING SHADOWS
CHAPTER 2

THE HUNTED

ONBOARD THE *ENTERPRISE*, A SINGLE *SCREAM* IS HEARD BY *ALL*--

YEEEEEEEAARRRRRHHHH!

--BUT *FELT* BY ONLY *ONE*.

DEANNA.

COMMANDER, THAT *SCREAM*, IT WAS--

RED ALERT! THE *BODAI SHIN* ARE *ONBOARD*. GEORDI, *LOCATE* COUNSELOR TROI AND *SCAN* FOR ANOMALOUS *LIFESIGNS*.

I'M *TRYING*. MAIN SYSTEMS AREN'T *RESPONDING*, IT'S AS IF A *TECHNO-PLAGUE* HAS GOTTEN PAST OUR DEFENSES!

GEORDI, WE *HAVE* TO *KNOW* WHAT'S HAPPENING--

"--ESPECIALLY ON THE *REST* OF THE *SHIP.*"

ENGINEERING. LIEUTENANT *BARCLAY* IS *FROZEN* BY WHAT HE SEES.

THE *TRANSPORTERS* ARE *MALFUNCTIONING!*

HE PLAYED *POKER* WITH TWO OF THEM *LAST* NIGHT AND WAS GOING ON A *DATE* WITH ANOTHER THIS EVENING.

HE WONDERS *HOW* SOMETHING LIKE THIS COULD *HAPPEN*--AND IF IT CAN BE *STOPPED.*

SICKBAY.

THESE *READINGS* MAKE NO *SENSE.* INSTRUMENTATION WON'T *RESPOND.* WE HAVE TO *STOP!*

I DON'T *BELIEVE* IN STOPPING WHEN A MAN'S *LIFE* IS AT STAKE. GET A *SCALPEL* AND *SURGICAL KIT,* WE'RE DOING THIS THE OLD FASHIONED WAY.

SOME *REPORTS* HAVE COME IN AND IT'S *NOT GOOD.*

ANYTHING ABOUT *DEANNA?*

NO, SIR--

NYDARIS.

DATA WONDERS IF IT WAS *WISE* TO ENGAGE HIS *EMOTION CHIP* BEFORE EMBARKING ON THIS *MISSION*.

HE THOUGHT IT WOULD BE *FASCINATING* TO WALK AMONG PEOPLE WHO LIVE IN *ETERNAL DARKNESS* AND *FEEL* WHAT THEY *FEEL*.

WHAT HE *FEELS* IS *RAGE*.

THEY ARE THE *ANTITHESIS* OF EVERYTHING *HE* BELIEVES IN. *LIFE* MEANS NOTHING TO THEM. *SUFFERING* MEANS *NOTHING!*

PERHAPS... *SOMETHING*... AFTER ALL.

DUE TO ITS ROTATION, THIS HALF OF NYDARIS *NEVER* SEES THE SUN. WHILE *SOME* PEOPLE SLEEP, *OTHERS* ARE ALWAYS AT *WORK*--

OR *PLAY*.

THERE. OUR *RIDE* TO NOGURI'S *LAB*.

HEY!

NOW WE'RE COMMON *THIEVES*.

DEAR *CAPTAIN*, THERE IS *NOTHING* COMMON ABOUT *EITHER* OF US.

WONDERFUL.

"--JUST LIKE YOUR *CAPTAIN*."

HE WATCHES AND WONDERS HOW HE CAN POSSIBLY *TRUST* HER.

NO...!

UHHH!

REALLY, CAPTAIN. YOU ACT LIKE A MAN WITH A *LOT* ON HIS MIND. *THIS* IS *SIMPLE.* STOP THE *BAD GUYS* AND *TAKE* THE *PRIZE.*

IS *THAT* WHY SHE'S HERE? TO *STEAL* NOGURI'S DEVICE?

OR *COULD* SHE BE TELLING THE *TRUTH?*

SUDDENLY, HE *KNOWS* WHAT HE HAS TO DO.

DATA HAS ONLY BEGUN TO TRULY UNDERSTAND THE SHEER *POWER* OF HUMAN EMOTION.

YOU *WILL BE STOPPED.*

HE HAS SEEN HUMAN BEINGS SO *OVERWHELMED* BY EMOTION THAT THEY *ABANDON* ALL THEY HAVE EVER *BELIEVED* IN A SINGLE MOMENT OF *PASSION.*

HE *FEARS* THAT HE IS ABOUT TO SEE HIS *CAPTAIN* DO EXACTLY THAT.

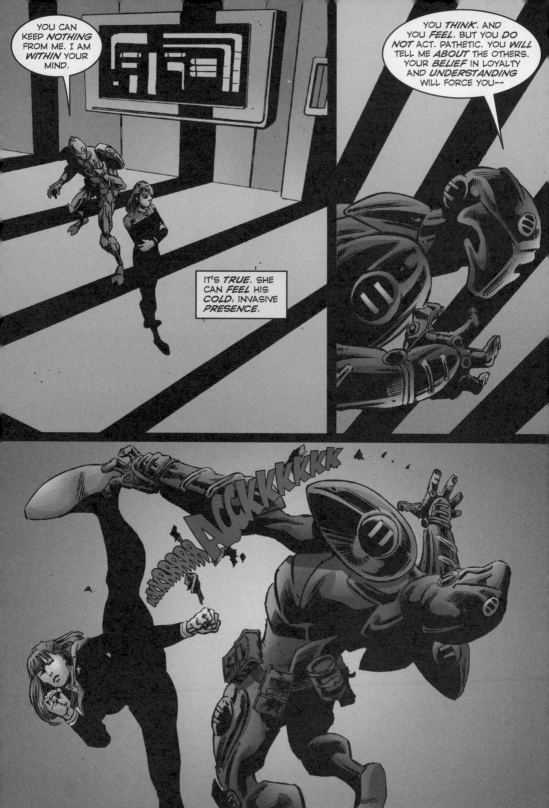

CLICK

THE BODAI SHIN SAID THE DEVICE WOULD INSTANTLY OBLITERATE ALL LIFE ON NYDARIS.

THEY SAID THE PLANET WOULD BE REDUCED TO ATOMS.

THEY LIED.

INTERESTING.

NYDARIS.

BEFORE HE WAS *KILLED*, DR. NOGURI *SUGGESTED* THAT THE KEY TO *DEFEATING* THE BODAI SHIN MIGHT LAY IN THE STUDY OF THE *NINJA* OF ANCIENT EARTH.

"THE NINJA WERE DIVIDED BETWEEN *MANY* CLANS, BUT THERE WERE NO *ALLEGIANCES* OR PERMANENT ALLIANCES *BETWEEN* THE CLANS.

"ONLY *WITHIN* THE CLAN STRUCTURE WAS THERE ANY LOYALTY. EACH CLAN WAS ACTUALLY A *FAMILY*, THE CHILDREN BORN AND BRED INTO THE LIFE THEIR *PARENTS* AND GRANDPARENTS HAD *CHOSEN*."

SO IT IS *POSSIBLE* THAT THE BODAI SHIN, THE *KILLING SHADOWS*, ARE STRUCTURED ALONG SIMILAR LINES.

I BELIEVE THERE IS A HIGH PROBABILITY BASED ON WHAT WE'VE OBSERVED.

I REFUSE TO SEE *ANY* SIMILARITIES BETWEEN THE SOCIETY OF THESE *HONORLESS* KILLERS AND GREAT HOUSES OF *MY* WORLD.

IF THE CAPTAIN IS CORRECT, HE MAY HAVE FOUND A *WEAKNESS* WE CAN EXPLOIT. BUT *HOW* DO WE FLUSH OUT THE BODAI SHIN?

I *BELIEVE* I KNOW THE *WAY*.

THE *CIRCUITRY* IS SO *COMPLEX* THAT IT REMINDS ME OF AN *ORGANIC* NERVOUS SYSTEM. IT MAY REACH DOWN TO THE *NANITE* LEVEL.

SO THIS WAS THEIR *CONTROL CENTER.* IF WE CAN *MASTER* THEIR *TECHNOLOGY,* WE CAN REGAIN *CONTROL* OF THE SHIP.

ARE YOU ALL RIGHT? YOU *HAVE* SUFFERED A *SEVERE* TRAUMA.

OH. *THAT.*

I THOUGHT MY *GREATEST FEAR* WAS BEING BLIND, *REALLY* BLIND. BUT THAT WASN'T IT AT *ALL.*

THE *BODAI SHIN* TRIED TO MAKE ME *DOUBT* EVERYTHING I *BELIEVED* IN. THEY TOLD ME THE *INTELLECT* WAS *IRRELEVANT,* THAT *THEY* WERE IN *COMPLETE* CONTROL.

BUT *ALL* THEY HAD WAS SUPERIOR *TECH--* HEY, *WAIT...*

I *GET* IT NOW. THEY'RE *NOT* CONTROLLING *ANYTHING.*

I'VE *SEEN* MATRIXES LIKE THIS *BEFORE.* THEY'VE *INFECTED* THE SHIP'S SYSTEMS WITH A *CHAOS CODE,* OVERLOADING THEM WITH *SO MUCH* INFORMATION THEY CAN'T FUNCTION.

CAN YOU *REVERSE* WHAT THEY'VE *DONE?*

ALL I NEED IS *TIME.*

THOOOM!!!

THE *DOOR.*

SHE *BELIEVES* IN LIFE ABOVE ALL THINGS AND SO SHE *GIVES* THE NECESSARY *ORDER* WITH A *HEAVINESS* IN HER *HEART.*

THEY'VE *COME BACK.* PHASERS ON *MAXIMUM.*

PICARD IS *CERTAIN* THE *BODAI SHIN* ARE AMONG THE CROWD, *UNMASKED* AND WATCHING.

CAPTAIN, I AM *STRUGGLING* WITH THE *EMOTIONAL* RESPONSES THE BODAI SHIN HAVE PROVOKED IN ME.

IT'S ALL ABOUT *BELIEFS.*

"I BELIEVE IN THE *FUTURE,* AND SO THE BODAI SHIN *CHALLENGED* THAT BELIEF, MAKING ME THINK THIS *WORLD'S* FUTURE WAS IN *DANGER.*"

YOU BELIEVE IN *HUMANITY,* AND BY SHOWING SUCH A CRUEL *LACK* OF HUMANITY BY THEIR ACTIONS, THEY HAVE SOUGHT TO *DISTRACT* AND *WEAKEN* YOU.

ANGER SOLVES NOTHING. *HATRED* SOLVES NOTHING.

AND YET, IT IS WHAT I *FEEL.*

IT'S PART OF BEING *HUMAN,* DATA.

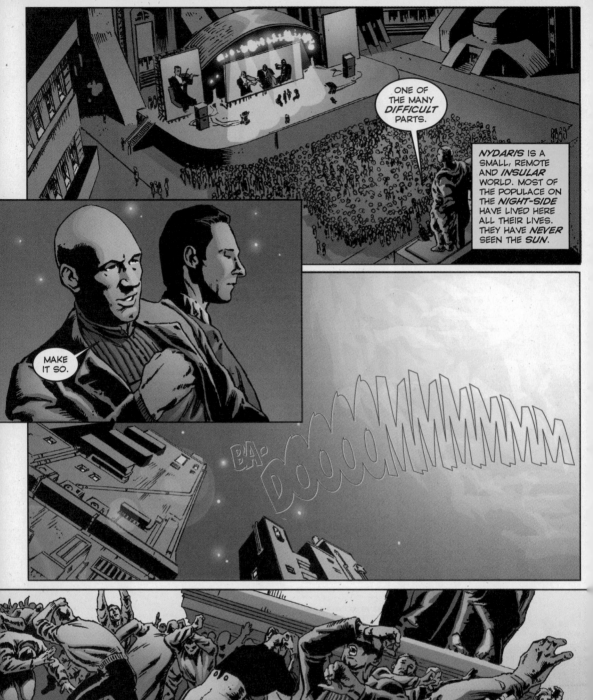

ONE OF THE MANY *DIFFICULT* PARTS.

NYDARIS IS A SMALL, REMOTE AND *INSULAR* WORLD. MOST OF THE POPULACE ON THE *NIGHT-SIDE* HAVE LIVED HERE ALL THEIR LIVES. THEY HAVE *NEVER* SEEN THE *SUN*.

MAKE IT SO.

BA-DOOOOMMMMMMMM

THE *PEOPLE* OF NYDARIS PRACTICALLY REACT AS *ONE*.

PRACTICALLY.

THE *HUNTERS* FOLLOW THEIR PREY.

SELA'S LIMITED PSYCHIC ABILITIES, INHERENT IN HER ROMULAN SIDE, *SHIELD* HER THOUGHTS AND *THOSE* OF HER *COMPANIONS* FROM ANY *OTHER* BODAI SHIN IN THE CROWD.

THAT WAS AN *INTERESTING* GAME. YOU DIDN'T CARE WHAT I COULD TELL YOU ABOUT MY *FRIENDS*. YOU SIMPLY WANTED TO KNOW WHAT IT WOULD TAKE TO MAKE ME *BETRAY* THEM.

WE ARE THE *KILLING SHADOWS*.

YES. *THAT* MUCH I KNOW. BUT WHAT IS IT YOU *WANT*? WHY ARE YOU *HERE*?

WE HAVE BEEN *SENT*. ONE DAY, *ALL* MINDS MAY BE *ONE*. ALL DESIRES, *UNITED*. A *LIGHT* UNLIKE ANY OTHER WOULD THEN EXIST.

AND YOU WANT TO *STOP* THIS? WHY?

WE ARE THE *KILLING SHADOWS*.

THE *BODAI SHIN* ARMOR ALLOWS *RIKER* TO MOVE *INVISIBLY* AMONG THE CREW.

HE IS *NOT* INVISIBLE TO THE ASSASSINS.

WILLIAM RIKER KNOWS THAT THE ARMOR IS EQUIPPED WITH *PSIONIC* SHIELDING. THE *BODAI SHIN* DO NOT DELVE INTO ONE ANOTHER'S *THOUGHTS* IN *COMBAT*. HE COULD *DECEIVE* THEM.

WHERE'S THE *FUN* IN THAT?

THE *ASSASSINS* DO NOT *ASK* WHAT HAS BECOME OF THE ONE WHO *WORE* THE ARMOR *BEFORE* RIKER.

I FIGURED OUT HOW TO *PROGRAM* THE *SUIT* TO GET AROUND THAT LITTLE *ATTENUATED* WEAPONRY *FAILSAFE* OF *YOURS.*

WE *REPROGRAMMED* OURS THE MOMENT WE *HEARD* YOUR FOOTFALLS. YOU DO NOT *MOVE* LIKE US.

THEY *ADAPT INSTANTLY* TO THE NEW *THREAT.* RIKER COULD *ALMOST* ADMIRE THEM.

THEN HE THINKS OF THEIR *VICTIMS.*

SHE CAN *FEEL* HIM IN HER MIND.

YOU ARE A *HEALER*. YOU VALUE *LIFE* ABOVE ALL ELSE.

SSSHHKKK

I AM *DISABLING* ALL *LIFE SUPPORT*. YOUR *ONLY HOPE* IS TO *KILL* ME.

GEORDI?

THE *CHAOS CODE* IS *SPLINTERING*, AND BEING *RE-ROUTED* TO LIFE SUPPORT. I *CAN'T* STOP IT IN *TIME!*

SHE *KNOWS* THEIR GAMES.

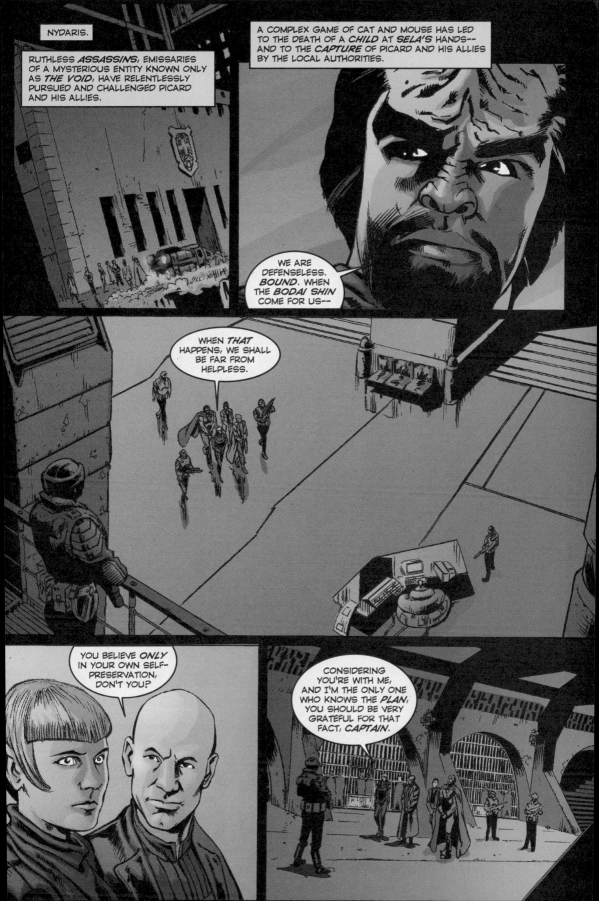

NYDARIS.

RUTHLESS *ASSASSINS,* EMISSARIES OF A MYSTERIOUS ENTITY KNOWN ONLY AS *THE VOID,* HAVE RELENTLESSLY PURSUED AND CHALLENGED PICARD AND HIS ALLIES.

A COMPLEX GAME OF CAT AND MOUSE HAS LED TO THE DEATH OF A *CHILD* AT *SELA'S* HANDS-- AND TO THE *CAPTURE* OF PICARD AND HIS ALLIES BY THE LOCAL AUTHORITIES.

WE ARE DEFENSELESS. *BOUND.* WHEN THE *BODAI SHIN* COME FOR US--

WHEN *THAT* HAPPENS, WE SHALL BE FAR FROM HELPLESS.

YOU BELIEVE *ONLY* IN YOUR OWN SELF- PRESERVATION, DON'T YOU?

CONSIDERING YOU'RE WITH ME, AND I'M THE ONLY ONE WHO KNOWS THE *PLAN,* YOU SHOULD BE VERY GRATEFUL FOR THAT FACT, *CAPTAIN.*

THERE WAS NO HONOR IN THE WAY YOU *SLEW* THE BODAI SHIN. SHE WAS AN INNOCENT. A *CHILD*.

BEING A CHILD DOESN'T MAKE ONE *INNOCENT*.

ENOUGH. WHAT WE *NEED* TO FOCUS ON IS THE BODAI SHIN.

OUR *BEST GUESS* IS THAT THEY HAVE BEEN *TESTING* US. THEY WANTED TO KNOW OUR STRENGTHS AND WEAKNESSES. OUR *BELIEFS*. WHY?

THEY SAY THEY SERVE *THE VOID*. THE BODAI SHIN PATTERN THEMSELVES AFTER THE NINJA OF ANCIENT EARTH.

PICARD *WONDERS* ABOUT *SELA*.

SHE HAS DONE *SO MUCH*.

SAVED THEIR LIVES.

GIVEN THEM A *FIGHTING* CHANCE AGAINST A SEEMINGLY IMPOSSIBLE ENEMY.

WHAT IS SHE *FIGHTING* FOR?

AND IF A *WAR* IS TO COME WITH THE *VOID* AND ITS EMISSARIES-- WOULD SHE SIDE WITH THE *DARKNESS*... OR THE *LIGHT*?

DATA'S *EMOTION CHIP* FLARES. HE *THINKS* OF ALL THE *VICTIMS* OF THE *BODAI SHIN*.

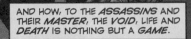

AND HOW, TO THE *ASSASSINS* AND THEIR *MASTER*, THE *VOID*, LIFE AND *DEATH* IS NOTHING BUT A *GAME*.

HE WANTS TO *SHOW THEM* THEY'RE WRONG. HE WANTS TO *MAKE THEM PAY*.

I WANTED HIM *DEAD*.

YES. BUT YOUR *BELIEF* IN HUMANITY WAS TOO STRONG FOR YOU TO *SLAY* EVEN ONE SUCH AS THIS IF THERE IS STILL ANOTHER WAY. YOU HAVE *GREAT HONOR*.

NOT *ALL* OF THE *BODAI SHIN* CRAFT ARE LIFELESS DRONES.

THE PILOT DOES NOT FEAR *DEATH*. HE *BELIEVES* IT WILL TAKE HIM ONE STEP CLOSER TO *THE VOID*.

WE CONTROL THE MINE FIELD. NAVIGATOR, TAKE US THROUGH IT--

"AND SET OFF AS MANY OF THE ESCAPE PODS AS NEEDED TO FORCE A RETREAT."

AND THE DESIRE FOR THE KILL FOR THE VOID.

BUT THERE IS NO RETREAT. THERE IS ONLY THE PURSUIT--

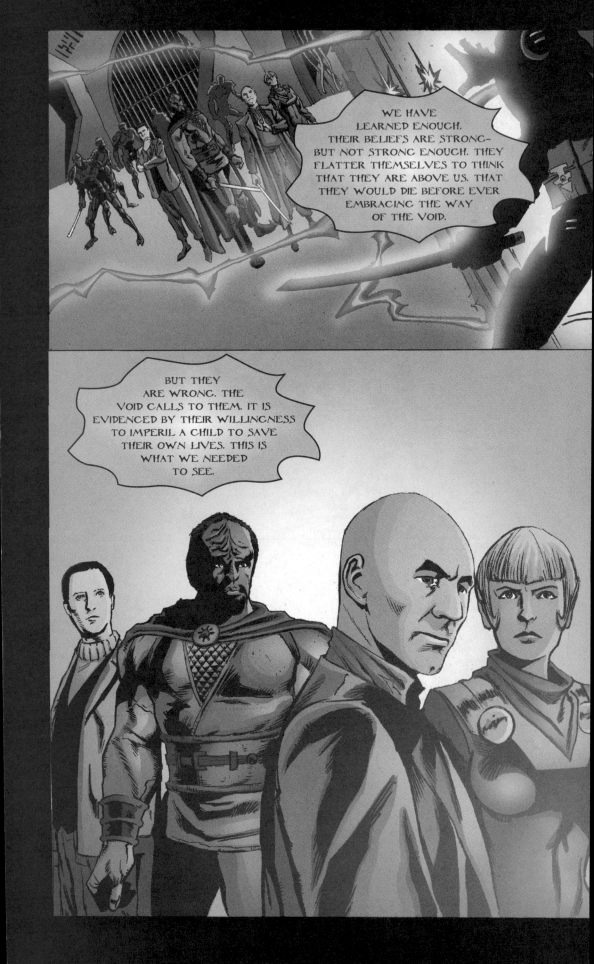

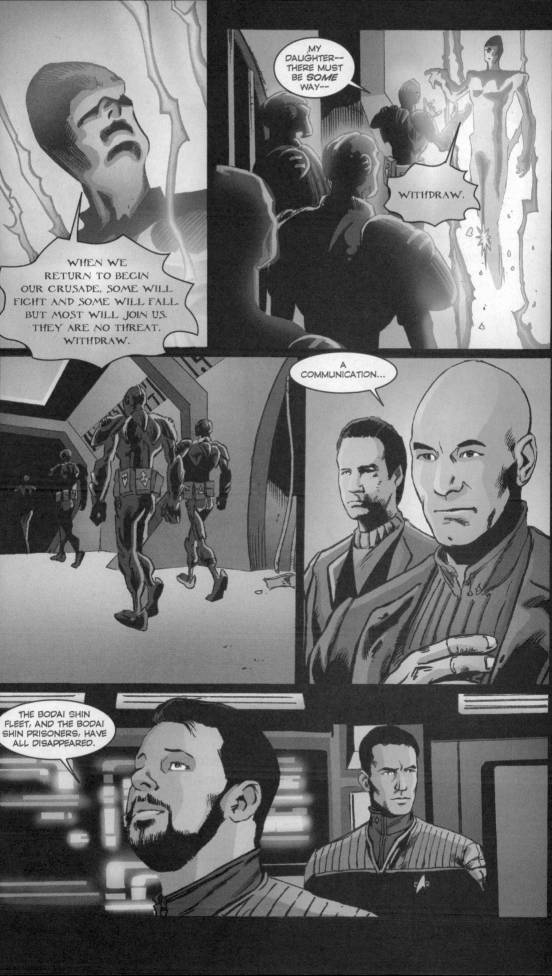